Reviews of
Reading the African Novel

"This is undeniably a radical and innovative work. It breaks a double mould in the world of African literary criticism. It rejects the anthropological analysis that sees African literature as a treatise on the customs and habits of the group of people, and it turns away from the school of criticism that rejects the role of culture in literature, concentrating instead on the form. Gikandi places the role of ideology in literature as a central and motivating force in both the creation of the work and in its success and in so doing has brought new life and new thought to the body of literary cirticism."   *New African*

"*Reading the African Novel* should prove to be one of the major works of criticism of the African novel."   *West Africa*

Reading the African Novel

Reading the African Novel

SIMON GIKANDI

James Currey
LONDON

Heinemann Kenya
NAIROBI

Heinemann
PORTSMOUTH N.H.

James Currey Ltd
54b Thornhill Square, Islington
London N1 1BE

Heinemann Kenya
Kijabe Street, PO Box 45314
Nairobi

Heinemann Educational Books Inc
70 Court Street
Portsmouth, New Hampshire 03801

British Library Cataloguing in Publication Data

Gikandi, Simon
Reading the African novel.
1. African fiction (English)——History and criticism
I. Title
823   PR9341
ISBN 0-85255-504-0

Library of Congress Cataloging-in-Publication Data

Gikandi, Simon.
Reading the African novel.
Includes bibliographies and index.
1. African fiction——History and criticism.
I. Title.
PL8010.6.G55   1986   809.3 .   86-14998
ISBN 0-435-08018-0 (Heineman)

Printed by
Villiers Publications Ltd.,
26a Shepherds Hill, London N6 5AH

*This book is dedicated to
my father and mother
who always allowed me to
play with books and words,
and to Henry Chakava
who, by taking the work
of a schoolboy seriously,
made me a writer and critic*

Contents

Contents

Preface

This book seeks to establish the relationship between form and content in the African novel. Most of our writers have acknowledged this relationship in their works, but most critics of the African novel have not always been able to utilize it meaningfully in their exegetic acts. More often than not, key African novels are either read as social documents which utilize the resources of fictionalization only superficially, or simply as decorative forms which seem to exist for their own sake. The relationship between form and content has, in fact, been the subject of numerous debates in African critical circles. And yet in spite of these debates we do not seem to have advanced very far in the search for a literary method, an aesthetic, that is expediential to the representation of the African experience in fiction, or, for that matter, the study of African literature. What is the essential function of literary criticism? We do not seem to have a common answer to this important question.

I do not believe that we can read the African novel meaningfully and effectively without bringing content and form into play as elements of literature which are equally significant, and my purpose in this study is to show why these elements cannot be mutually exclusive. Needless to say, I do not share Chinweizu's (and his co-authors') view that most African criticism of the novel has avoided the genre's 'vital function' by concentrating on the 'explication of themes and obscurities of texts and attempts to invent meaning where often there is none'.[1] Nor do I agree with Iyasere's contention that our critics have 'become overly concerned with the socio-cultural traditional aspects of the works and have used this information as the basis for evaluation without considering how these elements function'.[2] Both critical schools tend to ignore the complex relationship between life, reality and experience in the African novel. Hence the disdain for either the explication of themes, or the socio-cultural aspects of our literature, and the negation of what Abiola Irele calls 'human life and consciousness' in our literature.[3]

ix

Preface

In *Reading the African Novel* I have tried to show how this 'life and consciousness' moves from the external reality of the African novel into its interiority and how it functions there. I have approached the African novel primarily through its narrative method in the belief that narrative is the essence of African literature. As Ngugi wa Thiong'o has aptly observed, although the African novel is a borrowed form, its greatest debt to our oral tradition is narrative.[4] I operate from a theoretical premise, explored by Seymour Chatman in *Story and Discourse*, which posits narratives as real or implied communication from an author to an audience: 'What is communicated is *story*, the formal content element of narrative; and it is communicated by discourse, the formal expression element'.[5] What marks out the novels I have chosen to examine in some detail is the synthesis of formal elements, content and authorial consciousness; there is no perfect fictional form, only an effective medium.

In hermeneutical terms, I am eager to examine the truth claims of these texts, or what Walter Benjamin would call their 'usefulness',[6] bearing in mind the novel's traditional function as an oracle which, in the words of Michel Zeraffa, 'confronts us openly with the issue of the meaning and value of our ineluctable historical and social condition'.[7] To the extent that the African artist is preoccupied with the question of what Soyinka calls 'self-apprehension',[8] one of my central concerns in this study is the functioning of the African novel as an instrument of understanding on the individual and socio-cultural levels. In this respect, literary form is more than a mute vehicle for mimesis; it has a logic of its own, is indeed what Frederic Jameson terms 'the working of content in the realm of the superstructure'.[9] The text is not mere content or mere form: it is the process of form recreating reality in the terms set by authorial consciousness, constituting a world which might resemble external reality, but is also the novelist's own universe.

Notes

1 'Towards the Decolonization of African Literature', *Transition*, 9, No. 48(1975), p. 34. The troika's theories have been elaborated in *Toward the Decolonization of African Literature* (Enugu: Fourth Dimension, 1980).
2 'African Critics on African Literature: A Study in Misplaced Hostility', *African Literature Today*, 7(1975), p. 24.
3 The concept is borrowed from Abiola Irele. See *The African Experience in Literature and Ideology* (London: Heinemann, 1981), p. 1.

4 'Though it is apparently borrowed,' Ngugi says of the African novel, '[its] essence . . . is the narative. And the whole area of African oral literature contains the essence of narrative.' See Phanuel Akubueze Egejuru, *Towards African Literary Independence* (Westport, Connecticut: Greenwood Press, 1980), p. 109.

5 *Story and Discourse* (Ithaca: Cornell University Press, 1978), p.31.

6 Benjamin has argued that usefulness has always been one of the key elements in storytelling: 'The usefulness may, in one case, consist in a moral; in another, in some practical advice; in a third, in a proverb or maxim.' In general, usefulness is determined by the storyteller's need to communicate experience. See *Illuminations*, edited with an introduction by Hannah Arendt, translated by Harry Zohn (Glasgow: Fontana/Collins, 1973), p. 86.

7 *Fictions: The Novel and Social Reality* (Harmondsworth: Penguin Books, 1976), p. 11.

8 *Myth, Literature and the African World* (London: Cambridge University Press, 1976), p. viii.

9 *Marxism and Form: Twentieth-Century Dialectical Theories of Literature* (Princeton: Princeton University Press, 1971), p. 329.

1

The Parabolical Narrative

Character and Consciousness in the
Novels of Camara Laye and Ayi Kwei Armah

We begin with established African and Western critical responses to the novels of Camara Laye and the later works of Ayi Kwei Armah and the interesting paradoxes they present. Although Camara Laye has been accused of too much romanticism and the kind of blind worship of the black self which is seen as his debt to the ideology of Negritude, his novels present a form which is familiar to the critic schooled in Western literary criticism, so that works such as *The African Child* and *The Radiance of the King* are praised for their familiarity rather than their innovativeness. In contrast, the later Ayi Kwei Armah (*Two Thousand Seasons* and *The Healers*) operates within what a number of critics consider to be a strange and disconcerting literary terrain; his works, far from confirming the claims of the literary tradition and the hegemonic culture of which they are an integral part, tend to disrupt conventional modes of literary form and thought. The above problem is weighed up in Soyinka's *Myth, Literature and the African World*. The critic embraces Armah's rejection of the 'Eurocentric incubus', but is discomforted by 'the actual language of confrontation and the dramatic devices in which the victims of the author's ire are trapped' in *Two Thousand Seasons*. On the other hand, argues Soyinka, the private mythology which Laye develops in *The Radiance of the King* utilizes 'credible norms of social relationshp'.[1] Soyinka is a sympathetic critic concerned with the effectiveness of the forms which Laye and Armah have chosen within the paradigm of value and meaning in their works. A less appreciative view of Armah's latest works is held by Bernth Lindfors. In a recent study of Armah, this critic has seized on what has come to be known as the racial factor in *Two Thousand Seasons* and taken issue with what he deems to be Armah's 'philosophy of paranoia': 'In place of a usable historical myth,' contends Lindfors, *'Two Thousand Seasons* overschematizes the past, creating the dangerous kind of lie that Fanon used to call a "mystification".'[2]

My intention in this essay is to show the effectiveness of Laye's private mythology and Armah's historical myths as instruments of interpreting the African experience and to underscore the functionality of the dramatic and narrative devices which both novelists utilize. I am concerned with the literary forms of *The Radiance of the King* and *The Guardian of the Word* on the one hand, and *Two Thousand Seasons* and *The Healers* on the other, as instruments of challenging established norms and social values and the readers' prior perception of reality. My concern is not so much with overt intentionality, but with the set of values and meanings which underlie the authors' reshaping of reality in their fictional universe. I am not implying that these novels are self-contained, internally derived, self-perpetuating entities; I am merely suggesting that while any external knowledge we may have about the historicism and social background of the world represented in these works affects our reading of them, our judgements should ultimately be determined by our responses to their fictional entity. There is a lot to be said for a mode of criticism that judges works of fiction according to the terms the author has set for himself. My primary intention, however, is to demonstrate how modes of narrative are, invariably, instruments of value and meaning in a work of art.

From a cursory glance, no good reason exists for any comparison of Laye and Armah. And yet both novelists conceive their role as that of the traditional African storyteller rather than the isolated novelist. In their latest works in particular, we have seen both novelists becoming increasingly concerned not only with the practical orientation of their work — what Walter Benjamin would call its usefulness[3] — but have also made the implied reader an important part of their narrative art. As Walter Benjamin has noted, the storyteller is differentiated from the conventional novelist (the writer of the *Bildungsroman*) by his reliance on an oral tradition which he shares with his audience. 'The storyteller takes what he tells from experience — his own or that reported by others,' observes Benjamin. 'And he in turn makes it the experience of those who are listening to his tale.'[4] In terms of narrative structure, the two novelists work with a series of motifs and a central structure which is designed to link the past with the present, looking forward to the future.

There are, however, certain fundamental differences in the way the two novelists interpret the African experience. Cast fully within the tradition of Negritude, Laye is cautiously involved in an act of cultural diplomacy, a mixture, in the words of Mbella Sonne Dipoko, of

The Parabolical Narrative

'revolt, dialogue and compromise'.[5] As I will try to illustrate in my discussion of the allegorical movement in *The Radiance of the King*, the narrative structure in Laye's novels moves the reader and hero away from a situation of revolt, through a process of dialogue and compromise, and ends with a dramatic synthesis of the formerly divided self, and the assimilation of the hero in the universe rejection of which triggered the dramatic conflict. Confrontation is what defines the works of Ayi Kwei Armah. The narrative movement in both the novels we are going to discuss in this essay is controlled by a 'righteous' narrator who is never in doubt about the 'rightness' of the cause he or she espouses. This narrator is not interested in moving the story towards any point of resolution (the other side is wrong and contagious and cannot hence be co-opted), but to the enhancement of the conflict between right and wrong in the hope that its nature and character will be understood. Armah's novels are thus built around a narrative structure which moves the reader and the characters from one level of confrontation to another, with the hope of resolution held up only in the distant future.

As interpreters of the African experience, both novelists see their works as depositories of knowledge and counsel. They are concerned both with the meaning of Africa to their readers, and with the relationship between the continent (as a historical and mythical reality) and the rest of the world. Laye's ideological premise is that the values that will rehabilitate Africa in the eyes of the world are buried deep in our history and the ideal of African unity is embedded in our past:

> If the peoples concerned, having each achieved political independence, open themselves up, as indeed they should, to external influences, if they seek each other out and make common ground, we may then witness the awakening of a new civilization, one so vital that within the next few decades the immense territories watered by the Niger will in many ways become unimaginably prosperous.[6]

It is an understatement to say that the ideal of African unity is the fulcrum around which Armah's latest works revolve; his novels have become a forum for advocating the unification of African cultures, of the bringing together of those value systems that inspired the continent in the past as a prelude to a future of true national independence:

> The greatest source of power and influence available to the African tradition is its acceptance and imaginative use of the archetypal dream of total liberation, the end of all conflict and injustice, the advent of utopian conditions of abundance and freedom, the thoroughgoing negation of the repressive facts of real life.[7]

The Parabolical Narrative

For both novelists, then, myth and utopia are integral elements in the realization and dramatization of the values they deem necessary to the total liberation of Africa. In the following sections, I will examine some of the devices Laye and Armah utilize towards this end.

The allegorical movement in *The Radiance of the King*

The form of *The Radiance of the King* and the allegorical mode of expression in general presuppose the existence of some kind of ethereal reality: Laye's narrative demands that we collate his characters' experiences with both their real-world situations and with a world that exists only in their imagination. Real and imaginary movement is another important element in the allegorical quest. This is intended to move the character from one level of awareness or ignorance to another, from a limited understanding of real-world situations and the values that underlie them to a full understanding of the same. In the words of Gay Clifford, the journey, quest, or pursuit in the allegorical narrative is the 'metaphor by which a process of learning for both protagonist and readers is expressed'.[8] The process by which Clarence undergoes the African experience, and the changes that come over him in the course of his journey, constitue the narrative structure in *The Radiance of the King*; the meaning of Laye's novel is embedded in the movement and transformation of the hero who is often defined by his actions and reactions towards new situations, and the motives that move him to these acts and actions.

Clarence, like Sundiata in *The Guardian of the Word*, is a character who is linked to a particular kind of destiny; he is moved and motivated by a force larger than himself, and is defined by something more than his human qualities, which are almost insignificant in the development of his total character. Both Clarence and Sundiata have definite missions which go beyond their basic needs: Clarence's goal is acceptance by the king, which is tantamount to salvation; Sundiata's objective is the subjugation of his human and superhuman adversaries. Clarence's quest is superficially personal — it is one man's quest for his godhead. But, on a higher level, this quest is linked to a general philosophical dictum: the ideal of assimilation, of cultural synthesis and a universal civilization. The one question that dominates Laye's white man is whether at the end of his quest he will be accepted by the king in spite of his colour. In another sense, Clarence functions as the author's instrument, a means of defining, exposing and experiencing, a second dimension of reality which is barely visible to the human eye. Clarence's journey is both through the African experience and through a world of what Laye calls 'hidden things and mysteries'.[9] The situation within which Clarence defines himself is, hence, a fusion of the real and hidden worlds.

Clarence's quest is first and foremost an attempt to understand his

4

world, to control events to suit his objectives. And yet, for most of the novel, he is the victim of a world that seems far beyond his reach. In his first confrontation with the massive esplanade, the symbol of the power and splendour of the juvenile king, we find Clarence trapped by the vast crowds, an insignificant character who is referred to merely as a whiteman. He would like to turn back to where he came from, but Clarence has no say in the matter; 'he seemed to have had no say in anything for some days now'.[10] There is an interesting irony in Clarence's feeling of helplessness and entrapment: Laye has deliberately inverted the traditional motif of the whiteman as a conqueror of new volunteers and a master of his own fate, so common in the colonial novel of Africa. The relationship between the whiteman and the black people in this situation is not that of master and slave; the people waiting before the esplanade, we are told, either seem unaware of Clarence's presence, or pretend he is invisible; the whiteman has hence found himself in a situation which his culture has not trained him for: he is the victim of a universe yet to be defined, trapped by the crowds, hypnotized by the odours of his new environment. This is a place where chances are not easily given to characters even when, as in Clarence's case, they believe that their race entitles them to certain privileges. Above all, this is an inverted situation which destroys all presumptions: values appear inverted, and many things, including the arrangement of characters before the esplanade are 'the exact opposite of what should have been the case' (p. 8).

Clarence has a clear notion of what and how things should be — being a colonial entails not only sharing the colonial *esprit de corps*, but also developing a stereotyped way of seeing things — but his experiences challenge his assumptions at every stage of his quest. He confronts numerous cosmological symbols which enhance the difference between his illusions and new realities, between things as they are and as they are anticipated by his imagination. The landscape seems to be defined by its abnormality: the big cloud over the esplanade, far from protecting the city from the sun, accentuates the steamy heat, giving it 'a kind of tangible presence, a massive and almost unbearable solidity' (p. 9).

The protagonist's relationship with this strange landscape is basically ironic. The whiteman finds himself in a situation where he cannot define himself except in relation to a world he considers 'uncivilized'. After he witnesses a native dance for the first time, we have the authorial narrator noting the irony of Clarence's reaction to this art form: 'The novelty and strangeness of this barbaric spectacle were such that he could not take his eyes away from it' (p. 9). The attractiveness of what he should, as a keeper of the colonial tradition, have found repulsive, expresses the white man's state of confusion.

The Parabolical Narrative

Since his psychological growth begins only when he adjusts himself and develops his ability to read new realities, Clarence cannot but be confused. Every gesture and observation he makes expose his inability to get out of his stereotyped attitude. His view of the native dance is typical:

> 'They are dancing well,' he said at last. One of the black giants at his side looked him up and down in an unfriendly manner.
>
> 'You call that "dancing"?' he said bitterly. 'I call it "hopping", nothing more.'
>
> 'Well, yes, they *are* hopping,' thought Clarence. 'They *are* hopping, but they're dancing, too; that must be their way of dancing.'
>
> 'They don't know the first thing about dancing,' the black man went on. 'They . . .'
>
> But he did not finish his sentence. He spat contemptuously on the red earth. (pp. 9–10)

We are not sure whether the black man is contemptuous of Clarence's ignorance or of the native dance, but the last sentence in the quotation above is a good example of the double-edged expressions which Laye uses to expose his characters' ambiguities. Sometimes ambiguous sentences are intended to illustrate the spontaneous nature of this universe, its refusal to be schematized into time patterns. When Clarence asks the black man when the king is expected, therefore, he gets an answer which is very typical — 'at the appointed time'.

The black man is not merely a nuisance on Clarence's path towards his destination, but a significant psychological barrier. But Clarence is not daunted by the black man's antics or destructive tactics because he believes that his colour guarantees him an audience with the king. "I am not just anybody," he tells the black man. "I am a white man.' (p. 10). The assumption that Clarence is the representative of a race, whose superiority he readily assumes, is one that is important in the character's final dénouement; it is also an arrogant supposition which the white man must renounce before he completes his transformation, because the people of this land do not recognize whiteness as a badge of superiority. The black man knows this only too well. Whereas Clarence assumes that his colour is obvious, the black man insists he does not recognize the others' colour, forcing Clarence to doubt his whiteness. "Am I not a white man?" wonders Clarence. The black man's response only adds to the protagonist's sense of dejection: "The white men do not come here, on the esplanade!" (p. 11). Clarence will soon discover that his colour, far from facilitating his meeting with the king, serves as a kind of impediment.

Psychological barriers in the protagonist's allegorical journey tend to serve two purposes: they force the allegorical character to reappraise his relationship with the alien landscape, and to question certain deep-rooted aspects of his character. Clarence is forced to admit the simple fact that he cannot be the representative of the white colonial class and yet expect to be received by the juvenile king. He may be white, but his initial movement away from the 'veranda' culture of the colonials was not instituted on the character's own volition; he was rejected by the other whites because of his poverty and manners. He hence finds himself in a position where he must choose between his old self and the promise of a new character who has been saved by the king:

> Only a week ago, he had been sitting on that veranda, playing cards and drinking brandy; he was calling his partners by their Christian names and ordering the black waiters around, free with his tongue, and bitingly witty . . . But now he was no longer at the hotel . . . Would he ever go back there? . . . No, he would never go back there, because if he did, they would all turn their backs on him. (p. 11)

As far as white standards go, Clarence is one of the low; poor, humiliated, and now isolated from his native culture, which was the only source, as far as he could tell, of the values by which he lived and judged others. Curiously enough, ostracization has not diminished Clarence: for most black people waiting to meet the king, the protagonist's arrogance is the quality that defines the white race. The narrator's awareness of the false claims Clarence makes for himself is an important source of irony in the novel. Laye draws the reader's attention to the weaknesses of Clarence's character by comparing his arrogance with the humility and moral superiority of the beggar, who is more familiar with the landscape and its culture, yet has no preconceived notions about the juvenile king and his mission. Even when he is forced to accept certain undeniable realities, the old colonial self in Clarence's character cannot allow him to come to terms with certain basic truths. His response to the mystical aura surrounding the king is typical:

> 'The king of kings?' asked Clarence. 'Well, he must certainly be the king of kings, after all this display, all these horsemen, this red and radiant cloud of dust, this vast cloud . . . And yet, and yet . . . he couldn't really be the king of kings: he could only be a negro king, a ruler of one of the negro tribes . . . Yet this cloud, this vast assembly . . .' (p. 18)

He is not privy to the inner codes which define the ideals of kinghood, and since he is confronted by a phenomenon which he cannot easily fit into the pigeon-holes of his colonial mind, he has to grow with his doubts.

The Parabolical Narrative

It is not by accident that Clarence's doubts revolve around the person and meaning of the boy king. But in spite of being the allegorical pivot in the novel, the figure of the king poses an interpretative problem. What is he? What forces does he represent?

Early in the novel, we have been informed that the king is both powerful and divine, human and weak. In general, the king is defined by his ambiguities. Clarence observes that the monarch is 'so extraordinarily frail' without his entourage that he seems almost intangible, but, as the beggar is quick to point out, 'at the same time he is very old, and very strong' (p. 21). The king's powers are largely invisible; like the gold that binds him and keeps him down to earth, these powers are a sign of 'the purest kind of love' (p. 21), and their meaning lies in another sphere of experience. The king's divinity is sometimes reflected in his personality. Take his smile, for instance: 'it was the sort of smile one sees on the faces of idols — remote, enigmatic — and which is composed perhaps as much of disdain as of benevolence; the reflection of an inner life, no doubt, but — what sort of inner life?' (p. 22). Clarence is not sure, neither is the reader. But if the reader's inability to understand the meaning of the king symbol in the novel has a lot to do with Laye's own lack of clarity about his creation, Clarence's inability to understand has a lot to do with his upbringing; he has not been trained to recognize and respond to a positive power that is identified by its blackness, which he initially associates with 'hurtful beastiality'. Later, when Clarence has conceded that blackness can indeed be associated with divinity, he sees the king's idol-like features as symptomatic of 'that very life which lies beyond death' (p. 22).

To the extent that Clarence's subsequent journey in search of the king involves the eventual denial of his old veranda identity, I share Adele King's contention that the white man's journey 'shows how the soul must gradually lose its feeling of individual importance, if it is to find God'.[11] Whether Clarence actually finds his deity is one of the questions I will return to later. What is suggested at the beginning of his quest is the possibility of life after death, and the king's face suggests the kind of enigmatic remoteness which Clarence finds so enticing in the course of his journey: it promises the kind of life we seek 'when all is lost, and everything departs out of our hands', a life which, in Clarence's mind at least, appears 'remote' and 'so fraught with uncertainty . . .' (p. 22). Clarence's quest is directed by the hope that he too has a divine purpose (to find his godhead) and a sense of fear that what he wants to achieve is actually beyond his reach.

But must the quest of the allegorical character be directed? Writing on the transformation of character in allegory, Gay Clifford has noted how the hero of this mode of narrative, having established his objectives, follows a controlled or directed process. 'The control is provided by the object of the journey, combat, or quest,' observes Clifford, and 'we interpret the significance of the motion of the characters and of the forces affecting them in the light of knowledge about the direction in which they travel.'[12] As we have already observed, Clarence's objective in *The Radiance of the King* is to serve the boy king and, in the process, achieve his divine status, too; it is against this objective that we must judge all his actions. Between the protagonist and his objective, as the old beggar reminds Clarence, there are certain obstacles to be overcome, not least Clarence's colour, which has now become a liability. Confronted by the black crowd that surrounds the esplanande, the white man wonders whether he can battle against the waves which symbolize the distance between him and the continent of Africa. ' "Everything's against me . . ." ' he cries at one stage. ' "As soon as I set foot in this place, everything turned against me.' (p. 27).

It is when he begins to view his world with a more open mind that Clarence finally begins to be transformed. The important first step is his transfer of authority to the beggar in the hope that 'perhaps a beggar would have access to places where others would have met only with curt refusals' (p. 28). While only a few moments ago he was treating the beggar with disdain, Clarence cannot even mumble a protest when the latter offers to put in a word for him at the hotel:

> . . . he had fallen so low, and looked on everything with such a worm's-eye view that this phrase from the lips of a negro beggar no longer exasperated him . . . Could there be any question of 'rights' in the sort of world he found himself in now? 'Not in this world, nor, perhaps, in any other,' thought Clarence. 'Viewed from the pit where now I lie, there are no such things as "rights".' (pp. 28–29)

A man who had fallen to the lowest rung of the white colonial culture now finds himself at the pit of African social values, and he cannot but accept the obvious — his whiteness entails neither rights, nor privileges.

Clarence's journey takes him (and the reader) through a world neatly balanced between dream and reality, a world which, as advocates of Negritude have insisted, cannot be explained simply in terms of common sense or dialectic.[13] Understanding this world is indeed one of the obstacles the character must overcome before he attains his godhead. Where does he, or the reader for that matter, draw the line between illusion and reality? This raises certain interesting questions about the form of *The Radiance of the King*.

The first thing to observe about 'understanding' in the novel is that even when Clarence tries to speculate about the nature of natural and human phenomena, he only succeeds in exposing the limits of his consciousness now deprived of its old stereotyped perspective. Because none of his conjectures seems to be on the mark, Clarence becomes convinced that this land cannot really be understood, that 'there was no way of knowing' (p. 36). He is increasingly forced to trust first impressions more than rational understanding because things tend to change every time. The esplanade, which he thought he had fully understood and assimilated in his mind, fades into different shades of colour, mirror images and shadows which he cannot account for; his hallucinatory state of mind indicates an inability to tame reality, so that we are now dealing with an 'innocent' character, one in a nascent state of consciousness. This is an interesting irony in the novel, bearing in mind that Clarence came to Africa as the representative of what he thought was a higher civilization, one with a highly developed consciousness. He finds himself falling back on superstitions to explain worlds he can barely comprehend; limited understanding draws attention to his loneliness, and he is reminded of that moment when he crossed 'the reef that barred the coast of Africa — a great foaming line like a festering weal' (p. 38).

Awareness of limited understanding breeds a mixture of fear and hope in Clarence. He struggles to develop a new set of values that will help him narrow the great cultural divide between him and his idol, and to discover those concepts that will help him perceive his realities. At the same time, the implied author or narrator has to develop what Clifford calls 'a hierarchy of value and dis-value',[14] by which the protagonist's objective can be judged. The white man is taken back to his old hotel to be humbled, a decidedly retrogressive step which is, nevertheless, essential if he is to come to terms with his moral and material debts, so to speak. It is, however, premature to assume the completeness of Clarence's humbling. The author's, or narrator's, attitude towards the protagonist's process of change remains ambiguous almost throughout the novel. This ambiguity allows the narrator room for ironic comment. In one scene at the inn, Clarence has an altercation with the inn-keeper, and his 'foolish bravado' is the subject of ironic authorial commentary:

He had suddenly forgotten his tiredness and had regained courage; he felt full of courage. He forgot that this courage was no more than foolish bravado which only a few days ago had urged him on to play for high stakes, when all he had to lose was his honour. And because he had recovered that feeling of reckless courage, he was no longer the man who had been expelled from the white men's hotel, nor yet the man who had not been able to get himself the wretched little job of drummer to the king; neither was he that wreck of a man who owed money to this negro inn-keeper whom he addressed publicly as 'old tosspot'. No, he was that man no longer, he wasn't the same man at all! But this insolent man, this blow-up blusterer, this would-be hero — was he any better? Wasn't he like a creature that has reached the depths of despair, a creature who cared as little for others as he did for himself, a creature whose only defence is sarcasm? . . . Is that what you call a man? . . . And supposing all men were like that? (pp. 44–45)

By building up Clarence's mock heroism, then dismantling it with bitter sarcasm, the narrator is insisting that the allegorical character has not changed much.

But the white man's circumstances have changed, nevertheless. He has to develop plans to meet new situations, re-adjust his way of seeing, and develop a perspective. This is not a challenge he meets too readily, and when he embarks on his journey to the South, the protagonist does not have any discernible measure of self-control. Unable to seize what the beggar calls 'opportunities', he yields to the odour of the land and makes his journey 'out of consciousness'. There is, at least in a superficial sense, some kind of rapport between the character and the landscape at this point. And yet Clarence cannot really establish a genuine dialogue with this land and its people. ' "Everything is turned against me, and everything will continue to be turned against me," ' he mourns before the judge. When the judge reminds Clarence that there is 'something which does not say much for your truthfulness', the protagonist's response is familiar — ' "They misunderstood me." ' (p. 76)

The gap between Clarence and the South is invisible; the novelist is imprecise about the nature of this division and the character of the landscape, assuming, in the tradition of allegorical representation, that meaning is profound when inaccessible. The barrier between character and landscape in *The Radiance of the King* is symbolized by a wall, or the forest. The meaning of these symbols is not, however, easily understood, since they exist as shadows in Clarence's mind; they are not tangible realities but reflections of his psychological fear of the South, of the hostility and indifference which he sees in the region. Merging in his mind, the wall and the forest create the 'general impression of two equally disdainful masses' (p. 95). The protagonist is never sure of the actuality of these barriers, though; just when he thinks he has decoded the nature of the South, he begins to doubt their very existence: has he been dreaming about the forest and the wall, or has the beggar made them up? The problem, suggests the beggar, has to do with Clarence's vision:

There *are* paths. If you can't see them — and why should you see them? — you've only got your own eyes to blame. A white man can't see everything: and he has no need to see everything either, because this land is not a white man's land. (p. 96)

The Parabolical Narrative

As far as the beggar is concerned, there are doors and paths to the African experience which demand specialized modes of perception, and Clarence must understand this if he is to understand the South at all.

Our assumption so far is that the allegorical character is defined by narrative action. This character is transformed into another personality the moment this action drives him to understand his situations better and profoundly. Clarence's first major attempt to understand himself in relation to the South begins when he tries to unravel the mystery of its odours. he realizes, as does the reader who is involved in the same kind of probe, that the odour of the South is not ordinary, that it is 'subtlety itself, a seductive perfume' (p. 98). Our contention, then, is that the odour is the key to Clarence's quest and its meaning, and the element that defines the South itself. And yet this contention is not one that can be backed up with a large measure of determinancy, for part of the interpretative problem in *The Radiance of the King* lies in Laye's evocation of mystery for its own sake, so that ideas and abstracts are not always connected in the narrative. But there is a sense in which our inability to decode the meaning of the South fully reinforces the landscapes' ethereal character. The reader, like the protagonist, finds himself in a situation where 'everything is shifting and moving, yet nothing moves', where 'everything opens itself to every other thing, where everything is penetrated by everything else' (p. 99). This state of instability puts Clarence off his track at certain crucial moments. It is one of these aspects of allegory which never seem to justify themselves because the novelist insists on making his places and experiences unreal and emblematic, yet insists that the same situations have a recognizable link with reality. The patterns of thought that dominate Clarence's mind, on the other hand, suggest greater meaning, but the reader is never really able to discover this meaning. The novelist tries to link ideas and abstract thought in a number of ways. First, he has the beggar define the South as something more than the Africa which Clarence cannot penetrate, as a land that is 'everywhere', thereby confirming the narrator's earlier reference to the region as 'this universal possession' and an 'inferno of the senses' which is, presumably, the property of the whole of mankind. Second, as Clarence begins to experience the odours of the South with greater intensity, the narrator shifts from the past tense to the present continuous tense, suggesting eternal and incessant movement. Finally, the South is shown to hold the promise of eternal fulfilment, 'an indescribable, gentle happiness' (p. 106).

Implicit in Clarence's allegorical journey is the suggestion that he cannot acquire eternal fulfilment until he has understood the mysteries of the South. For most of the narrative, however, there is no suggestion that the white man can really achieve the kind of transformation he seeks: he seems to fall asleep just when he thinks he has grasped the meaning of the South, and his quest seems to lead nowhere. His movement for a large part of the novel is in circles. This circular movement is finally broken when Clarence meets Akissi, who is not only a composite character of all the women of the land, but also the vital link between the protagonist and the landscape. Even at this stage in the narrative, Clarence's transformation is represented with some ambiguity. When the eunuch Samba Baloum tells the white man that he is now 'a different person altogether', he is ostensibly referring to Clarence's new function as the stud of the Naba's harem; but he is also raising the possibility of real assimilation now that the stranger has been married to a daughter of the land and is also the father to some of the chief's children. Reflecting on his earlier experiences in the forest and at the esplanande, Clarence acknowledges the changes he had undergone:

> If anyone who had known him in those days could have seen him now, smoking and drinking, crouching in the manner of black men under the arcade, and dressed in a *boubou* like a black man, he would have appeared quite unrecognisable. (p. 159)

But there are a number of reasons why Clarence's metamorphosis is never complete. Underlying his new perspective are remnants of his old colonial mind ('it was not easy for Clarence to tell one black face from another' [p. 166]); and what appears to be an inability (one shared by the reader, no doubt) to understand what is really happening to him. For these reasons, the protagonist lives in a divided state of mind. This is a divisiveness we find manifested in his actions, too: he lusts for Akissi, and yet abominates this lust; he knows that nudity is natural in Aziana and would make him equal to the people of the South, but is ashamed of his own nudity during the day.

A greater divisiveness is evident in Clarence's consciousness as he tries to redefine his objectives and his chances of achieving them. What began initially as an ill-defined search for the boy king has now become the quest for cultural and social transformation and assimilation. If he begins to observe the traditions and customs of Aziana, he speculates, will he not become one of the people of the South in spite of his colour?

> 'It's the soul that matters,' he kept telling himself. 'And in that respect I am exactly as they are.' And was it not better that way? Was it not better than being Clarence? And that was why he was pursuing the downward path, the one the people of Aziana

preferred, though it was not his own? But what exactly was 'his' path?

'I have no particular path,' he said. (p. 168)

Clarence realizes that one does not become a subject of the king merely by wearing a *boubou* when he comes across the ascetic smith Diallou, who has been waiting for the return of the king all his life. Diallou is more than the force that shapes metals and tames fire; he is also an example of those values which Clarence must assimilate if he is to be accepted into the service of the king — honesty, morality, modesty and patience. Ironically, this knowledge comes to the white man after he has lost his innocence in the Naba's harem, hence his agonizing:

> 'Oh, to be a child again! To be a child, a little child again!' he whispered to himself. And he blushed violently; he was all at once the child who would blush at the sight of the man he had become; he felt himself burn all over with shame, burn as the incandescent iron was burning. For the man he had become no longer existed; that so-called man was now a beast — cock! (p. 212)

The protagonist's anguish is understandable: the divine motive behind his quest was salvation and purification, but his journey seems to have led him deeper into sin.

Clarence's journey towards salvation is marked by repeated reversals. He takes this particular one to heart because he thinks he should have been able to interpret the obvious signs that he was being used as the Naba's stud. Henceforth, the protagonist is involved in a battle of wills with the elements that typify the South, but he knows that his only hope of salvation is a personal gesture of expiation from the king himself. The latter prospect does not augur well for Clarence. By the time the return of the king becomes inevitable, Clarence's status in the South is at its lowest ebb. He is portrayed as a 'poor white man' (p. 243), a character of pity who is in the same situation he was in when he began his quest at the esplanade. In fact, the protagonist's journey has merely brought him back where he started, and the implied question here is whether his circularity is a completion of one life cycle or merely a repetition of the old sins. Whether Clarence actually makes any physical journey to the South, which by the beggar's definition is 'everywhere', is irrelevant. What we are concerned with here is Clarence's journey of mind and whether his experiences have prepared him for acceptance by the king.

But who is the king? His return is similar to the second coming of Christ, a point underscored by Laye's constant use of Christian imagery. We know, for example, that one cannot really be fully prepared for the return of the king because he comes without warning. We also know that the king has come to deliver all people, not to save one man. But if the king has not come to save Clarence, the white man has come to be saved by the king, hence the protagonist's inability to comprehend the Naba's decision to bar him from the ceremonies at the esplanade. If the king does not receive him, Clarence contends, then he will become a slave of the South, to which he has now given his all, wittingly or unwittingly:

> And he had the feeling that all was lost. But had he not already lost everything? . . . The boys could give him as many pregnant looks as they liked, he would not go near the royal presence; he had the measure of his own unworthiness. He could remain forever chained to the South, chained to his hut, chained to the naba and to the harem, chained to everything he had so thoughtlessly abandoned himself to. Oh! if only he could have his life again! (p. 282)

And yet the unworthy man, the sinner, is ultimately received by the king, proving that in spite of the reversals that accompany the allegorical movement, the protagonist's objective is a prophecy that must be fulfilled.

Clarence's perspective has changed at the end of his quest, but the system of values established by the implied author have been fixed all along. This element of fixedness is characteristic of the allegorical narrative which, in the words of one critic, expounds 'cosmic or political systems that are hierarchical and conservative',[15] The abstract nature of *The Radiance of the King* conceals Laye's conservatism, especially his attachment to old, traditional systems of thought and values, and the mysteries of the African past.[16] This attachment is dramatized most vividly in his last major work, *The Guardian of the Word*, an epic based on the Sundiata legend.

The epic hero in *The Guardian of the Word*

For Camara Laye, the griot's narrative voice elicits fixed truths and values on two levels; every form of oral literature is, in the same vein, made up of two truths — 'a first truth, consciously created and peripheral, intended to amuse the audience; but on the reverse side of the first truth there is a second truth, profound, close to the truth, to reality, but in a different way that the layman finds difficult to detect: that is the historical truth'.[17] The duality of truth and reality is, as we have already seen, central to the meaning of in *The Radiance of the King*. But the griot is more than an instrument of truth and an agent of discourse. In *The Guardian of the Word*, the griot functions as an interested narrator, an important member of an 'ancient, clearly defined hierarchical society' that is feudal in character. His loyalty is hence not merely to an abstract truth, but also to the values of this ancient hierarchy which Laye finds admirable in 'our ancient traditions' (p. 31). In strictly formal terms, the epic narrative reinforces the hierarchical position of the artist and the feudal structure of the community within which he situates his drama. Laye posits himself as the transcriber of a tale told by a traditional griot, but his neutrality as an implied author suggests a certain acceptance of the values celebrated in the narrative itself. And although *The Guardian of the Word* is a narrative about the life and times of Sundiata, it is not by accident that most of the saga is centred more on the values that inform the community in which the hero is born than the activities of the *dramatis personae*. Later in the narrative, when the whole saga is dominated by the character of its hero, Sundiata's personality and activities become direct celebrations of the values of the 'ancient hierarchy' of which the griot is a spokesman.

The direct relationship between the hero of the epic and the values of his community and social class has been the subject of some elaborate discussions by literary critics. The epic narrative presupposes the establishment of a social pattern within which the activities of the hero can be placed and a stage for the actualization of the hero's character. In other words, the narrator places the hero in a mythical context which the reader finds relevant (bearing in mind Northrop Frye's contention that myth is part of a society's knowledge of itself,' the understanding of its traditions, its customs, its situation in the world').[18] The irony, of course, is that this kind of narrative is anchored by a narrative agent or character who is larger than life, and is a form of discourse set above the people whose values the epic hero is supposed to represent; the epic itself operates within the realm of myth while claiming historical accuracy. In the world of the griot, however, myth and history are complementary. As Isidore Okphewo has noted, 'history for the unlettered artist is both what has actually happened and what is fabled to have happened. For him myth has considerable historical value; because it has been told all too often, it bears the stamp of truth'.[19]

Our concern in this section is the development of Sundiata as a character who represents certain mythical–poetic ideals and their implication within the broad context of the narrative. The narrative opens with an appraisal of the values to which the hero will be born: in tracing Sundiata's maternal roots, the narrator underscores his mother's ugliness, not merely as a physical quality, but also as a symbol of disadvantage. Ugliness makes Sogolon a social outcast, but also marks her out as the chosen one. It is important that the hero be born of the lowest stock, so that his achievements and transformation can be spectacular. The hero's maternal roots are planted deep in animism, while his paternal side is inspired by Islam; for Laye, the union of the two religious traditions is part of the vitality that propels the hero on his predicted path to power and glory.

Because the hero is introduced very late in the narrative, one of the devices which the narrator uses to create anticipation is prophecy; this provides us with details of episodes central to the hero's development long before they happen. In the epic narrative, as in allegory, characters have been selected to fulfil certain spiritual or social roles and are hence prophetic. There is an important difference in the use of prophecy in the two modes of representation, though: in allegory, neither the implied reader nor the narrator are aware of the consequences of the actions the characters take, or will take; in the epic narrative, on the other hand, the narrator is aware of his characters' destiny and is more willing to share it with his audience. Prophesies in *The Guardian of the Word* are pronounced with great authority. When the griot tells the king of the Manden, Maghan Kegni, of the imminent arrival of Sologon in the kingdom, he does not say that the girl is arriving in person, but as a spirit: 'The dread guardian spirit of a powerful kingdom is about to emigrate into our own kingdom in the person of a young girl.' (p. 74). Of the girl's future role, the griot is equally certain: 'She will bring into the world a son who shall extend his power over all the lands of the savanna.' (p. 75). So the hero's role has been predetermined and our interest is centred not so much on the attainment of his objectives, but how this role is dramatized in the narrative. The circumstances in which Sundiata is conceived and is born are as extraordinary as his personality: he is preceded by portentous, unexplained events, including a violent meeting of cyclones over Niane:

> They tangled and formed an enormous whirlwind that lifted the roots off the huts and decapitated the mango trees. Were they the local spirits of Dô and the Manden? Perhaps. Perhaps, too, that unleashing of fury was nothing other than the nuptial procession of the buffalo–panther of Dô and the lion of the Manden, and now, perhaps, they were consummating their marriage. (pp. 112–113)

Sundiata is hence born through the agency of multiple, natural forces.

It is an understatement to say that the heroic epic is about the hero and his heroic exploits; everything else is secondary to these and has no relevance unless it has a direct bearing on the character's transformation. Sundiata's physical characteristics are symbolic of the role he is born to play, his actions are pathways to his destiny, and other characters exist only to facilitate him. Above everything else, the hero's development cannot be stifled, nor can his role be diminished by ordinary mortals. For this reason, young Sundiata is called Nankama, 'he who has come to fulfil a heavenly mission' (p. 115). And yet Sundiata is born a cripple, casting doubts on his ability to play his heroic role:

> With his tormented and taciturn air, looking rather like an idiot, the son of Sogolon had a particularly long and difficult childhood. By the time he was five years old, he still could not stand upright: his legs seemed as if paralysed, and indeed they were really paralysed. And probably it was this infirmity that had always made him drag himself along the ground like a crocodile crawling on a sandbank. (p. 124)

The hero then, has no power to carry out his mission, and the reader is supposed to share his parents' sense of betrayal. But the narrator knows better: Sundiata's infirmity is but a temporary inconvenience, for he still retains the guardian spirits that are the real source of his power. What the reader is asked to witness is not really the transformation of the hero, but the reawakening of the guardian spirits within him. We know, on good authority, that the hero's fate must come to pass; our concern now is how Sundiata transcends the obstacles that lie between him and his destiny.

From the foregoing, one might be tempted to conclude that the hero of the epic narrative is not important as an agent of narrative movement. This contention needs some qualification. The hero is not merely a passive instrument of fate: his physical bearing, his sense of moral superiority, and his determination to meet the challenges of his times — all these are important in the movement of the heroic epic. Sundiata's personal determination to walk and to exert his will is also the initiation of great dramatic moments in *The Guardian of the Word*:

> Diata lowered his head as if examining his feet still trailing on the ground. When he lifted his head again, he saw nothing but the bar before him. The next moment, his muscles swelled, his biceps bulged. Now, embracing the bar, he boldly hauled himself up, his head completely thrown back, and his eyes half closed so that his view would not be obstructed by the sweat drenching his body. The faint smile that had played on his lips a moment before had completely vanished.
> When he judged that he had climbed high enough, his knees, which for the first time he tried to brace, began trembling frantically, like a field of corn whipped by the harmattan. Suddenly, in a supreme effort, he gradually managed to stretch himself completely upright, planted on his own two legs! But the great iron bar had become twisted and had taken on the form of a bow. Was it Diata's strength that had bent the bar? Perhaps, too, it had been done simply by the combined forces of the buffalo and panther of Dô and the the lion of Manden. (pp. 134–35)

The Parabolical Narrative

This dramatic gesture defines the hero in a number of ways: through this performance Sundiata establishes his own domination over his universe and asserts the power that is very much part of his *raison d'être*; at the same time, he uses this moment of 'supreme effort' to fuse his human side with his supernatural spirit, thereby proving that he is the man chosen by the deities to carry out their will. The most significant change in the hero's personality is discernible in the attitude of his community towards him — he becomes the object of 'universal admiration' (p. 137).

It is during the moment of total exertion that the hero raises himself above his environment of which he was, until now, a victim. From this moment onwards, Sundiata is portrayed both as the agent of the deities and their equal, or at least one of them; no one can influence his actions: 'One could only watch them turning, watch the wheels of destiny turning: the destiny of Diata, thanks to his three ancestral totems, was to become a big man!' (p. 138). The rise of the hero from a cripple to superman dispels his people's fears that he has been betrayed by fate. His subsequent exile is hence merely a device used by the narrator, either to cast new insight into Sundiata's character, or to prepare him for his final act of triumph. As his reaction to his banishment order indicates, Sundiata knows that his exile does not hold back his movement towards his destiny:

> Diata, before retiring, looked the king sternly in the eye, then cried, in a threatening manner:
> 'You do not want us? Very well then, we shall depart far from here, but we shall return, do you hear me? We shall return!'
> The tone of his voice was so authoritative and so categorical that the king took fright. He was so terribly frightened, he started trembling all over. (p. 145)

Sundiata's temperament is typical of all heroes in the epic narrative: it indicates his impatience with a world too small to contain his bursting personality. He sees his exile as unjust because it postpones his reckoning with destiny; but, on the other hand, his banishment is taken as inevitable, as part of his growth, for it is in exile that the hero (as an agent of right and justice) confronts Sumaoro Diarrasso, the agent of evil.

It is interesting to note how the narrator controls our response towards Sundiata's opposite. Sumaoro Diarrasso is, like the hero, born in supernatural circumstances: 'But perhaps,' conjectures the narrator, 'in the womb of his three mothers the foetus of Sumaoro Diarrasso was already a wizard of the highest abilities and an exceptionally gifted magician.' (p. 166). Diarrasso has a character which is built around force and violence, a quality which he no doubt shares with the hero, but his reign is presented as tyrannical. The narrator, as we observed at the beginning of this section is not neutral; he presents Diarrasso as 'a veritable wild beast that had to be killed' (p. 177), and predicts his inevitable demise numerous times. The tyrant is described as 'he who is condemned to death by destiny'; he has committed sins against his family and the cosmos which cannot be 'effaced, that nothing can redeem' (p. 177). But, as we have already observed, secondary characters are only important in the narrative if they facilitate the hero's movement towards his objective, and Diarrosso is the man who creates a final role for Sundiata:

> The city of Niane was wiped out by Sumaoro. Therefore the Manden, without a king and in full rebellion, was seeking out its new destiny. The kingdom's soothsayers were unanimous in saying that only the prince with the triple baptismal name and the triple totem could bring the country out of chaos, restore its dignity and even extend its frontiers . . . (p. 178)

Sundiata triumphs over the forces of evil in a final re-enactment of the now too familiar theological battle between right and wrong, and the feeling we get at the end of the narrative is that the movement of the epic has followed lines which have been predetermined with a certain inevitability.

Narrative voice in *Two Thousand Seasons*

Armah's greatest qualities as a storyteller lie in the way his narrators maintain a consciousness of themselves as storytellers, and their function as the mediating consciousness between reader and writer. In *Two Thousand Seasons*, in particular, the narrator presupposes an audience which he seeks out to influence or persuade. The primary function of this narrator, as Robert Fraser has observed, is to 'enable the envisaged audience to get its bearings, to achieve a sense of direction preparatory to the supreme task of reconstruction'.[20] The practical orientation of the collective narrator in *Two Thousand Seasons* makes him a spokesman of his racial group on the one hand, and of the visionaries who make up Armah's fictional universe on the other hand. It is important to observe that, although this is a self-conscious narrator, he is never on the defensive about his role; he asserts truths which he considers common, while waging a rhetorical war against what he sees as the distortion of the African experience.

Equally important to the narrator's rhetorical scheme is the existence of an implied verbal and historical antagonist. The novel begins from a simple premise which the narrator sets out very clearly in the preface:

our history has been distorted so much that the issues must be debated in public if the visionaries' objectives are going to be realized:

> The air everywhere around is poisoned with truncated tales of our origins. That is also part of the wreckage of our people. What has been cast abroad is not a thousandth of our history, even if its quality were truth. The people called our people are not the hundredth of our people. But the haze of this fouled world exists to wipe out knowledge of our way, the way. These mists are here to keep us lost, the destroyers' easy prey.[21]

This is a summary of the key themes in the novel: the distortion of African history, the disunity of our people, and the loss of their Eden-like ideal. The narrator presents himself as our authoritative guide through the mists of time. This role demands that the narrator adopt a dual character: he is both the author of this narrative, with a prior knowledge of the events about to be recreated and a key character in the drama itself, influencing, or being influenced by, other characters and events. In this respect, Armah's narrator is *interested*, not *neutral*. But unlike Laye's griot, who serves classes and institutions, the narrative voice in *Two Thousand Seasons* is part of a group which represents ideals and goals yet to be realized. The narrator is placed at the crossroads of time: behind him lie one thousand seasons of the African experience, years which have seen the rape of the continent by foreign invaders; before him lie a thousand seasons which promise greater challenges, with the hope of a better future in the distance. What Armah promises us in *Two Thousand Seasons*, as in *The Healers*, is an incomplete fictional movement; he does not offer his readers easy salvation, for if the present movement of our history is like that of a spring flowing into the sands of the desert, which knows no giving, then we cannot find any useful lessons from this history. The past, which is dominated by predators, and destroyers, is not one of inspiration, it is infertile. Neither does the present narrative offer much hope, since the flow of time is still towards the direction of death. The narrator has learnt (through some of the bitter experiences related in the narrative) that that which cannot be changed must be destroyed. The preface is marked by a set of absolutes which remain unshakeable throughout the novel, which are indeed justified by some of the experiences the narrator and his friends undergo, so that one of the questions any reader of *Two Thousand Seasons* must address himself to is the extent to which the novel is subordinated to predetermined and fixed authorial positions.

Two Thousand Seasons is a novel of absolutes. The spring that chooses to flow to the desert has, by this choice, preferred extinction over regeneration: the nature of those who have chosen the way of death cannot be changed, so they should be abandoned to their death; in fact, disillusionment with the way of death is not necessarily a love of life. Such fixed truths are often expressed through formulaic symbols: 'it is the nature of the spring to give; it is the nature of the desert to take' (p. xii). The question then is this: What gives the narrator the authority to make such absolute assertions?

It is in the first chapter of the novel that the narrator really justifies his authority by either falling back on his knowledge of a past already lost to his implied audience, or drawing on his learned understanding of Anoa's prophecy and its implications. At this early stage in the novel, the narrator adopts a retrospective stance, highlighting events that will be dramatized in subsequent chapters. As a rhetor, the narrator is actually engaged in the art of invention, seeking out evidence to set the case he wants to defend in the novel. He is interested in setting up a body of feelings and values which are common to him and his implied audience. At the same time, the narrator acts as the custodian of his people's communal values and their mythical ethos, what he calls' 'the way'. He is also the reader's guide along a time trail that can sometimes be confusing: the man who knows the difference between the past when black people were one, and a past when they were the victims of the destroyers and predators; an agent of historical understanding who knows fully the dangers of present time:

> We wander along steep roads declining into the whitest deaths. Along these highways whatever we may do will fight against our self — how could there be other possibilities? For seasons and seasons all our movement has been a going against our self, a journey into our killers' desire. (p. 2)

The narrator's objective, then, is to convince his implied audience about the suicidal implications of their present trend. The starting point is the reaffirmation of the close relationship between the people and their ancestral lands, and the drawing of distinctions between historical movements within the continent itself, movements designed to enhance the unity and survival of African peoples, and those movements initiated by foreign interests whose desire is the fragmentation of black people. The narrator's assertiveness is brought out by his categorical rejoinder to his invisible detractors:

> This land is ours, not through murder, not through theft, not by way of violence or any other trickery. This has always been our land. Here we began. Here we will continue even after the thousand seasons' groping, though the white death sometimes openly, often

covertly, seductively now, brutally at other times, changes means but always seeks one end: our extermination. (p. 4)

Where necessarily, the narrator's ornate style gives way to plain, didactic statements of fact: 'Our fears are not of motion. We are not people of dead, stagnant waters. Reasons and promptings of our own have urged much movement on us — expected, peaceful, repeated motion.' (p. 5).

In relating the people's experiences to the needs and demands forced on them by their natural environment, the narrator is offering a rejoinder to the argument, very pronounced in colonial historiography, that the movements of African peoples have essentially been motiveless. The narrator's contention is that the movements of peoples within their own cultural orbit and natural environment are natural, and he uses numerous examples to show the rationale behind such movements and their consequences: Brafo moves with his new bride Ajoa to escape from his father's greed; the people of Antobam leave their ancestral lands in search of more fertile land. Such movements differ from subsequent ones in one important respect — they do not lead to social alienation or disruption. Before Anoa's prophecy, observes the narrator, 'our migrations were but an echo to the alternation of drought and rain' (p. 6).

The image of the pre-colonial African community the narrator is setting up is not entirely perfect: characters have natural human foibles, there are occasional disputes and tensions among the people; but so long as they are in control of their land, the natives of Anoa have developed mechanisms to rectify their weaknesses. Foreign invaders must hence bear full responsibility for the total disruption of African communities. Since the narrator is aware of the existence of a body of opinion that questions the above assertion, he moves fast to influence his readers, using the question-and-answer technique (*rogatio*) to bring his audience round to his way of thinking:

You do not understand how the destroyers turned earth to desert? Look around you. You are ignorant of death, but sleep you know. Have you not seen the fat ones, the hollow ones now placed above us? These the destroyers have already voided of their spirits, like the earth of its fertility. Barren, unproductive pillars have been driven into their brains. Then, left to walk the land, they do their zombi work, holding up the edifice of death from falling in vengeance on the killers' heads. (p. 7)

This kind of narrative technique is functional in a number of ways. First, the narrator reminds his implied audience that, although most of his story is set in the past, we are still victims of historical events.

The Parabolical Narrative

Second, the use of *rogatio* assumes broad agreement between the narrator and his audience (which is hence not entirely innocent) and some measure of empathy, underlined by the use of 'you'.

Despite the broad agreement between the narrator and his assumed audience, the former always exists above the latter, privy to historical secrets which the reader is not aware of until the narrative is almost concluded. As a character in the narrative, however, the narrator is primarily the spokesman of the group of visionaries who have borne the ideals of 'the way' through different phases of the historical process, and have witnessed the prophecy of Anoa come to pass. But what past is the narrator talking about? It is important to recognize the existence of different historical time periods in *Two Thousand Seasons*, otherwise we will fall into Lindfors' mistake of asserting that there are no conflicts in Armah's community.[22] There exists a painful past of greed and lust, a past when men were parasites living on the labour of women, a past full of so many tensions and rivalries that when the predators finally invaded Anoa, the people were weak and tired. The narrator uses various examples from history, myth and fable to illustrate these tensions and their consequences.

Characters in *Two Thousand Seasons* are primarily narrative devices who embody either the ideals of 'the way' or the forces that work against them; as agents of drama, such characters also function as archetypal figures who bring the tensions and conflicts in the community to life. Yaniba, for example, is the archetypal character of myth who helps her community to struggle against hostile nature. Anoa is a still more important archetypal figure because, in a world where the power of the gods does not affect human activities and is indeed dismissed as mere supersition, she is the embodiment of 'the way', its seer and visionary. As the narrator observes, Anoa is marked out by her insights even as a child: 'an intensity of hearing, a clarity of vision and a sharpness of feeling marked her character' (p. 14). Her spirit clamours for the highest peaks of communal endeavour, the colour of her skin typifies the beauty of her race, and her movements are like those of a goddess. In terms of rhetorical form, her prophecy is predicted action; it suggests the possible movement of the story and the probable course of its characters:

> Slavery — do you know what that is? Ah, you will know it. Two thousand seasons, a thousand going into it, a thousand crawling maimed from it, will teach you everything about enslavement, the destruction of souls, the killing of bodies, the infusion of violence into evey breath, every drop, every morsel of your sustaining air, your water, your food. Till you come again upon our way. (p. 17)

The Parabolical Narrative

Because of the moral authority with which her character is endowed, we have no option but to believe Anoa's utterance; the rest of the narrative is the dramatization of the conflicts raised in the first chapter of the novel, in general, and the structuring of the ideas contained in her prophecy, in particular.

In traditional rhetorical terms, the second chapter of *Two Thousand Seasons* constitutes the arrangement: here the experiences of the visionaries, the children of Anoa, are used to illustrate and exemplify some of the assertions posited in the first chapter. The mode of communication between the narrator and his readers is, however, sustained in an almost unchanged manner through most of the narrative. In other words, the narrator never loses consciousness of himself as a narrator, even when he is involved in the drama. He is the voice that draws our attention to the key issues in the visionaries' quest for the way; often he will even draw the reader directly into the centre of the discourse, as the first few lines of the second chapter show:

> The predators, their first appearance among us was that of beggars. Haggard they came, betrayed and lonely in their hunger of soul and body. We pitied them, for is it not a part of the way that the stranger shall be given sustenance and helped along his road? But the way is not a partial remembrance only. How was it forgotten then that it is also part of the way, inseparable from every other part, that the guest who turns contemptuous is a guest no longer but a parasite? How was it forgotten that hosts who spread a welcome for parasites prepared their own destruction? (p. 19)

This paragraph, typical of many in the novel, is a good example of how the narrator in *Two Thousand Seasons* exercises control over his materials and his readers. First, the narrator shapes the reader's reaction to the predators by casting them in a negative way; at the same time, he puts the audience on guard by reminding it that a review of the past must of necessity be complete and unsentimentalized. Second, the last two rhetorical questions establish agreement between the narrator and the audience by raising generally-accepted truths.

The reader's initial view of the predators is confirmed by their activities, presented by the narrator through a selection of episodes which are both bizarre and derogatory; sexual images and symbols expose the decadent character of the invaders which, curiously enough, is inherited by the Zombis. To a large extent, the narrator is not bothered by the credibility of the episodes he represents or describes; the descriptions belong very much to the language of abuse perfected by the late Okot p'Bitek in *Song of Lawino*. Where a certain phenomenon needs further probing, though, the narrator's voice becomes more retrospective and less dramatic: the time after the defeat of the predators, for example, is 'a time of attempts to understand the things that had happened' (p. 26).

In Armah's novels, the quest of characters is never complete if they have not learnt from their experiences. The narrative voice is hence an instrument of understanding in a situation where episodes have no real meaning except in relation to consciousness. For the people of Anoa, the period of occupation by the predators is one of trying to understand experiences their minds are not yet ready to confront:

> Our thoughts were not yet keen enough to cut the roots of schism. Against the inner causes helping our destruction, against the uncreative splitting of our people, against the turning of the one half against its twin, against this we had lost our defence. (p. 26)

The greatest effect of conquest is the birth of the slave, and the slave mentality, whose orientation is 'forever conditioned against himself, against our people' (p. 26). As a retrospective commentator, the narrator understands the motives and justifications of the slave who exists as a threat to liberation or the possibility of liberation. He is also able to pre-empt the consequences of the people of Anoa's decision to leave the slaves among them alone — 'a generosity we lived to regret' (p. 27). Left on their own, the slaves, or 'individual cripples,' regroup in the desert and return to the community with religious zeal, eager to play the role the predators trained them for:

> They came back with minds somersaulting in the potency of religious madness, bursting with a zeal to impose on their people the slavery their conquerors had first forced upon themselves. For these people's destruction was for the predators not an end in itself but a trial. After its success the victims had one aim: to help destroy their people, forcing the yet undestroyed surroundings into unison with their lost selves. (p. 29)

The Zombis and Askaris constitute a new buffer class between the people of Anoa and the predators; they are an instrument by which the conqueror can continue his conquest by default. Even when the predators have been driven away from the land, the effect of their reign of terror is imprinted on the psychology of the people; they cannot return to 'the way' without a thorough cleansing.

Because the argument set up in the preface of *Two Thousand Seasons* is repeated often in the course of the narrative, the whole novel tends to develop very slowly. But as we have tried to show so far, every stage in the rhetorical argument presents the debate in a different light. The third chapter, for example, is expository: the author examines the

alternatives open to the people of Anoa after the predators have liter-
ally wreaked havoc on them. Because the rise of a slave class has
disunited the people, they rule out any further resistance and decide to
migrate from their homes in search of a new land where they can
develop the ideals of 'the way':

> . . . we would move again . . ., move after so many thousand sea-
> sons in which our distances breathed peace, thousands of seasons
> when movement was about the desire for something to be found at
> the destination, not fear of destruction at the point of departure.
> (pp. 38–39)

Since this particular movement is central to the development of the
narrative and its meaning, the narrator takes time to explain the rationale behind it:

> Our way, the way is not a random path. Our way begins from
> coherent understanding. It is a way that aims at preserving knowl-
> edge of who we are, knowledge of the best way we have found to
> relate each to each, each to all, ourselves to other peoples, all to our
> surroundings. If our individual lives have a worthwhile aim, that
> aim should be a purpose inseparable from the way.
>   Our way is reciprocity. The way is wholeness. Our way knows no
> oppression. The way destroys oppression. Our way is hospitable
> to guests. The way repels destroyers. Our way produces before it
> consumes. The way produces far more than it consumes. Our way
> creates. The way destroys only destruction. (p. 39)

This is a catalogue of the values associated with the way: consciousness, self and group identity, and communality. Naturally, the
predators are antithetical to these values: they clamour for violence
and destruction, they are anti-consciousness.

The danger facing a mode of discourse built so much around a
pattern of images and debates that are repeated constantly is superflu-
ity. To overcome this danger in *Two Thousand Seasons*, Armah tries
to give simple symbols and images greater meaning by shifting their
contexts. In the fourth chapter, then, we have the visionaries reaching
the coast for the first time after their initiation into adulthood, and the
pervasive water symbol becomes almost synonymous with their new
way of life. The flow of the river into the sea becomes symbolic of the
harmonious life the visionaries have led as a group, but the meeting of
the river and the sea creates 'a terrible beauty' whose meaning is so
strange that they are not exactly sure what it portends. If the silent
waters of Anoa reflect the visionaries' state of innocence, then the sea
waters represent their loss of innocence, their inevitable confrontation

with a wider world. As the fundi cautions the young adults, the waves at sea symbolize a new form of violence:

> He told us of the danger of the violence of the waves. He warned us not to pit ourselves directly against the power of the waves — for that would exhaust our strength — but to watch the water's rise and fall and to rise and fall with it, conserving strength. (p. 76)

The waves' image is paradoxical, though: the waves protect the visionaries by breaking the destroyer's ship, yet bring the two protagonists together where the river meets the sea.

The ambiguity of such images as the wave and the water is reflective of the characters' state of mind. They are neither sure of what is happening around them nor definite about the meaning of Anoa's utterance: the activities of the destroyers reach them through the grapevine, embellished by fables, almost untrue; Anoa's prophecy has not yet been understood beyond its 'mere sounds'. As for the narrator, he has learnt the drawbacks of an undeveloped consciousness the hard way:

> The things that happened after the coming of the white destroyers have all been heavy, monstrous things. At the time these things were happening our understanding was still infant. And most of the events took place in such a way, at such times and in such places that their meaning was hidden from our knowledge until we ourselves had had our souls forced into the heaviest knowledge of the world the white destroyers came to make. (p. 78)

The subsequent movement of the visionaries through slavery, the middle passage, uprising and return, is paralleled by a marked growth in their consciousness; their quest for 'the way' is a trudge through a foliage of half-truths, illusions and the 'whispers of time' towards the 'hidden meaning' of their history.

It is an understatement to insist that ignorance is one of the major handicaps the characters in *Two Thousand Seasons* have to struggle against. They are naïve about the nature of the slave ship: 'In the ship's immobility and ours on it the sun burned us with a hostile intensity that made some ask again why we were kept up here away from the shade below.' (pp. 123–24). Naïvety is confounded by the strangeness of their setting, which makes any conscious reaction against enslavement initially impossible: 'We sank into a leaden silence and lived in it for days we had not learned to count, our spirits numbed with the immensity of separation from each other, separation from our land, separation from our people and our way.' (pp. 124–25). It is not until they have acquired a unified perspective that the visionaries are able to overcome their captors and continue with their search for the way.

The Parabolical Narrative

The visionaries' struggle to define and test their beliefs constitutes the narrative centre of *Two Thousand Seasons*. The crucial section in this regard is Chapter 6, when the narrator sets out to prove that his characters cannot develop a true sense of values without developing a high state of consciousness through three processes. First, the narrator takes his characters through a series of debates or 'conversations of discovery', during which the visionaries discuss their options after escaping from the slave ship. There are those visionaries who prefer to return to Anoa; others prefer to stay at the coast; and a third group opts to seek refuge in the fifth grove, 'the secrecy of seers, refuge of hearers, keeper of the utterers', where they will make 'a beginning to destruction's destruction' (p. 149). But these options are not real; as the controller of the discourse, the narrator does not leave us in doubt that only one option is tenable. The visionaries who prefer to stay at the coast are implicitly criticized for being afraid of the past and the future, but are given the benefit of the doubt; those who choose to return to Anoa are harshly attacked for their lack of foresight; the third alternative is then presented, through a common question-and-answer technique, as right and unquestionable:

> Far less than a third of us were left to drink in the meaning of the third voice. What was the meaning of this voice that called us?
> Its farthest meaning, that meaning large enough to hold all other meanings, was the meaning of the way itself: the call to reciprocity in a world wiped clean of destroyers, innocent again of predators. What was the meaning of the call to the way? Its closest meaning: the search for paths to that necessary beginning. (p. 149)

The third alternative is presented as the path to the destination promised both in the preface and invention of *Two Thousand Seasons*.

The experiences of the characters in the fifth grove, and their struggle with the destroyers and their agents soon after, are meant to exorcise their doubts, to test the level of their consciousness. The inner doubts among some of them pose the greatest dangers to the unity they have forged over a long period; despair, loneliness, and the opportunism of the lumpen element among the visionaries tempt some of them from 'the companionship of the mind' built over a period of struggle. But once the visionaries have triumphed over their own weaknesses, they become a tool of conscience in their community, involved in the 'work of persuasion, work of remembrance, work preparing paths to the way again' (p. 192). The end of this particular episode is not an achievement of the objectives set out clearly at the opening of the narrative, but a kind of beginning:

> Soon we shall end this remembrance, the sound of it. Soon it will

end. Its substance is what continues. The ending of our remembrance should give greater force to the continuation of the beginning flow in search of our way. (p. 204)

Although the task of the visionaries remains incomplete, any form of consciousness that brings us closer to the dream of the way is a stage closer to the mythical – poetic dream of total liberation, '[b]ut still, in the present what a scene of disintegration, what a bloody desolation the whites have stretched over this land! What a killing of souls!' (p. 206). The narrator's cry of anguish is an appeal to the reader's pathos from one who has seen it all happen, and remembers.

History and character in *The Healers*

The position of the narrator in relation to experience is central to the form, value and meaning of the historical novel. The narrator is the link between characters, their individualized experiences, and the larger historical event which is being dramatized in the novel. As Georg Lukacs has observed in *The Historical Novel*, 'if the historical novelist can succeed in creating characters and destinies in which the important social–human contents, problems, movements of an epoch appear directly, then he can present history "from below", from the standpoint of popular life.'[23] The narrative voice in *The Healers* functions as a link of one event to another, of moments of time, and even the pattern of ideas being explored in the novel. The narrator is also what I will call an agent of particularization. He is the person who pins the events of the story down to a particular period (the British invasion of Asante), and a specific geographic area (the stage of the drama is Esuano, situated between the Nsu Ber and Nsu Nyin rivers).

In spite of its particularization, *The Healers* shares a common vision with *Two Thousand Seasons* — a belief in the eventual unification of African peoples, symbolized by the ritual games:

> They were not so much celebrations as invocations of wholeness. They were the festivals of a people surviving in spite of unbearable pain. They were reminders that no matter how painful the journey, our people would finish it and thrive again at the end of it, as long as our people moved together.[24]

The drama is, however, set in a period of disruption when the dream of wholeness invoked by the ritual games is threatened by internal and external factors, and the narrator is keen to underline the gap between the desired dream and historical realities. 'The hard realities of our scattering and our incessant wandering had long disturbed the oneness these fetivals were meant to evoke, to remember, and to celebrate'

The Parabolical Narrative

(p. 5). The narrator's act of remembrance is characterized by a duality: memory of a past of oneness and fears of a fragmented present. In *The Healers*, as in *Two Thousand Seasons*, the narrative moves from a distant ideal, through a contemporary state of fragmentation, towards a future recapitulation of the first ideal. The community's movement away from its ideals is characterized by the changes that come over the ritual games:

> Time passed. Circumstances overwhelmed meaning. At Esuano the ritual games continued. But their meaning was no longer what it had been meant to be. In the circumstances of fragmentation, the meaning of unity had not been destroyed, perhaps. But it had been torn to shreds. (p. 5)

Throughout the novel, then, the ritual games and how different classes perceive them are an important yardstick of the people of Esuano's deviation from the ideals of their ancestors. The games also function as a medium of selectivity, setting the heroes apart from the villains, as it were. Densu, who is opposed to the competitive spirit of the games, prefers to keep out of the violent wrestling match; his friend Appia refuses to press his advantage against Kojo Djan because of the brutality this would entail. For both boys, the price of victory is too high in social and human terms; the very idea of competition enhances social divisions by setting one individual apart from the rest.

Change is a significant theme in *The Healers*. As the manipulator Ababio aptly notes, Esuano is in the throes of a moment of great change, the kind of change that comes only once in several generations. 'The world,' he tells Densu, 'has changed in ways some people do not yet understand.' (p. 29). This is also the moment when the people of Esuano must make choices about the future development of their society. What makes this moment of change particularly dramatic, though, is the introduction of an external force in the form of the white invaders; this factor makes the need for making choices more urgent, since the people themselves are no longer solely responsible for the tempo and pace of historical change. The choice, as Ababio observes in an incisive discussion of the mechanics of colonialism, is between collaboration and resistance. He has chosen the former course of action because it provides him with an easy path to power and privilege. 'If we help the whites get this control [over the land], we stand to profit from the changes,' Ababio tells Densu, trying to sell him the line of collaboration. 'Those foolish enough to go against them will of course be wiped out' (p. 31).

But Ababio also knows that resistance, which is tortuous and lacks many material benefits, has a lasting appeal to many people because it is the only guarantee against subjugation and the loss of human dignity. Densu typifies this appeal: his wish to join Damfo and the other healers in the eastern forest is almost as inituitive as his revulsion at Ababio's manipulative tactics. Because Densu is forced to make his choice by historical events, without reflecting on their implications, *The Healers* becomes, in the end, the story of his growing consciousness against the background of events central to the evolution of his community. Densu makes the appropriate choice, but until much later in the novel he does not know why he makes this choice. When Ababio asks him if he would accept power if it was offered to him, Densu has a gut feeling that he wouldn't — something inside him rejects the notion of power as an instrument of manipulation — but he is not able to articulate this feeling. Soon after, when Ababio suggests that the boy has compromised himself by listening to the manipulator's plans, the boy is confused: 'What is it I must do?' he asks his would-be mentor. Ababio's insinuations pain him, but he cannot provide a well-argued rejoinder; the only thing he is really sure about, at this stage, is that he would like to be different from Ababio and the other manipulators in Esuano.

To his credit, Densu understands the limits of his understanding; he spends sleepless nights trying to pattern his disparate thoughts, aware, like most Armah characters, that he can only be whole if he understands himself within his socio-historical context. The issues that trouble him at this stage in the narrative are not new: 'In the past they had been confusing, a mixture of feelings and thoughts, hard to grasp completely.' (p. 39). The games function as an instrument of self-search, of reaching into the heart of his community and the values that inform it:

> He did not hate the games and the rituals. But he wished he had found rituals that could have given life a better meaning. The ceremonies, rituals, and games that could satisfy the yearning inside him would have to be ceremonies, rituals, and games of cooperation, not of competition. The present games made him uneasy. Nothing they offered gave an answer to his soul. (p. 39)

An understanding of the wide gap between historical realities (as represented in the ritual games) and the yearning of the character's soul provides the key motives to Densu's thoughts and actions. He seeks to break away from the acquisitive society in the belief that there 'should be something better' (p. 40).

One of the interesting questions about character and historical movement in *The Healers* is the narrative function of Densu. Does he exist merely as a character of thought, an instrument of comprehending the issues and ideas that concern Armah in the novel, or is he the Lukacsian hero of the historical novel, who raises common experiences 'to a higher level of historical typicality by concentrating and generalizing them'.[25] The former role suits Densu better: he is not a historical figure in the sense that he does not overtly determine the movement of historical events in the same way as Asamoa Nkwanta; his contemplative nature, on the other hand, places him in the centre of the movement of thought in *The Healers.* Ordinary human experiences are seen, and acquire greater meaning, through Densu, but the problem of placing a contemplative character as the moving consciousness in a historical novel is obvious: the ruminations of this type of character, and the subsequent internalization of his experiences, are always in danger of diverting attention from the central historical conflict in the novel. Because Densu is not drawn into the centre of the historical conflict between the forces of Asante and the foreign invaders until late in the novel, his presence tends to draw the reader's focus from the major historical movement, although the character's thoughts are themselves always being drawn to the meaning of experiences. Densu's character does not, however, connote a passive role as an agent of fictionalization: he tries to transcend limited experiences, to place himself in an appropriate historical context, and fuse the past with the present and future. Ultimately, Densu is not so important for what he does, but for what he thinks: his thoughts and actions seem significant to the extent that they trigger, shape or control the readers' perception of events in the novel.

There is of course a strong conflict between Densu and his social/historical context. After the festivities in Esuano have come to a close, we find him overwhelmed by thoughts 'he did not choose to think':

> A feeling of loneliness, intense and hurtful, came over him and threatened to overwhelm him. He tried again to find escape from it in sleep, but he failed. He turned his mind upon the feeling, determined to understand it. He knew inner pain was often a sign he had not understood something happening within himself. He knew also such pain would persist until he achieved understanding. Then it would vanish as pain, becoming just a calm awareness, the feeling of reality finally understood. (pp. 48–49)

Densu's loneliness and distance from the ethos of his time has some significant bearing on the nature of Armah's narrative: because he is not socially active or involved in Esuano, he cannot, in the tradition of the prototype historical figure, carry his community with himself towards the ideal of unity which constitutes the leitmotif of *The Healers.* He is an alien in the Esuano court, repulsed by the antics of the ruling class, clamouring for 'distance, a great distance' from Ababio and his creed. But Densu's desire to get away from Esuano does not imply a rejection of the community and its values. Beyond his immediate repulsion of the manipulators is a greater desire — 'a potent urge to seek people whose ways were an antidote to all the petty poisons which were food to the men of power he had known' (p. 49). Understanding the motives behind Ababio's actions offers Densu 'good possibilities' for further growth.

Densu's meeting with Ajoa reinforces his sentimental attachment to the ideals of the healers. Ajoa's character is realized in almost mythical terms. When Densu first meets her, she is a small, fragile child, 'but already her skin had that darkness that was a promise of inexhaustible depth, and her eyes were even then liquid, clear windows into the soul within' (p. 63). The power of her eyes beckons Densu to the eastern forest 'with a strength whose source he felt within himself' and she functions as the instrument of his 'sights far beyond the present moment'. Densu's relationship with Damfo, the healer, begins through Ajoa, in an accidental way which, on closer examination, seems to reach deeper into himself and his quest for understanding:

> Deeper than the surface he could see connections; he could sense natural links between his love for Ajoa and his long search for understanding and knowledge, the search that brought him, all alive with conscious purpose, to Damfo. (p. 66)

In Armah's histories, there are natural links and historical connections, but never accidents. The inter-relationship of characters helps them illuminate one another as they move towards total understanding.

Densu's relationship with Araba Jesiwa brings out other aspects of his character. She typifies the kind of transformation that makes a person whole, and serves as an exemplar of what the healers can do to a maimed body and soul. In this respect, the role of the healer is to help a character discover his, or her, truest self; healers function as agents of seeing, hearing and knowing on both an individual and social level. Healing is hence a commitment to 'wholeness' and a special kind of universal knowledge:

> Those who learn to read the signs around them and to hear the language of the universe reach a kind of knowledge healers call the shadow. The shadow, because that kind of knowledge follows you everywhere. When you find it, it is not difficult at all. It says there are two forces, unity and division. The first creates. The second destroys; it is a disease, disintegration. (p. 82)

As Densu learns later, the healers' art goes beyond the fusion of the body and the soul, towards a larger task — 'the bringing together again of the black people' (p. 83). It is his understanding of this dimension of healing that finally convinces Densu that his life has changed. His long dialogue with Damfo brings out the range, and the full implications, of the division between his inner self and the creed professed by the court at Esuano. But in spite of the changes that come over him, he is not yet able to understand the changes taking place outside himself fully, nor find 'a welcome into the world his soul desired' (p. 83). He is trapped in a double vision which is, nevertheless, important to the movement of his thoughts; it gives him 'a strange kind of heightened consciousness of his own actions, and an increased sensitivity to the how and why of everything he found himself doing' (p. 86). From this point onwards, he feels he can question his motives and actions and 'the ways of Esuano and the wider world it belonged to' (p. 87).

The third and fourth sections of part three of *The Healers* weaken the dramatic movement in the novel considerably. After the stages of growth Densu has been through so far, culminating in his conscious decision to break from the court at Esuano, his long, discursive conversations with Damfo do not advance the narrative. Having developed the kind of consciousness which these dialogues are intended to trigger, these sections cannot be anything but redundant. They are at best an interlude between the main narrative (Densu's movement of thought) and the trials and tribulations of Asamoa Nkwanta, which constitute a tertiary narrative.

There is an extent to which Densu's journey back to Esuano (which leads to his capture by Ababio and the death of his friend Anan) defeats the purpose of Damfo's dialogues. After the death of Anan, Densu's relationship with the real world becomes imbalanced, his body is detached from his mind, and the universe that imposes itself on his consciousness is described as 'chilly' with 'no refuges he could recognize' (p. 131). This state of mind eventually verges on despair. Even when Ajoa's beckoning — 'it was a beckoning that said life should be worth surviving for, in spite of everything' (p. 133) — helps his doubts. Densu's mind does not acquire its equilibrium for a long time. Thoughts of death come over him with a devastating effect because they seem to indicate the futility of a life which only a while ago offered him great possibilities. What worries the youth after the discovery of Araba Jesiwa's body is not whether she is alive, but if her body contains conscious life. 'I don't understand anything,' he tells Damfo later; and this inability to understand is symptomatic of his lack of the kind of inner thought which, in the healer's view, can come only from absolute belief.

There is, of course, another source of power in *The Healers*: the natural environment, especially the trinity of the river, the forest and the sky, which symbolizes the wholeness of life. When he goes out into the fields of Praso to work for the female healer Nyaneba, Densu's

mind is moved back to an infantile past when he could barely understand what was happening around him. Contrasting that time of limited knowledge and now. Densu has hopes and fears for the future,
especially a future that transcends a single lifetime. The healer's ultimate objective — the unification of all black people — is terrifying in
its magnitude, he reckons:

> The vision was terrifying even in its hopefulness, but with greater
> understanding the terror of his own impotence dissolved in the
> knowledge that if he worked well he would be part of the prepara-
> tion for generations which would inherit the potency that should
> bring people back together. (p. 159)

Densu's fear of death remains central to his growth as a character.
Death is a powerful image that looms in his mind, sometimes driving
him into reckless actions (such as when he goes to the rescue of the
victims of the Asante ruling class's ritual murder). In the later situation,
he does not reflect on the viability of his actions; 'all he was aware of
was the unbearableness of what was happening' (p. 167). Damfo predictably sees this irrational act as a weakness which Densu must overcome in his quest for full understanding, for the healers operate in a
world in which the best ideals are not always realized. Thinking,
Damfo argues, can reconcile Densu to what is real and attainable.
When Densu asks the healer whether being realistic (accepting that we
cannot stop men from being brutes because there is an element of evil
embedded in their characters) means there is nothing we can do to stop
the manipulators, Damfo replies that we have to be reflective first, 'find
out what can be done, how to do it, how long you'll have to work in the
direction you see, and how paltry the results will look to your impa-
tient eyes' (p. 171). Densu's consciousness thus demands focusing. As
the water-gazing ritual makes it clear to the youth, the image he has of
himself and the world is confused; he can only attain full growth of
mind by entering into relationships with people of a similar orientation, which will carry him beyond present historical realities (and
imperfect images) to a utopian world yet to be born.

Ironically, since the character's mind seeks symmetry with a world
that is 'not yet entirely present' (p. 229), full consciousness cannot be
achieved, In this respect, as Densu learns when he returns to Kumase
with Asamoa Nkwanta, doubts have a positive effect on the growth of
character. The boy is no longer troubled by his ignorance: 'Knowing he
would be seeing and hearing things he had never in his life heard nor
seen gave him a keen, anticipatory thrill.' (p. 236). This new state of
mind prepares the youth for his painful exodus through the Asante
country after it has been devastated by the colonial invaders. Hope

does not, however, preclude his sense of bitterness — 'He had seen so much destruction' (p. 297) — which is contrasted with Ababio's dance of joy, typifying, at least in the present time, the triumph of brutal power, manipulation and the slave mentality. But the ending of *The Healers* is deliberately ironic: Ababio is destroyed by the forces he so eagerly served, while the black people brought from other parts of the world to help the colonizer dance a new dance. The dance signals the end of an era, but as the old healer Ama Nkroma notes, it also offers new possibilities for the healers' ultimate dream — the unity of all black people.

One of the major criticisms made against Armah's characters is that they are too elitist, that they stand above the very people they are supposed to serve. This is ironic in view of the motive force behind Armah's novels: the novelist believes that individuals are only relevant within the group. As we have already observed, Densu does not find his true self until he is co-opted into a community that shares the ideals of wholeness which he finds lacking in Esuano. And yet the youth, like the other healers, is set apart from the mainstream of the community to which they minister, isolated like high priests. These characters are saintly, aloof, solitary, misunderstood. They do not seem to live the lives of common men. The most apparent contradiction in a novel like *The Healers*, which lays claims to historicism, is the detachment of its characters from the vagaries of common experience. Characters like Densu and Damfo are thus cast more in the fabular mode than the historical one; they are righteous men, and as Walter Benjamin has aptly noted, 'the righteous man is the advocate for created things and at the same time he is their highest embodiment'.[26]

There is one character who comes closest to functioning as a conventional figure of the historical novel in *The Healers* — the Asante general Asamoa Nkwanta. He is the symbol of a power which can be enhanced for the advancement of historical ends, but when we meet him, he is a rebel against such power. He is relevant to the historical movement in the novel not because he functions as any kind of central consciousness, but as a character whose personal feelings and grievances affect the future of his people. He thus offers the healers what Damfo calls 'great possibilities'. The general's search for understanding under the tutelage of the healers is an attempt to distinguish between a power that is committed to the self-aggrandizement of one social class, and another form of power that is in the service of communal ideals. 'I've spent my life fighting to make Asante strong,' Nkwanta tells Damfo. 'If the past was a time of unity, then must I see my entire life as wrong?' (p. 177). By the time he resumes his command, the general has been made to understand the difference between the needs of the Asante nation and its royals. The irony, of course, is that once he leads the Asante army into war against the colonial invaders, the general finds himself serving royalty once more. In this respect, his function as a healing force is limited; he is a servant of an infrastructure and class that stands in the way of African unity, a point confirmed by Nkwanta's betrayal and irreversible despondency.

Finally, a comment on Armah's treatment of the colonial invader Glover in *The Healers*. Glover is a real historical figure who is cast in a mock-heroic mode to expose the vanity of the imperialist. He stands for, and represents, racist arrogance and paternalism which, together with greed, are the motive force for the colonial invasion of Africa. In the following mock-heroic presentation of the colonial frontiersman at work, the presumptions of the invaders of Asante are indicted as much as the man himself:

> Here indeed was the white man in action. Glover the godlike. Glover the white man descended among the black people to do magnificent wonders. The white man looked immensely happy, fulfilled this Saturday morning. Why should he not be? Here he was a god, a god among mere men, a beloved father-god among infant-men.
>
> Here he was, the white man who was known to have travelled through the lands beside the river even greater than the Firaw, the lands of the long, immense Kwarra to the east. Here he was, the man who had gone along the mysterious Kwarra and done what no mortal white man had ever hoped or dared to do even with help from thousands. Here he was, the man who knew himself a true magician when it came to getting black people to fight other black people for the profit of white people. Here he was, the one white man who could boast he could tell black men to do anything, no matter how difficult, and they could do it immediately out of love for him, Glover. Here he was, Glover the father of the Hausa fighters, protector of loving slaves. Here he was, Glover, he whose word was alone sufficient to inspire thirty thousand black men to rush delirious into the open jaws of death. Here he was, Glover the glorious, boastful one, Glover for-every-five-black-men-any-white-can-raise-I-can-raise-will-raise-hundreds. Here he was, the great white man. No need for the searcher to tire himself searching. Glover was visible as the sun this Saturday morning. (p. 255)

The satire here is double-pronged: it is directed both at Glover and his pretentiousness, and those blacks who allow themselves to be used as tools of pacification. In the next essay, I will try to show how irony and satire have been used by the African novelist to examine and indict the colonial situation.

Notes

1 *Myth, Literature and the African World* (Cambridge: Cambridge University Press, (1976), p. 110.
2 'Armah's Histories', *African Literature Today* 11(1980), p. 90.
3 'Usefulness,' Benjamin tells us, is a general characteristic of story telling. But this usefulness is not fixed: 'The usefulness may, in one case, consist in a moral; in another, in some practical advice; in a third, in a proverb or maxim.' See *Illuminations*, ed. with an introduction by Hannah Arendt, trs. Harry Zohn (Glasgow: Fontana/Collins, 1973), p. 86.
4 *Illuminations*, p. 87.
5 'Cultural Diplomacy in African Writing' in *The Writer in Modern Africa*, ed. Per Wastberg (Uppsala: The Scandinavian Institute of African Studies, 1968), p. 59.
6 *The Guardian of the Word* (Glasgow: Fontana/Collins, 1978), p. 15. Further references to this edition will be cited in the text.
7 Ayi Kwei Armah, 'African Socialism: Utopian or Scientific?' *Présence Africaine* 64 (1967), p. 8.
8 *The Transformation of Allegory* (London: Routledge and Kegan Paul, 1974), p. 11.
9 See 'The Soul of Africa in Guinea' in *African Writers on African Writing*, ed. G.D. Killam (London: Heinemann, 1973), p. 160.
10 *The Radiance of the King* (Glasgow: Fontana/Collins, 1965), p. 7.
11 'Camara Laye' in *A Celebration of Black and African Writing*, ed. Bruce King and Kolawole Ogunbesan (Zaria & London: Ahmadou Bello & Oxford University Presses, 1975), p. 117.
12 *Transformation of Allegory*, pp. 14–15.
13 See 'The Soul of Africa in Guinea', p. 161.
14 *Transformation of Allegory*, p. 11.
15 *Transformation of Allegory*, p. 7.
16 See 'The Soul of Africa in Guinea', pp. 159–161.
17 See his preface to *The Guardian of the Word*, p. 25.
18 Northrop Frye, 'Literature and Myth' in *Relations of Literary Study: Essays on Interdisciplinary Contributions*, ed. James Thorpe (New York: MLA of America, 1967), p. 27. Daniel Biebuyck makes the same point: 'The content of the epic constitutes an encyclopedic inventory of the most diverse aspects of a people's culture. There are direct and indirect statements about the history, the social institutions, and social relationships, the material culture, and the system of values and ideas.' See 'The Epic as a Genre in Congo Oral Literature' in *African Folklore*, ed. Richard M. Dorson (Bloomington: Indiana University Press, 1972), p. 267.
19 *The Epic in Africa: Toward a Poetic of the Oral Performance* (New York: Columbia University Press, 1979), p. 66.
20 *The Novels of Ayi Kwei Armah: A Study in Polemical Fiction* (London: Heinemann, 1980), p. 104.

21 *Two Thousand Seasons* (London; Heinemann, 1979), p. 1. Further references to this edition are cited in the text.

22 Lindfors criticizes Armah's 'Garden of Eden' myth as untenable, an example of 'xenophobic oversimplification'. See 'Armah's Histories', p. 90.

23 *The Historical Novel*, trs. Hanna and Stanley Mitchell (London: Merlin Press, 1962), p. 285.

24 *The Healers* (London: Heinemann, 1979), p. 4. Further references to this edition are cited in the text.

25 *The Historical Novel*, pp. 285–86.

26 *Illuminations*, p. 104.

2
The Biographical Narrative

The Irony of Experience in Mongo Beti's
Mission to Kala, Ferdinand Oyono's *Houseboy*
and Cheikh Hamidou Kane's *Ambiguous Adventure*

In this chapter we are concerned with the form and meaning of three novels from francophone Africa which have been acclaimed as some of the most incisive and personalized examinations of the colonial situation and its ramifications on both the social and individual levels. Some of the key issues in Mongo Beti's *Mission to Kala*, Ferdinand Oyono's *Houseboy* and Cheikh Hamidou Kane's *Ambiguous Adventure* are not radically different from the central themes in the works of Laye and Armah discussed in the previous essay. In general, the central contextual movement in these novels is the transition of the African community from a tranquil communal past to turbulent neo-colonial times. But whereas Armah and Laye work with broad social canvases and large, sometimes indeterminate periods, the world of Beti, Oyono and Kane is more confined. Often, the latter novelists are concerned more with the effects of colonialism on the individual's psyche than the strictly historical and ideological ramifications of this process. I am not of course suggesting that ideology and history are insignificant in the three novels I am going to discuss in this essay. What needs to be stressed is the nature of the relationship between individual characters and the historical backdrop, which in these novels is markedly different from anything we have discussed so far. The obvious point to note here is how the main characters in these novels move from their limited experience towards larger social themes, and from being isolated from their societies to becoming submerged in the issues of their time.

The journey from self to community is a process of education. The movement from home into the world of colonialism is, for these characters, a confrontation of the realities of a European imperialist culture and its *raison d'être*. But just as not all grown-up people are mature, characters who have undergone the processes which Medza, Toundi and Diallo experience are not necessarily enlightened. The incompleteness of the hero's education in the *Bildungsroman* was best summed up by Hegel in his *Aesthetics*, where he observed that the end of the character's apprenticeship was essentially the formation of a proper perspective towards the world:

> . . . the subject sows his wild oats, educates himself with his wishes and opinions into harmony with subsisting relationships and their rationality, enters the concatenation of the world and works out for himself an appropriate attitude.[1]

As I will try to show in my discussion of *Mission to Kala*, this kind of hero strives to draw the whole world into his limited consciousness, but at the end of his adventure he accepts the impossibility of this assimilation. The development of an appropriate attitude is really the hero's awareness of what we will call the irony of experience.

The three novels we are going to discuss are bitter denunciations of the culture of colonialism and its material base. And yet Beti, Oyono, and particularly Kane, have been influenced by the ideology of Negritude, whose advocates are not famous for taking an uncompromising stand against colonialism and its instruments of domination and exploitation. To what extent, then, do the three novels reflect the distinctive style and vision of Negritude? As Abiola Irele has shown in a recent study of African literature, the ideology of Negritude is founded on a general sentiment — the fact of being black in a colonial situation; it differs from other modes of nationalism in its concern with colonialism as 'a community of blood'.[2] In the tradition of Negritude, the anti-colonial writer concerns himself with his characters' inner state of being and existence; he is armed with an absolutist ontology which assumes the totality of the black race and its uniqueness. This kind of writer is inevitably obsessed with the identity of the black man within a colonial situation whose mechanisms present themselves as emblems of white supremacy. The colonized black man's search for his true sense of self is mediated through what Senghor would call a spiritualist vision. Senghor and other scions of Negritude thus see their works as a significant contribution to the continuing search for a black epistemology: the principle underlying their anti-colonial works is that, in the colonial situation, there is a 'spiritual maximum-being' beyond the materialistic ideology that motivates most forms of nationalism. For Senghor, this maximum spiritual being — expressed through 'the overflowing of the soul, of the intelligence and of the heart' — is the ultimate goal of most human activity.[3]

The above assumptions affect the nature of the narratives in several ways. The three novels we are going to discuss in this essay have a strong biographical element: Beti, Oyono and Kane present the lives and times of characters seeking self-understanding, against the back-drop of an oppressive culture, from first-hand experiences. On another level, however, these authors would like to present their personal experiences as typical. The disillusioned African assimilados in *Mission to Kala*, *Houseboy*, and *Ambiguous Adventure* often posit themselves as symbolic figures, illustrations of what colonialism has done to a whole generation of Africans. In formal terms, the novelist tries to structure his novels in such a way that the experiences of the individual character illuminate the creed underlying the colonial domination of Africa and its consequences.

Cheikh Hamidou Kane speaks for the other novelists when he says that there are several parts in *Ambiguous Adventure* 'which are my own history and there are certain things which are not mine, but the history of the people of my generation who are placed in the same historical and intellectual situation as myself'.[4] There is another dimension, however, in this relationship between the colonized intellectual and his history — the white colonizer. The white colonizer exists both as a character and force in these novels, and as part of the implied audience. In spite of their hostility towards the agents of colonialism, Beti, Oyono and Kane are involved in an act of cultural diplomacy: they strive to restore to their people a sense of dignity, and at the same time convince the colonizer that these people are worthy of this dignity. Kane's case is, again, typical. He sees his novel as a private mediation on his position as a cultural half-caste, and a response to the political demands of a time when we had 'at some point, to make ourselves felt'.[5]

Irony and the transmutation of character in *Mission to Kala*

Many critics have assumed the completeness of Jean-Marie Medza's journey at the end of *Mission to Kala*, implying that he comes out of his adventure with a full understanding of himself as a colonial. Although Abiola Irele concedes that Beti's novel ends in 'a situation of total disorientation in which it is impossible to discern any positive perspective', he still insists that Medza's journey 'acquires the value of a quest ending with self-discovery and inspiring a final gesture of self-affirmation'.[6] It is perfectly true that Medza assumes the unity of the experiences he is recreating in *Mission to Kala*; the novel, in the tradition of the biography, thus covers a temporal sequence 'sufficiently extensive to allow the emergence of the contour of life'.[7] There is, however, a marked distance between the vision that assumes this unity (the vision of the adult Medza, the endless wanderer) and the perspective of the young man who returns from his mission to Kala to discover that he has grown too big for the small world prescribed by his father.

There are, in fact, three perspective in *Mission to Kala*. First, there is the self-conscious, often parodic vision of Jean-Marie, the failure who adopts the quixotic illusion of a conquistador to escape from realities he cannot deal with. Second, there is the semi-critical perspective of the young man who is tamed and educated by the 'primitive' people of Kala; this is the character who, in the course of the narrative, is transformed from an uncritical medium of colonial platitudes into an interpreter of the culture of the colonized. Finally, we have the perspective of Medza, the adult implied writer of this novel, who gives past experiences some kind of pattern.

At the heart of the biographical narrative is a conscious process of self-interpretation. Medza's writing of his past experiences is motivated by a desire to understand what he has become after his mission to Kala. And although this novel is a dramatization of events as they occur, memory is an important ingredient in Beti's narrative technique. Medza's adult life is psychologically conditioned by memories of his youth, especially that one period in life when he thought he had discovered his natural bent. But as I will try to show in the course of this discussion, there is no suggestion in the novel that Medza ever resolves any of his contradictions as a cultural half-caste, nor the larger social problems that affect him as a colonized African. Even years after the event, Medza's recollection of the mission to Kala is determined not by one linear, informed vision, but by an impulse which, on his own admission, 'absorbs every mood: romantic nostalgia, indifference, the lot'.[8] The reader is left in no doubt about the degree of the youth's maturity after Kala; and yet Medza is not able to master his impulses and deal with the emotions of his youth in a rational, sustained manner. The narrative itself is evidence of the character's ability to pattern his past experiences, to link his impetuous 'slave' past with the rebelliousness that turned him into a perpetual exile, but I do not think he has developed the psychological reinforcement necessary to deal with this or any phase of his life. He concedes that most of his youth has been melted by what he calls 'the scorching light of maturity', so that the mission to Kala is only memorable in the vague sense that it was the turning point in the hero's life.

The Kalan experience refuses to vanish from Medza's mind: its recapitulation is a belated attempt to understand the past so that the exile can situate himself in the future. If the biographer of this life is aware of the incompleteness of the mission to Kala, as I will insist below, remembrance is a quest for completeness in the future. Medza asks his reader (in the prologue) whether there was some special significance in his Kalan adventure which he has failed to unravel, and we cannot but conclude that this is a rhetorical question: he would not be replaying this portion of his past if it was not central to his growth. And yet the question is very pertinent as far as the implied reader is concerned, for this narrative is addressed to Medza's former friends and classmates, and to his generation of Africans in general. The character hence assumes that his narrative will only be meaningful if he can draw this implied readership into the orbit of his private experiences by typifying them, and thus, learn lessons from the mission to Kala and its consequences. Medza assumes that his readers have travelled along a similar road, as it were, and that 'this fragment' of his life will stir 'some familiar echo' in their minds. In other words, the cultural context of *Mission to Kala* is one shared by both the implied author and reader. At the beginning of the adventure, for instance, Medza addresses himself specifically to a former classmate, whom he asks to remember where and how the mission began, and tries to link his own disappointments in life with his generation's 'betrayal' by the colonizer. After this invocation to the spirit of his old classmates, Medza moves the narrative back in time and presents the events as they really happened.

There are a number of explanations for this fast shift in time. Beti is trying to deal with two problems associated with temporality in the autobiographical narrative, i.e. the effectiveness of temporal transfer in a work where past, present and future influence each other almost interchangeably; and the question of hero–reader identification. Some theorists of the novel have argued that a novel in the first person rarely succeeds in fusing the illusion of presentness in the novel and the immediacy of the dramatized action, that the reader is not able to identify with the experiences of the hero because they seem remote in time, part of a past that is no longer part of his personality. The essence of this kind of novel, insists A.A. Mendilow, 'is that it is retrospective, and that there is an avowed temporal distance between the fictional time — that of the events as they happened — and the narrator's actual time — his time of regarding those events'.[9] Beti tries to surmount this problem by minimizing retrospection in *Mission to Kala*. He only draws on his protagonist's adult perspective where he thinks the young protagonist's actions should be placed in context, or linked with his future development as a character. The structural irony in the novel is constructed around young Medza's ignorance of the consequences of the actions he takes, and his later awareness of this irony.

Young Medza is at his most vulnerable when he is not able to discern the ironies of his experiences. At the beginning of the novel, for instance, he is a victim of his self-delusion and Beti's sense of parody: there is a mock-heroic element in the protagonist's resolution to pass his time profitably during his vacation, and his struggle to control what he calls his evil genius. The solemnity of his tone — 'Unfortunately, my evil genius had decided to give me no respite, I was to be forced to admit his absolute powers over me' (p. 2) — is undermined by the comic presentation of the old bus struggling in the mud as a great event in itself. During this stage in his life, Medza's perspective is an admixture of his tendency to see things in terms larger than life, and his colonial education. The former exposes his superficiality; the latter highlights the limitation of his education, a theme we will return to later in this section.

At this point, we have to observe that the autobiographical narrative has a perspective which is prescribed by the presence in the novel of a hero who is not merely the major character in the drama, but also the historian of his own thoughts and actions. Because the 'I' figure cannot see beyond his own experiences, he is trapped in his own knowledge and understanding; he cannot, by the same token, analyse his unconscious reactions to these situations. This is why Beti uses irony as an instrument to expose the nature of Medza's character which the hero himself is not aware of. Medza's 'Homeric argument' with the Greek bus driver and his self-appointed role as his people's spokesman are a case in point. We find him defending the French colonial system in what he calls 'logical terms' which amount to nothing but humbug, yet he is adored by the other passengers in the bus as a learned game cock. This is of course the most consistent irony in the novel: considered as a failure by the colonial system, Medza is hailed by his people as an authority on the culture of colonialism. One of the most problematic questions in the novel, though, is whether Medza puts on the mask of the educated colonial to cover up his failures, or is actually locked up in the myth of civilization as presented to him by his colonial educators. As a character, he exhibits an engaging sense of playfulness; as a narrator, he is very unreliable in relation to the norms he sets for himself and also in terms of his potential deceptiveness.[10]

As we have already intimated, Medza's role as a conscious narrator is conditioned by his need for self-enhancement. This involves a certain degree of self-manipulation which the reader is not always aware of; the narrator's act of self-interpretation involves both self-revelation and deception. Early in the novel, in particular, Medza is keen to manipulate the reader in such a way that his failure in the colonial school will appear minimal compared to the ignorance of the villagers of Vimili. As a man who has travelled, one with a condescending view of those who have not been closer to the colonial masters, Medza thinks Vimili's claims to 'main town status' are laughable. But far from making the hero more admirable to the reader, Medza's over-reliance on platitudes only makes us aware of his prevasive sense of failure. He may spite Vimili and its people for their self-delusion, but as the village appears closer to Medza, his psychology is dominated by his awareness of the consequences of this failure, especially 'that dreaded interview' with his father. As he soon learns from his aunt, Amou, failure is the matrix by which his village and family will henceforth judge him. 'All we knew in the village,' Amou tells Medza, 'was that you'd been failed' (p. 6). Such uncomplimentary statements are important in balancing Medza's usually inflated sense of himself; sometimes they remind him what other people actually think of him, and this exposes his deceptiveness as a witness to his own actions. After casting himself as a game cock at the beginning of his journey home from school, for example, he is later forced to admit that his reputation in school 'had really been low, one way or another' (p. 5).

For most of the early part of the novel, however, Medza's self-characterization is not marked by any measure of modesty. His attitude towards other people is the best indication of how a colonial education has not only alienated him from the mainstream of his community, but also reinforced his slave mentality. His view of his family and neighbours is only minimally determined by any real contact with, or knowledge, of them; he sees them the only way his colonial masters have taught him to see them — in a patronizing and derogatory manner, which is reflected in his language and style. Although he is to undertake the mission to Kala (the only meaningful mission he has ever undertaken) as a representative of his kinsman Niam, Medza knew 'this chap' about 'as well as I did any of my cousins, which means hardly at all; (p. 7). Implicit in this assertion is the protagonist's acceptance of his ignorance, but it is when he tries to explain marital relations among his people in a stilted anthropological way that we realize the full extent of his alienation:

> Still, you must bear in mind that normally these affairs are restricted to members of the same tribe; they are, so to speak, a family affair. The seriousness with which any adultery is regarded is in exact proportion to the physical or social 'distance' between the two tribes — those, that is, of the cuckolded husband and the intrusive lover respectively. (p. 8)

Medza has already adopted the role his education has predetermined for him: he is an outsider among his own people; the posture he adopts is that of a detached explorer reporting his findings to his home audience. As an explorer, Beti's character is not content with surface observations, hence his unsuccessful attempt to explain things in a way that brings out his learnedness. And yet, this failure without any real knowledge of his people and their traditions is sent on a mission to Kala to retrieve Niam's wife and restore some happiness in his life. This is the first major irony in the novel.

The Biographical Narrative

But Beti's sense of irony is marked by its dialectical, paradoxical and recurrent nature. There is never a single object or subject of this irony at any one time in the novel; it is an irony which attacks everyone and everything almost simultaneously. When the people of Vimili decide to send Medza to Kala, he is the only one who objects because he is aware of the false premise on which this choice was made. 'Now the one thing I wanted to do at that precise moment was to sleep off my little set-back,' he observes. 'Not the sleep of the just, perhaps, but the sleep of a failed exam-candidate, which was almost as well-deserved' (p. 11). The more the villagers highlight Medza's qualifications for the mission to Kala, the more he is reminded of his failure in school and his loss of confidence in himself. In such moments, he falls on philosophical catch-phrases which act as a bulwark against the villagers' assumptions, and yet reinforce their view that he is the right man for the mission. Medza knows that Niam's performance is a meaningless charade based on the kind of misunderstanding he should be protesting against, but he has the audacity to pass the villager off as Demosthenes. He knows that old Bikololo is overstating the point when he declares that young Medza just needs to make a trip to Kala and 'put the fear of God into those savages' (p. 13), but since he will not own to his inabilities in public, he falls back on 'the arsenals of my Cartesian dialectic'. The mode of ironic play in this scene is made more tantalizing by Medza's uncle when he provides the reasons why Medza has not yet comprehended what he is being asked to do:

> Why not explain the situation to him a bit more clearly? You can't expect him to understand it just like that, can you? Use your common sense. He's away at school most of the time. He only comes home occasionally. The real surprising thing is that he's still familiar with our tribal wisdom and customs at all. (p. 14)

Without realizing it, the old man has presented the reader with two good reasons why Medza should not undertake the mission to Kala: he does not understand his role within the social group as a whole, and is no longer in touch with his people's traditions and customs. Old Bikololo does not, however, see the issue in the same way: Medza's 'special thunder' does not derive from his understanding of his people's customs, but from his certificates, learning and mastery of the French language.

At this stage in the novel, Medza's situation is typical of the marginal would-be assimilado in the colonial situation: he has neither mastered the colonial instruments of domination fully (hence his failure in school), nor has he retained any real knowledge of his people. And yet his failure is conceived as a kind of knowledge by those of his countrymen who exist on the fringes of the colonial situation — he is elevated to a position of leadership on the basis of his pseudo-assimilation. We must remember, though, that Medza does not undertake the mission to Kala because his kinsmen succeed in convincing him that he is the best man for the job. He simply allows his imagination to run away with him:

> The ploughed student was transformed into a brigand chief, a pirate, a true Conquistador. My fancy settled firmly for the Conquistadores. The thought of being adopted into this exclusive clan elated me: my promotion had indeed been rapid. (p. 16)

It is this kind of self-inflicted irony that distinguishes Medza from both Toundi in *Houseboy* and Samba Diallo in *Ambiguous Adventure.* While the last two characters experience the rigours of the colonial situation with great earnestness (and suffer for it), Medza's attitude towards his adventure, and his function within it, is never more than half-serious. He is constantly involved in play-acting; even when he lurches into his fantasies, he is aware of their unreality.

Indeed, Medza builds his life around the balancing of illusions and his half-education. Sometimes such illusions mask his real function as a colonial who has been elevated to the position of 'the coming man of the tribe' (p. 18). There are even moments when he subordinates realities to illusions. He certainly finds it easier to deal with fictionalized realities, but in many cases it seems to me that he is aware of his role as a fictionalizer. On the way to Kala, to mention just one of many examples, the land appears to him as a 'vast panorama lying open to my future exploitation', but he knows that this is not true, hence the interjection that this 'vast panorama' was 'for the most part restricted to a seedy vista of tree-trunks lining the road, oppressive in the most literal sense' (p. 20). It is my contention, then, that critics who take Medza to be a picaresque hero merely accept his illusion of a quixotic adventurer as the real basis of the protagonist's character. This inevitably leads to another error of critical judgement — the assumption that Medza's emotional, intellectual and psychological journey begins from a position of innocence.[11]

To insist that Medza embarks on his journey with a far greater understanding of his position than many critics are willing to acknowledge, and with a fuller ability to discern illusion and reality, is to underscore the incompleteness of his enlightenment at the end of the novel and its effect on the nature of the narrative. Why do I think the question of Medza's education in the course of the novel central to its overall meaning? The question has to do with what I consider to be the motive of every biographical narrative — the transformation of the hero in the course of the story. In the words of Jean Starobinski, it is 'the internal transformation of the individual — and the exemplary character of this transformation — which furnishes a subject for a narrative discourse in which 'I' is both subject and object'.[12] If the internal transformation of Medza does not appear as dramatic as his prefatory note would make us believe, this has much to do with his playfulness. This is not to say that he does not grow or change. As an observer of life in Kala, and as a player in the drama of social life in the village, Medza has to keep on changing his position vis-à-vis his subjects. New experiences help him dispense with some of his illusions even when the Kalans reinforce them. We can hence judge Medza's growth both by the increasing seriousness of his tone and his involvement with the Kalans.

The potential conflict between earnestness and game in Medza's transformation is apparent in his initial reaction to the Kalans. On his arrival in Kala, Medza strikes the pose of an explorer and uses anthropological clichés to explain the villagers' ball game: 'It was not the setting which struck me so much as the primitive savagery which animated every participant in the business' (p. 2). His condescending tone is only matched by his arrogant assumption that he knows the power behind his cousin's tussle with the giant ball. But these are the views of Medza, the play-actor, the temporary conquistador who is not responsible for his actions and utterances. The real Medza's reaction to Zambo's power is 'instinctive fear and repugnance . . . perhaps because the weak are naturally terrified by strength, and therefore come to hate it' (p. 24). Zambo's heroic demeanour reminds Medza of the unreality of his conquistador pose: 'All I wanted to do at that moment was get back into my ordinary clothes and put my best suit away in the wardrobe again' (p. 24). The 'ploughed student' wears ordinary clothes; the suit belongs to the non-existent 'coming man of the tribe'. And because Medza is perhaps the only person in the novel who knows the real man behind the conquistador image, he ultimately finds resentful the adoration of the Kalans, who seem to venerate him for the things his family spite him for not acquiring ('my learning and diplomas' [p. 27]).

But if Medza is not entirely ignorant of himself at the beginning of his mission, his cousin Zambo and the people of Kala are his first real teachers and, in narrative terms, instruments of his ironic dénouement; they enhance his self-interpretation. Kala is important in another respect, too: it is a social terrain with such depth and breadth that the outsider must grow to understand it. As the protagonist observes, Kala gives him 'a simultaneous impression of savagery and security': 'it was as though one was on a small island, pounded by heavy seas and yet safe from drowning' (p. 30). And yet Kala begins by reinforcing Medza's false image of himself: Zambo refers to his cousin as 'the good fortune' that has befallen Kala, and is proud of the fact that 'he sits on the same benches as the sons of white men' (p. 31). At this stage, we realize that the Kalans are locked in the colonial myth probably more than Medza. Their situation is comically tragic in one respect: while the hero knows that their image of him is false, the Kalans seem to believe it. Medza objects, silently of course, to Zambo's 'brisk little comedy' because he knows that his cousin is earnestly touting the image he is trying to reject, but he soon realizes that it is only by accepting this false image that he can cover up the insubstantiality of his character, which his ironic attitude has exposed. At the same time, the adoration of the Kalans seems to justify Medza's patronizing attitude towards them. The Kalas, though, are not entirely ignorant of the real Medza.

We cannot, of course, tell for sure whether many Kalan believe the things they say about Medza because they have no independent perspective of their own in *Mission to Kala*. In other words, the only view of the Kalans we have is that effected through Medza's perspective. The complexity and ambivalence of the ironic mode in this novel is largely due to the absence of an implied author independent of the hero, since Medza is both the instrument of irony in the novel and its determinant. But as we have suggested, irony in the biographical narrative is more than an element of characterization — it is a mode of introducing a different point of view in a situation where our attitude towards the hero is determined by a narrator who is also the main character in the narrative. Ambivalence tends to augur well for this kind of irony because it implies different possibilities of meaning. As Muecke has observed, the reader's sense of irony involves the ability to see ironic contrasts and to shape them in the mind, to identify the ironic intent and to activate the ironic situation. In this respect, notes Muecke, real meaning in irony 'is meant to be inferred either from what the ironist says or from the context in which he says it; it is "withheld" only in the weak sense that it is not explicit or not meant to be immediately apprehensible'.[13] A salient aspect of Beti's ironic technique in *Mission to Kala* is the exposition of Medza's limitations through the making of pronouncements and assertions whose ironic nature he (Medza) is not aware of; this is how he inflicts irony on himself. For instance, responding to his lionization by the Kalans, Medza makes the following, almost innocent observation: 'I had become a kind of universal mascot for the whole of Kala: not only a strange animal, but an animal that they liked to examine at close quarters and hear roar, or howl, or bray, or whatever.' (p. 47). Superficially, his assessment of the situation is correct. On another level, however, he is an animal, not to be admired, but to be used, for without his knowledge some Kalans are enriching themselves at his expense.

However, to the extent that Medza is the chief instrument of irony in the novel, he is not entirely oblivious to his ironic situations: he is aware of the basic misconception around which other people have built their perception of him; he also knows that his acts and gestures are an impediment in his search for an essential truth about himself. His city/ school image is a barrier against any real involvement with the people of Kala:

> If only they wouldn't treat me just as a 'scholar' and nothing else! I'd have given all the diplomas in the world to swim like Duckfoot Johnny, or dance like the Boneless Wonder, or have the sexual experience of Petrus Son of God, or throw an assegai like Zambo. I wanted desperately to eat, drink and be happy without having to bother my head about next term, or such depressing things as revision-work and orals. The very least I could do was to conquer my fear of women — even divorcées. (p. 59)

This affirmation is Medza's frist step in dispensing with his illusions; it is the first act in his quest for what he calls his 'natural bent'. But he also knows that his colonial education acts as a barrier against any hopes of being assimilated by Kala.

> Without being aware of it, I was no more than a sacrifice on the altar of Progress and Civilization. My youth was slipping away, and I was paying a terrible price for — well, *what?* Having gone to school, at the decree of my all-powerful father? Having been chained to my books when most children of my age were out playing games? (p. 63)

Medza's growth can at least be judged by his awareness of his typicality: he becomes experienced enough to place himself in context, to admit his previous inexperience and to reject the role his father has created for him. By presenting an alternative way of life, Kala enhances Medza's self-undertanding.

But the Kala that releases Medza from his past also overwhelms him; he finds himself living in circumstances which he has not been trained to meet, and he is no longer capable of understanding his own reactions. When the chief imposes her daughter on the young man, the latter finds himself acting against his better judgement: love, a newly discovered emotion, puts him in a state of mind which he had never anticipated, so that he can no longer see or ignore what he calls the 'inevitable pattern of my real existence' (p. 160). At the end of his mission, Medza discovers that Kala has provided him with the instruments by which he can reach into the deep layers within himself. But has it taught him how to deal with real-life situations in his own world, the world determined for the youth by a powerful, domineering father?

Medza's father is a colonial agent per se: he runs his home according to the totalitarian rules imposed on the rest of the country by the imperialist power that governs the country. It is important to understand the political function of the father figure in *Mission to Kala* to appreciate why Medza associates him with the forces that have stultified his growth. The boy's image of his father is that of a relentless oppressor: 'he was like a bloody policeman — no, worse: a private dictator, a domestic tyrant' (p. 164). More significantly, Medza's father uses the colonial school as an instrument to control his son and bend his nature to his greedy purpose. The parallel between the paternal dictator and the colonial system of oppression is uncanny: Medza's father imposes his will on the family through violence — 'his naturally violent personality took everything to extremes' (p. 165) — and tries to sacrifice his son to a system of oppression whose goals he believes are right. In the latter regard, Medza's father is presented as an archetypal figure — 'the quintessential Westernized native of one generation back' (p. 166).

Although Kala has paved the way for his revolt against the tyranny of his father and the colonial cultural machine, Medza cannot turn his rebelliousness into anything more than the kick of a colt that 'can't bear the restraining authority of the bit' (p. 164). He thus ends up being an aimless wanderer, searching for the elusive dream represented by the purity of his would-be wife, Edima, but always aware of its unattainability. In retrospect, the protagonist sees his journey to Kala as a quest for 'many truths' —

> not least among these was the discovery — made by contact with the country folk of Kala, those quintessential caricatures of the 'colonized' Africa — that the tragedy which our nation is suffering today is that of a man left to his own devices in a world which does not belong to him, which he has not made and does not understand. (p. 181)

And yet in spite of this discovery, Medza's knowledge of himself must remain incomplete for two reasons. First, he is not in a position to do anything to change his situation and must therefore keep on searching for ideals which are lost to him forever. Second, while both the Kalans and the colonizers have made their world to suit their needs, and hence understand the motives for their actions, Medza belongs only partially to either world, and must live with his half knowledge of both. This is what it means to be an exile.

Irony and perspective in *Houseboy*

Irony and satire pose a number of specific critical problems in Ferdinand Oyono's acclaimed study of the psychological and physical destruction of the colonized African. Some critics have argued that the relationship between the colonizer and the colonized in *Houseboy* — which is set in stark black-and-white terms — rests on what John Reed has called 'comic misunderstanding'.[14] Reed goes on to assert that Toundi's vision is presented to us naked, and is more dangerous than tragic 'because his disillusioned innocence lacks dignity and the forces which he brings down on himself are themselves sordid'.[15] Abiola Irele, on the other hand, contends that although the novel is written in a satirical vein, it is 'far removed from comedy in its total effect'.[16] Another critic is disturbed by the nature and dimension of Oyono's satire: 'Once he starts to be amused at those on the receiving end of injustice,' observes Leonard Kibera of Oyono's satire, 'he finds it difficult to stop and begins to contrive situations to accommodate his largely one-sided satirical vision'.[17]

Whether we consider the satirical vision in *Houseboy* misdirected or not, we have to examine some of the assumptions underlying its usage. I would like to suggest that the problem of interpretation in Oyono's novel has much to do with the instrumental use of irony in the novel, i.e. its function as an aspect of satire, and its use as a element of meaning. The crucial question here has to do with Toundi's development as a character, since he is the only perspective in the novel: does he inflict satire on himself, or are his ironic pronouncements just offshoots of his naïvety? In a novel like *Houseboy* where the author is entirely absent from the narrative, only irony enables the reader to mediate the consciousness of the character, the subject and object of irony, and to relate it to the larger world. The subject of this kind of novel is what Georg Lukacs calls 'a free object of free irony'.[18] He seeks a new perspective of life through the establishment of a connection between the independent parts of his life and the totality of the world that inflicts suffering on him. In *Houseboy*, where there is no other narrator except the writer of the diary, the experiences which the hero undergoes cannot be mediated by his adult perspective. The diary form does not allow for retrospection: the writer of the diary concentrates on his immediate experiences because he has no knowledge of either the consequences of his actions or the ending of his narrative. The relationship between his inner and outer world can only be ironic, since hindsight is necessary for any organic or conceptual linkage of different phases of the protagonist's life.

As we will see in Toundi's violent encounter with the agents of colonialism, the hero of the diary does have a subliminal awareness of the implications of his actions; in Seymour Chatman's view, he can only have apprehensions and make predictions, and 'suspense derives from our curiosity about whether or not his hopes or fears materialize'.[19] It can also be argued that since a diary is written for the author's eyes only, it's success or failure does not depend on the reader's response. And yet the reader of the diary ultimately functions as an active agent in the story: he does not affect the arrangement of the author's materials, his editorial role being limited, but his reading of the diary is a re-enactment of the protagonist's life. Through our reading of Toundi's diary, then, we try to make his suffering in the past appear close to us in the present. Even when the diarist is writing for his eyes only — the diary form always assumes a private discourse — his work is only meaningful if it can affect the reader's way of seeing things.

The reader of Toundi's diary sets the illusions which the protagonist's experiences help him dissipate: he presents himself as a Frenchman and minimizes the violent relationship between the colonizer and the colonized by shrugging it off as 'a little strain'.[20] But this contented colonial lives under the violence inherent in the process of colonial pacification, and he recognizes a common fate in Toundi's death. Ironically, the contented colonial and the brutalized victim of colonial violence have no identities of their own — they are recognized merely as subjects of a colonial power. Like *Mission to Kala*, *Houseboy* is a novel about one man's quest of his identity as a victim of the colonial culture of silence and violence. The diary is the answer to the question which Toundi poses to the reader before he dies: 'Brother, what are we black men who are called French?' (p. 7). What began as a quest for assimilation into the colonial set-up has become, for young Toundi, a nightmare. Note that the reader of Toundi's diary had never confronted the question of his identity before: 'I was young then and thoughtless,' he observes, 'I felt myself grow stupid.' (p. 7). But young Toundi knows who he is now, and fully understands the consequences of his previous actions: 'I am a Maka . . . I'd have made old bones if I'd been good and stayed at home in the village' (p. 7). Toundi accepted his death sentence the moment he decided to abandon his family and seek sanctuary in Father Gilbert's church; as the reader of his diaries notes, the boy was 'already rotten before he died' (p. 8).

We have already seen how Medza's journey in *Mission to Kala* leads to a better perspective of the world and enables him to make certain choices, the consequences of which he can live with. In contrast, Toundi's movement away from home is retrogressive. He develops a better understanding of the relationship between master and slave in the colonial situation, but his character does not grow in any positive way. Once he has entered the world controlled by the colonizer, he begins life without the benefits of previous knowledge or experience. He must begin to understand everything anew without either the foreknowledge of a Samba Diallo *(Ambiguous Adventure)*, or the hindsight of a Medza. His identity is created for him by others. Father Gilbert, his 'master and benefactor', teaches him a few lessons in history as seen from a colonial point of view: his ancestors were cannibals, and the white man is the agent of civilization. And we have to remember that Toundi is not forced to leave his parents' home: he is attracted by Father Gilbert's trinkets on the eve of his induction as a full member of his group, and seeks to make his break from his people irreversible. Not even his mother's pleas can force the boy to turn back. He sees in Father Gilbert's motorcycle the intoxicating symbol of a new way of life which offers great promise:

> I was going to learn about the city and white men and live like them. I caught myself thinking I was like one of the wild parrots we used to attract in the village with grains of maize through their greediness. My mother often used to say, laughing, 'Toundi, what will your greediness bring you to . . .?' (p. 17)

Toundi is aware of his fatal flaw — his greediness — very early in his encounter with the colonizer, but he does not try to pre-empt actions that might lead to the kind of tragic fate that overtakes him at the end of the narrative. There is an extent to which he is only partially responsible for his actions: he seems hypnotized by the promise of a new life which colonialism holds out for him, and he allows himself to be led to his tragic end with little or no resistance. He has no sense of importance: he relates to events only as they occur and cannot place his experiences in a context of significance in which every act has it possible consequences. He allows Father Gilbert to shape him into whatever the priest wants, and is proud of his passiveness. Toundi sees nothing demeaning in being treated like a pet animal, and mistakes the priest's patronizing attitude for love and fondness; his greatest moments are when he is presented to visiting whites as Father Gilbert's 'masterpiece'. He takes a long time to develop the kind of perspective that will enable him to make value judgements that are based on a clear understanding of the motives behind his, and other people's, actions.

But Toundi's identification with his masters is never absolute: the more he becomes familiar with the colonizer's culture, the more the boy is able to distinguish illusions from realities. When Father Vandermayer brings five more women to the Sixa, Toundi makes a significant aside: 'If they knew the work there is waiting for them here, they would have stayed behind with their husbands' (p. 18). He sees his knowledge of what actually happens in the Sixa as an important weapon, and uses his *igün* perspective to expose the false assumptions of which he was, and continues to be, a victim. Toundi is certainly never totally naïve. But can we ever be sure about the range of his knowledge? What appears to me to be the character's unawareness of his ironic vision confuses the reader, who cannot but rely on Toundi as his authorial guide. Denied any real knowledge of an irony of which he is largely the victim, Toundi cannot rely on this irony to correct his false perception of the colonial relationship. When Father Gilbert dies, Toundi makes a statement which is symptomatic of the problem I have in mind: 'I have died my first death' (p. 23). This statement can mean a number of things: Toundi has either identified with the priest so closely that part of himself has gone to the grave with his master, or the death of his protector has left him exposed to the violent colonials, as subsequent events prove. A statement like the one above can also be simply ironic. When Toundi becomes the Commandant's 'boy', he describes himself as 'the king of dogs' (p. 24), and the reader is left wondering whether this is just a bland description of the boy's position in the hierarchy of colonial house servants, or a deeper understanding of his role as the potential scapegoat. The problem with this kind of irony is that the victim does not recognize it, and the reader is not aware of its ironic nature until it is confirmed by subsequent events in the narrative. Because he has not developed the resources to discern the irony of the experiences he undergoes, Toundi cannot use it to expose the contradictions in the colonial *esprit de corps.* In this respect, Olusola Oke's contention that Oyono's total reliance on Toundi's point of view 'leads to the absence of direct irony in the novel'[21] is valid. Irony is only direct if its subject and object recognize it.

When we move into Toundi's relationship with the events that destroy him, we find ourselves in another problematic area. There are two hermeneutic problems here: First, to what extent are Oyono's characters involved in, and responsible for, their tragic fate? Irele has argued that Oyono's characters are 'denied any initiative and, faced as they are with a rigid situation, can only be passive sufferers of their fate.'[22] Oke describes Toundi as a spectator in the life that unfolds before him, but insists that he is an important spectator because he is always at the scene of the action, and neither hides what he sees, nor exaggerates what he observes.[23] The second problem is hinted at by Gakwandi, who accredits Toundi with a more active role, and asserts that he is disillusioned with the colonial process and hence rebels against it. Does Toundi embark on any conscious rebellion against the colonial order?

We have already suggested that there is a degree of rational choice in the steps Toundi takes, especially in his initial rejection of home and tradition. But we have also contended that he does not seem responsible for his actions once he has entered the world of the colonials: his understanding of, and participation in, the events that shape his life seems marginal; the notion of rebellion in Toundi's actions is very limited indeed. Characters such as Sophie understand the working of the colonial machine and its agents better than Toundi, but they do not contemplate revolt. Sophie only seeks crevices in the colonial set-up which she can exploit for her own purposes: her acceptance of her place within the colonial hierarchy is different from Toundi's acquiesence; she does not step out of bounds, and when she does, she flees for her life, leaving Toundi to bear the consequences.

As Toundi becomes disillusioned with the colonial relationship, he begins to appreciate the values of the tradition which he rejected: he seems to believe that, by asserting the moral superiority of his people's culture, he can resist the physical and psychological violence directed at him by the Commandant, his wife and her lover. The discovery that the Commandant is not circumcized is ostensibly a weapon the boy can use against his master:

> I was relieved by this discovery. It killed something inside me . . . I knew I should never be frightened of the Commandant again. When he called me to bring his sandals his voice sounded far-off. I seemed to be hearing it for the first time. I wondered why I used to tremble in his presence. (p. 33)

Although such discoveries reinforce the boy's moral centre, they cannot constitute modes of revolt in themselves. Even Toundi's sense of moral superiority is false: Toundi ran away from home before his circumcision, and we have no evidence that he has undergone the rituals of initiation. Most gestures of revolt which he makes are internalized, ineffective, and the Commandant continues to call the shots to the very end. And yet the boy is destroyed because he refuses to yield to the psychological demands of the colonial tradition; his sense of moral superiority is, therefore, evidence of a certain measure of triumph over the Commandant.

There is, however, possible confusion between Toundi's naïvety and Oyono's satirical vein. For most of the novel, Toundi is cast in the role of the *ingénu*, an ironic *naïf* who makes observations and asks questions without understanding their full import. The best example of this function is Toundi's relationship with Madame. He is infatuated with her at first sight: he sees her as the spirit that gives him a new lease of life after Father Gilbert's death, and the mere touch of her hand electrifies him:

> My happiness has neither day nor night. I didn't know about it, it just burst upon my whole being. I will sing on the banks of the river, but no words can express my happiness. I have held the hand of my queen. I felt that I was really alive. From now on my hand is sacred and must not know the lower regions of my body. (p. 56)

But Madame is the cause of Toundi's death, hence the ironic implications of his words. He does, in fact, have a presentiment about

Madame's attraction: her looks warm his heart, but he is afraid of himself. He sets his hopes high, nevertheless; he genuinely identifies himself with Madame, so that when she begins to live out her life as a colonial, the boy is really hurt. 'She had forgotten I was there,' he writes about her changed attitude. 'As I write these words I feel even more unhappy than I felt at Father Gilbert's funeral (p. 56).

In the final analysis, Toundi is destroyed because he neither yields to the demands of the colonizers fully, nor revolts against them completely, once he has exposed the insubstantiality of their moral claims. He never really goes beyond his immediate situations to understand the rules of the game, so to speak; he seems to believe that his exposure of what he deems to be the weaknesses of the whites is enough to protect him from the wrath of the Commandant and M. Moreau. He thus finds himself in a situation where he willingly acts as the liaison between Madame and her lover, yet adopts a patronizing attitude towards the couple. 'These whites,' he observes of the lovers, 'once their passions get a hold, nothing else matters' (p. 75). The boy's detached tone is false: he has invested some measure of sentiment in the affair, as if he was the other lover in this romantic triangle. When M. Moreau visits Madame when the Commandant is at home, Toundi is furious with himself. And he wonders, 'How can I get rid of this ridiculous sentimentality which makes me suffer over matters which have nothing whatever to do with me?' (p. 82).

Eventually, Toundi learns to read the world of the colonial when he witnesses Ndjangoula beating prisoners under the supervision of M. Moreau in a foreplay of his own treatment later in the novel. This time, the boy sees the colonial system for what it really is — violent, ruthless and racist:

> I could not hold myself from shaking as I watched. It was terrible. I thought of all the priests, all the pastors, all the white men, who come to save our souls and preach love of our neighbours. Is the white man's neighbour only other white men? Who can go on believing the stuff we are served up in the churches when things happen like I saw today? . . . (p. 87)

Toundi's movement away from total acceptance of the colonial creed, his scepticism and doubt are real enough, but unsatisfactory for a number of reasons. He does not look back on his past and reappraise his previous attitudes in the face of new experiences. The diary form of *Houseboy* eliminates a reflective distance from the narrative. Categorical statements against the colonial order constitute Toundi's only visible mode of revolt, but they are undermined by his inexplicable attachment to the characters responsible for his demise.

Toundi places himself in a situation where he cannot accept his subservient role any more — in Madame's words, he creates the impression that he is doing a houseboy's job 'while waiting for something else to come along' (p. 65) — but he cannot reject his servitude because it holds the promise of success in the colonial situation. Toundi tells Madame that his goal in life is to lead the same kind of life as the whites; this implies a rejection of what the French woman sees as his preordained rank. The boy seems to believe that, having gained insights into the social life of the whites, he can choose those aspects of it which he thinks will better his lot, while leaving out the more decadent aspects of the colonial culture. He is, however, aware of the limits of his range of choices; having seen through certain things in the colonial régime, he cannot stop 'living through them over and over again' (p. 88). The other Africans know when to stop knowing too much about their masters because they know that the whites will never respect their humanities; in the cook's words, 'you are only alive to do their work and for no other reason' (p. 100).

Toundi's greatest illusion is possibly his naïve belief that his knowledge of the affair between Madame and M. Moreau has admitted him into the whites' inner circle. Kalisa puts it more aptly when she tells the boy the reason why the Commandant is harsher on him than the adulterous wife and her lover are. She compares Toundi to the eye of the witch 'that sees and knows', and adds that a 'thief or any one with a guilty conscience can never feel at ease in the presence of that eye . . .' (p. 115). As the eye that sees into the dirty life of the colonials, Toundi hence functions as what Kalisa calls the 'representative of the rest of us':

> because you know all their business, while you are still there, they cannot forget about it altogether. And they will never forgive you for that. How can they go on strutting about with a cigarette hanging out of their mouth in front of you — when you know. As far as they are concerned you are the one who has told everybody and they can't help feeling you are sitting in judgement on them. (p. 116)

Madame and the Commandant are reconciled for the sake of the colonial *espit de corps*, and Toundi is sacrificed on the altar of colonial solidarity.

It is not fair to argue that Toundi's vision is so naked that he cannot avoid the kind of lethal knowledge that costs him his life: having rejected his native culture for the new dawn of colonialism, he is right to insist on undressing the world of his masters fully; as soon as he has been condemned on the altar of colonial solidarity, he knows he must pay the full price for this choice. Toundi suffers his fate silently for two reasons: he knows he cannot return to the people he abused when he decided to side with the colonial masters; he also sees his silent suffering and punishment as a means by which he can triumph over the Commandant, Madame and M. Moreau. What one finds cannot be explained in *Houseboy*, then, is not so much Toundi's suffering of his fate, or his inability to break away in good time, but his vague belief, against all existing evidence, that the colonials can treat him as one of them, can allow him to share in their secrets. His violent death is Oyono's way of disabusing the assimilados' faith in the redeeming powers of any system of exploitation.

The irony of experience in *Ambiguous Adventure*

Kane has called his novel a récit, defined by Abiola Irele as 'a narrative that is barely removed from a direct reporting from fact'.[24] But to term *Ambiguous Adventure* straight reportage is to ignore some of the nuances of discourse in the novel, particularly the convergence of views between the implied author and the protagonist. This convergence allows author and character to mediate the key themes that inform the narrative in a lucid, discursive manner, and allows for a balance between telling (diegesis) and showing (mimesis). In other words, the author and character divide these two functions between themselves. Debate is a key stylistic and thematic element in the novel. As we will see later, the whole discourse revolves around a debate on life, death and change, which is not only concentrated in character, but is played anew at every stage of the narrative. *Ambiguous Adventure* has a basic unity of mood built around the principle of sorrow. As the implied author notes in one of his rare moments of intrusion into the narrative, happy memories are excluded from the narrative because they 'would bring gaiety to this recital of which the profound truth is wholly sad'.[25] Samba Diallo's memory is hence geared towards the remembrance of sorrow, but the novel is itself retrospective only in a minimal sense: it is a story remembered by the implied author, but lived out by the protagonist. The use of a second-person narrative voice allows the author to explore not only the subconscious thoughts of his main character, but to compare and contrast his (i.e. the protagonist's) vision with that of the other characters. By allowing himself scope to draw other strands of thought into the centre of his narrative, Kane is thus able to explore in a broad context the ambiguities that haunt Samba Diallo.

The limited presence of the implied author allows the real author to take the reader out of his protagonist's mind and to see him and his world from the vantage point of a character who takes a different view. This contrast of thoughts, views and motives creates the irony of the novel, which is not the irony of tone or narrative method, but of the larger universal experiences the characters are caught up in. At the opening of the novel, for instance, the irony of the moment is built around a simple fact — Thierno, the teacher, has punished Samba Diallo, although the boy knows his sacred verses; the teacher is demanding total perfection from his student, and an acknowledgement of the need to suffer and the mastery of this suffering. The teacher, a symbol of life and divinity in the village, is associated here with pain, suffering and death. The irony of this situation is further confounded by the characters' and the author's unawareness of its existence. The teacher sees suffering, pain and death as elements that enhance life, and thus cannot recognize the distance between his beliefs and practices. Neither can Samba Diallo recognize the irony, since he has been taught to believe fervently in the teacher's creed and not to question it. The word for which the boy suffers martyrdom is emblematic of this acceptance: 'It was a word which demanded suffering, it was a word come from God, it was a miracle, it was as God Himself had uttered it' (p. 4).

The reader is the activator of the irony in the novel because he is the only one who is able to develop a dual attitude towards the main players in this drama about death and suffering. The author posits himself as a partial observer keen to balance all the views expressed by his characters and cannot be relied upon to expose their contradictions. In another sense, the implied author neutralizes the reader's temptation to take sides too early in the debate. As the teacher metes out his punishment and we watch Samba Diallo's little body 'burning with fever', we are forced to sympathize with him; but when the boy accepts and justifies his suffering, our attitude towards the teacher becomes less than overtly hostile. The word for which the boy suffers is presented as a force that edifies him: 'The word of God flowed pure and limpid from his fervent lips. There was a murmur in his aching head. He contained within himself the totality of the world, the visible and the invisible, its past and its future.' (p. 5). In this respect, the author functions as the controller of the reader's sentiments towards the characters. He justifies the teacher's harshness as necessary for the boy's wellbeing, while underlining Samba Diallo's shifting, unformed view of the world. If the teacher appears singular and dogmatic to the reader, it is because he represents forces which are deeply entrenched in the traditions of the Diallobé; the threat of the encroaching forces of historical change have forcibly put the teacher on the defensive. In contrast, Samba Diallo is caught between the forces of traditionalism on the one hand, and the world of colonialism on the other hand; he is the 'gift from God' that will be central in determining the future direction of the Diallobé. At this moment of change and choice, Samba Diallo must learn to do things which, in the Most Royal Lady's words, 'we hate doing, and which do not accord to our customs' (p. 41).

The Biographical Narrative

The implied author also functions as Samba Diallo's guide through his ambiguities. As an agent of debate and discourse, the young boy has not developed the understanding and experience needed to place those ambiguities in context, and the author intrudes into the narrative when it is necessary to link the boy's limited actions to their larger implications. For example, Samba Diallo is overwhelmed by the French school, but only the implied author knows what this institution really means to the colonized:

> The new school shares at the same time the characteristics of cannon and of magnet. From the cannon it draws its efficacy as an arm of combat. Better than the cannon, it makes conquest permanent. The cannon compels the body, the school bewitches the soul. Where the cannon has made a pit of ashes and of death, in the sticky mould of which men would not have rebounded from the ruins, the new school establishes peace. The morning of rebirth will be a morning of benediction through the appeasing virtue of the new school. (p. 45)

This is the implied author's view of the process of colonization: he sees the school, the cultural wing of imperialism, as permanent and profound because it changes the nature of the colonized community almost irreversibly; and yet the process of pacification which accompanies colonial conquest has a redeeming quality — it establishes 'peace' among the colonized.[26] Even with his limited understanding, Samba Diallo does not share the implied author's faith in the redeeming features of imperialist domination, nor the benedictory qualities of the French school. His doubts are reflected in his elegiac tone and demeanour.

The burden Samba Diallo has to bear, indeed the source of his sorrow and the cause of his eventual death, is that of reconciling two divergent individual and communal needs: he must mediate between the forces of traditionalism and modernization, and also divide his inner self between the demands of life and death. The boy's growth as a character is reflected in his ability to understand both paradigms. He shares a theological belief in life after death. He is, in fact, convinced that the teacher of the Diallobé and the traditions he represents will remain 'more than a love and memory' after their death. At the same time, however, Samba Diallo is not sure about the master's effectiveness after death:

> The teacher, Samba Diallo was thinking, has a body so fragile that already it seemed to be scarcely there. But, in addition, he has the word, which is made of nothing corporeal, but which endures. He has the fire which runs like flame through the disciples and sets the

heart aglow. He has that restless concern which has more force than his body has weight. The disappearance of this body — could it negate all that? (p. 58)

This allegorical presentation of the meaning of the teacher and the word has some interesting corporeal implications. One of the questions the protagonists in *Ambiguous Adventure* are concerned with is whether the culture and traditions of a people (their soul) can outlive the expropriation of the nation's material base (their body). Samba Diallo foresees the possibility of the word surviving without the body, and, as he sees it, the challenge facing him in the French school is to prove that he can be physically assimilated into the culture of the West without yielding the Diallobé spirit in him to European materialism. The feeling that comes over him on the night of his Koran recital is that 'the Diallobé would not die in him' (p. 66). But the night that marks his full initiation into the Islamic tradition is also the night that signals the end of the teacher's epoch. During the night, Samba Diallo glorifies the stellar world of his fathers, but the voice that springs from the depths of the ages, within him, is that of 'a long love which today was threatened' (p. 67): 'For a long time, in the night, his voice was that of the voiceless phantoms of his ancestors, whom he had raised up. With them he wept their death; but also, in long cadence, they sang his birth.' (p. 67). What then, is the nature of Samba Diallo's death and rebirth?

Samba Diallo's father, the knight, typifies some of the most obvious contradictions of synthesizing the Western and African traditions. He represents the uneasy attempt to draw a line between the material and spiritual effects of colonial domination, which is at the heart of the debate on change in *Ambiguous Adventure*. To his credit, the knight has a deep insight into the irreversible effects of colonial domination, at least on the cultural level. The knight believes that his son's enrolment into the French school marks the completeness of the foreigner's victory. He presents this conquest or 'solar burst' in negative terms as 'the midday burst of an exasperated civilization' (p. 62). It is not merely the realization that his own family has succumbed to the temptation of the West that makes the knight suffer so much, but the knowledge that his people's race 'headlong into the future' is a suicidal 'blind contest' (p. 62). The Diallobé cannot be anything but victims of Western civilization because they neither control its movement, nor have they been party to its evolution. The culture of the West, argues the knight, is built around the dissociation of spirit from matter, whereas that of his people is a fusion of both. But however much he appreciates the ontology of the Diallobé, he knows that his people are no longer free and can maintain their traditions only at the cost of their material progress.

The Biographical Narrative

Underlying the knight's argument is a key negritudist concept — that culture is a balance between man's divine state and his milieu. In Senghor's ontology, therefore, being is identified with life, which is defined by the individual's consciousness of the sacred. The African, contends Senghor, 'communes directly with nature and with the elements, and through these, with the absolute fountain-head of vital force, of God himself.'[27] We can discern the measure of Samba Diallo's alienation from this vital force by the degree of doubt he develops about the cosmic unity between matter and spirit. In the Glowing Hearth, he did not see any contradiction between prayer and life — although it was apparent to the reader, the agent of irony in the novel, that prayer emasculates the bodies of those who indulge in it — the young man is prompted by his Western education to view life and prayer as cosmological oppositions. He sees the presence of God in his father as emasculating. 'All the profane exuberance of life must certainly be burnt out of this man by his profound prayers,' he observes at one instance. 'My father does not live, he prays . . . (p. 86).

We have to remember that Diallo has been brought up in a cosmology that allows no room for doubt in matters of faith; in his father's words, the act of faith is an 'act of allegiance': 'There are those who believe and those who do not believe; the division is clear' (p. 93). In the negritudist *ouevre*, modes of thought and belief which do not owe allegiance to a spiritual being cannot enhance life.[28] This is the standard the knight sets for his doubting son before the boy goes to university in France.

Once in France, Samba Diallo finds himself at the centre of an educational system which is built around scepticism; he also has to live in a culture that no longer takes religious faith for granted. This is one reason why he wears his religion as a cloak, or as M. Martial observes, waves his profession of faith 'like a banner in the wind' (p. 103). His religion is not so much an affirmation of his Diallobé spirit, but an instrument of struggle against forces which he believes, rightly or wrongly, are undermining the foundations of his belief. The nature of the youth's transformation has already been hinted at by the knight, who sees in Pascal's journey from doubt to belief an inevitable miracle which ends like an act of grace. But if Samba Diallo's fate in the West is inevitable, he is not consciously aware of this inevitability; he is only able to reflect on the possibilities of his fate. Will he return home or will the Occident assimilate him entirely? This is a question which Diallo ties to his metamorphosis and the possibilities it offers:

It may be that we shall be captured at the end of our itinerary, vanquished by our adventure itself. It suddenly occurs to us that, all along our road, we have not ceased to metamorphose ourselves, and we see ourselves as other than what we were. Sometimes the metamorphosis is not even finished. We have turned ourselves into hybrids, and there we are left. Then we hide ourselves, filled with shame. (p. 104)

Despite his concern with the metamorphosis of the colonized intellectual, Diallo never leaves his spiritual source, except in a physical sense. He never seems to be an integral part of the situations in which he finds himself in France or elsewhere; he is either forced into such situations by other people, or is forced to adopt particular stances by circumstances. If he is taken to the Glowing Hearth at the request of the teacher and into the French school at the insistence of the Most Royal Lady, then we have to ask ourselves whether he ever functions as an agent of his own free will.

Samba Diallo's spiritual instability must, of course, be compared with the dogmatism of the teacher. The latter is an epitome of absolute faith, 'old, emaciated, withered and shrunken by mortification of the flesh' (p. 6). His character is driven by a deep spiritual force, propelled by his devotion to labour, unshaken by the kind of doubts that plague some of his pupils. If prayer has strengthened the teacher's spiritual centre, it is also a gesture of extreme pain, and a symbol of his acceptance of this pain as an instrument of transcendentalism. Prayers are not only a form of communication between the teacher and his supreme deity, but also an example of his fortitude: 'Old age and rheumatism had made of this gesture — still repeated twenty times a day — a grotesque and painful exercise which the watchers, moved and breathless, were following' (p. 109). This observation by the implied author assumes a degree of sympathy with the teacher's choice; in any case, no criticism is directed at this agent of traditionalism, some may say reaction, by the narrator.

The authorial position in *Ambiguous Adventure* is one of sympathetic observance. The implied author seems particularly sensitive to Samba Diallo's struggle with his ambiguities within the cultural context of a civilization that is hardly sympathetic to his quest. In Paris, Diallo is tempted to heed the call of the teacher and withdraw from the corporeal arena of 'their confused desires, their weaknesses, their flesh' (p. 117). He tries to convince himself that he is solely responsible for his actions. But this is not, of course, true, for Diallo is the Diallobé's cultural frontiersman in the West. His momentary recognition of a part of himself — what he calls 'myself' — which is not necessarily a possession of the Diallobé, does not mark any real change in his total vision. After all, Diallo sees his adventure in the West not so much as a break with, or alienation from, the culture of the Diallobé, but a significant shift in the way he perceives it. As he confesses to Marc, he does not see things fully in the West — he never feels anything 'directly':

> It seems to me that in coming here I have lost a privileged mode of acquaintance. In former times the world was like my father's dwelling: everything took me into the very essence of itself, as if nothing could exist except through me. The world was not silent and neuter. It was alive. It was aggressive. It spread out. No scholar ever had such a knowledge of anything as I had, then, of being. (p. 139)

As in the case of Medza and Toundi in the novels we examined in the previous two sections, Samba Diallo's adventure in the West is a quest for an understanding of himself as a colonized African.

Because of the highly discursive nature of Kane's novel, characters in *Ambiguous Adventure* are only relevant as illustrations of some of the key themes informing the narrative. One of the major criticisms made against this novel is Kane's subordination of his characters to his philosophical attitude. Rarely is Samba Diallo presented or defined in terms of himself and his needs as an individual; he often exists as the physical and verbal expression of philosophical dictums, even when these are larger than his personality. When Diallo is discussing the idea of God with his father, to cite one example, the peace that reigns in his heart is also heavenly peace: 'Samba Diallo was not existing. There were innumerable stars, there was the earth chilled anew by the coming of night, there was the shade, and there was the simultaneous presence.' (p. 96). Similarly, captured in the entrancement of prayer, the teacher is not merely an old man who has subordinated his corporeal self to his faith, but the embodiment of total faith. His whole character has no meaning except in relation to the 'word' — as he puts it, 'my voice claims to be swollen in the universal outflowing' (p. 110). Even interpersonal relationships exist to express the multiple aspects of the debate on change and modernization which is the leitmotif of the novel. Such relationships are either fused or juxtaposed to create an association of ideas rather than persons. For the teacher, who believes that the exaltation of man cannot be the basis of faith, the Diallobé can have some hope if he can turn Diallo into 'such a man as the country's great past has produced' (p. 21). Opposed to the teacher's creed is the Most Royal Lady, who epitomises 'everything that 'the country treasured of epic tradition' (p. 19), and yet believes that, if the Diallobé are to survive, they must go to the colonial schools and learn how to 'join wood to wood'.

The teacher's stand on the colonial school is categorical: it cannot function as a preserve of the Diallobé's past because the learning it will offer is also a form of forgetfulness. The question he poses in this regard is crucial to the whole debate about change in the novel: 'can one learn *this* without forgetting *that*?' (p. 31). The Most Royal Lady counters this debate by an equally significant assertion: if the Diallobé do not go to the new schools, how will they live in a world which they no longer control? Her contention is that the teacher's regimen is already out-dated because, in the new world in which the Diallobé are victims rather than masters of their own destiny, her people will have 'to do with a world of the living, in which the values of death will be scoffed at and bankrupt' (p. 24). So whereas the teacher is absolute in his belief that the colonial school cannot teach the Diallobé the values and meaning of a spiritual existence, the Most Royal Lady is adamant in her insistence that her people will have to learn from their conquerors how to survive:

> We must ask them: we must go to learn from them the art of con-quering without being in the right. Furthermore, the conflict has not yet ceased. The foreign school is the new form of the war which those who have come here are waging, and we must send our élite there, expecting that all the country will follow them. It is well that once more the élite should lead the way. (p. 34)

The knight takes the debate further when he sees his son as the bearer of a common destiny between the colonizer and the colonized. His argu-ment is that 'the era of separate destinies has run its course', but 'from our long and varied ripenings a son will be born to the world: the first son of the earth; the only one also' (p. 73). His son is hence a pledge to what the Negritudists would call a universal civilization.

The assertion that the Diallobé can indeed contribute to the building of a universal civilization rests on the assumption that the colonial masters and their victims can relate on the basis of equality. And yet, as the teacher very well knows, the Diallobé must yield the basis of their spirituality for the sake of the new child. The teacher is tormented by the nature of this yielding precisely because he cannot comprehend how the Diallobé can enter into a functional relationship with the colonizers and yet maintain the sanctity of their soul. Pre-empting Samba Diallo's disillusionment with the West, the fool is categorical in his belief that cultural synthesis is not possible. He remembers the unmistakable anguish that came over him once he had stepped on European soil during his visit to France. The glitter of European materialism — symbolized by the pavement — appealed to him from a distance, but he was 'vaguely aware of an incongruity' (p. 82). The fool's revolt against the culture of the West seems to come from the deepest reaches of his soul: 'What I felt went deeper than the mere revolt of my body. This trembling, which was again subsiding now that I was sitting down, seemed to me to be my body's fraternal echo to an inward disturbance.' (p. 83). For the fool, the world of machines and cold pavements is one of total dissociation, 'completely dehumanized, empty of men' (p. 85) — it cannot be the source of a new birth.

Even Samba Diallo, who has been pledged to the two worlds (traditional Africa and the West), cannot come to terms with the Occident — his experiences there only confront him with his alienation. He knows he has been severed from the spiritual centre of the Diallobé when death becomes strange to his *oeuvre*: whereas there was an intimacy between him and death while he lived among his people, he now no longer considers dying as a form of transcendentalism or the key concept in his cosmology. 'When I search for it in my thought,' he observes, 'I see only a dried-up sentiment, an abstract eventuality, scarcely more disagreeable for me than my insurance company' (p. 139).

Death, then, has been the symbol of Diallo's identity as a Diallobé. The meaning of this death though, is open to various interpretations. W. S. Shriver suggests that death in *Ambiguous Adventure* is a reference to 'spiritual life', which he defines as 'an intuitive grasp of the divine intention reinforced by the word [which] has given the structure of [Diallobé] culture their permanent validity, which is ontological, not historical'.[30] Death in the novel is positive in the sense that it enhances life; it has a redemptory function which allows a person to discover what the teacher calls the 'essential truths of existence'. From the teacher's or knight's point of view, death becomes a way towards a profound reality, not what Wole Soyinka has called a 'temporal illusion'.[30] And yet, once Diallo goes to the West and tries to apprehend reality through death, he cannot but find existence as meaningless, for in Western thinking the conquest of death is the triumph of life. No wonder he remains an outsider even when he has mastered the codes of Western culture. 'The shadows are closing in on me,' he says in a final invocation to the teacher, 'I no longer burn at the heart of people and things' (p. 15). His alienation is not so much a movement away from the culture of the Diallobé, but from its cosmology, centred on the idea of death.

Ambiguous Adventure is a novel about the spiritual effects of colonialism on one African people; it negates the material foundations of this alienation and posits it as a phenomenon with no cause-and-effect link with historical processes. But this is not unexpected. As we have already observed, the creed or ideology of Negritude sees its uniqueness in its quest for an African ontology beyond the apparently real. But a negation of the material conditions of culture also points to the incompleteness of the discourse on colonialism in Kane's novel. The fool demands that Diallo should submit to God and the position which the former represents, a tradition which by Kane's own admission is 'conservative and regressive'.[31] But Samba Diallo cannot submit to God because he has lost his fundamental belief in death, so the fool kills him. What then, is the meaning of this death? Is it a form of transcendentalism that completes Diallo's ascendance towards his godhead, or an indefined 'mystical act'?[32]

Kane has said that death enables Diallo to overcome his ambiguity, and hence serves as the opening up to the negritudist dream of cultural synthesis between Africa and the West. But can there really be any opening up in Diallo's forced act? Having returned in haste from the West (whose traditions he could not assimilate), Diallo cannot return to the hearth and continue the teacher's quest where he left off; his stay in the West has affected his perception of death; denied him total understanding of his cosmos. As for his transcendentalism — typified by his mystical fusion with the teacher, and, by implication, with the traditions of his ancestors — it has no real relevance to his ambiguities, which are placed in an ordinary, real-life context. In this regard, Kane is right when he describes the protagonist's spiritual death as a form of escapism which 'proves that all the problems are still there'.[33] In the next chapter, we will see how the problems of a double consciousness and social alienation are tied to their social and historical basis in the African novel.

Notes

1 Quoted in *The Modern Tradition: Backgrounds on Modernist Literature*, ed. Richard Ellmann and Charles Feidelson Jr. (New York: Oxford University Press, 1965), p. 740.

2 *The African Experience in Literature and Ideology* (London: Heinemann, 1981), p. 70.

3 Quoted in *The African Experience*, p. 79.

4 In Phanuel Akubueze Egejuru, *Towards African Literary Independence* (Westport, Conn.: Greenwood Press, 1980), p. 149.

5 In *African Writers on African Writing*, ed. G.D. Killam (London: Heinemann, 1973), p. 152.

6 *The African Experience*, pp. 155–56.

7 Jean Starobinski, 'The Style of Autobiography' in *Literary Style: A Symposium*, ed. Seymour Chatman (London: Oxford University Press, 1970), p. 285.

The Biographical Narrative

8 Mongo Beti, preface to *Mission to Kala*, trs. Peter Green (London: Heinemann, 1964). Further references to this edition are made in the text.

9 *Time and the Novel* (London: Peter Neville, 1952), p. 106.

10 For a general discussion of the concept of the 'unreliable narrator' see Wayne Booth's *The Rhetoric of Fiction* (Chicago: University of Chicago Press, 1961), pp. 211–34.

11 See, for example, Eustace Palmer, 'Mongo Beti's *Mission to Kala*: An Interpretation', *African Literature Today*, omnibus edition (1968–72), pp. 27–43.

12 'The Style of Autobiography', p. 289.

13 D.C. Muecke, *Irony and the Ironic* 2nd ed. (London: Methuen, 1982), p. 35.

14 'Between Two Worlds', *Makerere Journal* 7(1962), p. 8.

15 *Ibid.*, p. 9.

16 *The African Experience*, pp. 156–57.

17 'Colonial Contact and Language in Ferdinand Oyono's *Houseboy*', *African Literature Today* 13 (1983), p. 92.

18 *The Theory of the Novel*, trs. Anna Bostok (Cambridge, Mass.: MIT Press, 1971), p. 75.

19 *Story and Discourse: Narrative Structure in Fiction and Film* (Ithaca: Cornell University Press), p. 171.

20 *Houseboy*, trs. John Reed (London: Heinemann, 1966), p. 3. Further references to this edition are made in the text.

21 'Ferdinand Oyono's *Houseboy* and Gustave Flaubert's *Un Coeur Simple*', *Black Orpheus* 2(1970), p. 44.

22 *The African Experience*, p. 167.

23 'Ferdinand Oyono's *Houseboy* and Flaubert's *Un Coeur Simple*', p. 44.

24 *The African Experience*, p. 167.

25 *Ambiguous Adventure*, trs. Katherine Woods (New York: Collier Books, 1969), p. 47. Further references to this edition are made in the text.

26 This seems to me to be the implication of Senghor's perception of the French language as an instrument of civilization. See his 'opening address' in *African Literature and the Universities*, ed. by Gerald Moore (Ibadan: Ibadan University Press, 1965), pp. 13–17.

27 Quoted in *The African Experience*, p. 77.

28 Thus Senghor sums the negritudist dissatisfaction with Marxism: 'What embarrassed us in Marxism was, along with its atheism, a certain disdain for spiritual values: this discursive reason pushed to its outermost limits turned into a materialism without warmth, into a blind determinism.' Quoted in *The African Experience*, p. 78.

29 W.S. Shriver, 'Hamidou Kane's Hero', *African Literature Today* 12(1982), p. 67.

30 *Myth, Literature and the African World* (Cambridge: Cambridge University Press, 1976), p. 84.

31 In *Towards African Literary Independence*, p. 148.

32 The term is Madame Gore's. See 'The Solitude of Cheikh Kane: Solitude as the Theme of "Aventure Ambigüe" by Cheikh Hamidou Kane" ', in *African Literature and the Universities*, p. 36.

33 In *Towards African Literary Independence*, p. 140.

3

The Subjective Narrative

Exile and Alienation in the Novels of
Wole Soyinka and the early Ayi Kwei Armah

The novels we are going to discuss in this essay tend to go against the tradition of continuity in African literature. This tradition, notes Kofi Awoonor, is concerned with 'a fundamental process of integration and survival, integration as opposed to a dichotomised process of evil and good, beautiful and ugly', and is opposed to 'an itemistic concern, a fragmentation . . .'[1] Although both Soyinka and Armah are opposed to alienation on an ideological level, they tend to confront it nakedly in their works. They seem to work under the assumption that we have to reaffirm reification to reject or transcend it. This attitude can be explained in a number of different ways. The novels we are concerned with here were written in the late 1960s and early 1970s when, confronted by the nightmare reality of neo-colonialism and the failure of national consciousness, the African novelist was reassessing his role as a would-be social visionary. Whereas a few years before that the novelist would fall back on his people's vision of a communal past to transcend alienation and reaffirm the need for national independence, in the post-colonial period he would have to confront the harsh realities of his time with a mixture of guilt and a sense of betrayal. As Emmanuel Obiechina has noted, some writers now believe that their previous concern with the past was diversionary: 'It is even being said that preoccupation with the past provided a cover for the post-independence élites to carry on irresponsibly and corruptly.'[2] And as we will see in our examination of Soyinka's novels, the past has itself become a target of the novelist's dissatisfaction with his people's experiences.

We cannot, however, explain the 'modernist' novel in Africa in simple socio-historical terms. There are novelists like Ngugi wa Thiong'o who share Soyinka's and Armah's dissatisfaction with the present, yet write radically different novels. We can describe the formal character-istics of the latter's novels as modernist, but, as Lewis Nkosi has recognized, this bracket classification can be deceptive, for whereas European modernism is identified by the writers' celebration of form and technique, Soyinka and Armah are not formalists. They are undoubtedly amongst the most stylish prose writers in Africa today, but they conceive form as an integral part of value and meaning in their novels. And yet the two novelists are not oblivious to the tools of European modernism and the philosophical assumptions underlying them. Modernism in these and a number of similar African Novels expresses itself most apparently on what Richard Ntiru has called 'the mediatic, thematic and *Weltanschauung* levels'.[3]

Soyinka and Armah are minority novelists. Their works dramatize the consequences of the rise to power of the African élite and its functions as a privileged, oppressive minority, but they effect this drama in a mode of discourse which is very exclusive. Their stylistic perfection mitigates against the establishment of a live dialogue with the majority of the people they speak for, and the central characters in their works are either artists or intellectuals who have detached them-selves from the mainstream of a way of life which they see as corrupt and contaminating. There is no evidence that the authors of *The Beautyful Ones Are Not Yet Born, Fragments,* and *Why Are We So Blest?,* and of *The Interpreters* and *Season of Anomy* have tried to shape their style to appeal to a wider readership. These novels seem to me to exhibit a consciousness of a minority readership which reminds one of Ortega y Gasset's prediction that modern art would always have the masses against it because it divided the public into 'two classes of those who understand it and those who do not'.[4]

Another modernist tendency in the novels we are going to examine in this essay is their concern with the plight of alienated characters struggling to salvage their sanity in a world with which they have little in common. The most interesting contrast between the early and later Armah has to do with the characters' relationship with their society or community. While *Two Thousand Seasons* and *The Healers* are narra-tives built around the striving for unity by a whole group of people, the novels we are going to discuss here trace the plight of one or two characters in a community that contradicts or spites the values they represent. In Soyinka's novels, the individual character has fellow suf-ferers, but these constitute a small social group which seems at war with the rest of the community. Alienation in these, as in other modernist novels, has a dual character. First, we have the spiritual alienation of an idealistic soul, the Hegelian contrite consciousness, which triggers the conflict situation in the narrative when it becomes conscious of the incompatibility between its true self and its 'own nothingness'. The contrite consciousness aspires towards what Hegel calls the 'changeless', but it also has 'the knowledge of the opposite, namely of its own individuality'. Second, we have the form of alienation which develops when human labour becomes external to the worker. In this situation, as Marx noted in the *Economic and Philosophic Manuscripts of 1844*, labour ceases to belong to the worker's 'essential being', so that in his work 'he does not affirm himself but denies himself, does not feel content but unhappy, does not develop freely his physical and mental energy but mortifies his body and ruins his mind'.[5]

The modernist novelist sees himself as the medium through which the alienated individual expresses his sense of fragmentation. In a world in which the worker is at war with his two selves and his labour, the novelist does not see himself functioning as the healer of souls or synthesizer of experience. He is too conscious of the gap between the ideals embedded in his ideology — especially the hope that reification can be overcome — and the ability of his characters to activate these ideals. These characters exist in a world which always seems beyond their practical abilities, so that understanding is no longer an instrument of dealing with real-life experiences; they prefer to withdraw from a world which they know only too well. In formal terms, the novelist tries to perfect symbols, images and narrative structures which will enhance the division within his characters' consciousness on the one hand, and between his heroes and their world on the other.

This kind of novelist rejects communal myths as illusory and prefers to confront the rotten under-belly of society. The form and meaning of these narratives is thus mediated by a Manichean vision which is particularly suited to the antinomies on which the dramatic structure in the modernist novel moves. Fictions mediated by the Manichean vision, observes Daniel J. Schneider, 'swarm in the mental world, but only in the mental world; they are "subjective", not "real" '.[6] Irony and empathy are juxtaposed with ease in these kinds of fiction: the latter is a mark of the writer's understanding of his world and its search for a sense of balance; the former is a badge of his detachment from this world. The structure of the novels we are going to examine below is, predictably, inward-looking, for as Fletcher and Bradbury have recognized, the modernist novel 'hangs on the border between the mimetic and the autotelic species of literature, between an art made by imitating things outside itself, and an art that is internally coherent-making'.[7] As agents of narrative, characters have been made to recreate their worlds in their minds, and this version of reality seems to matter to them more than surface reality, although the latter exists to confirm their view of the world and to justify the Manichean vision.

The Subjective Narrative

We have already observed that the most common type of character in the modernist novel is an artist figure who adopts the status of an internal exile, looking back on his past with a mixture of irony and pity. This character 'takes on shape as a spirit, a voyager into the unknown arts, and an embodiment of the difficulties in the form which surrounds him, taking his place in the complex perspectives of the writing itself'.[8] For this reason, the shape of the modernist novel is determined closely by the protagonist's point of view. What distinguishes the African modernist novel from its European counterpart, though, is the protagonist's defensiveness about his status as an exile; he does not celebrate his loneliness or isolation, nor does he seek to deny his real world as a tangible universe. If we find these characters melancholic, it is because they are aware of their ineffectiveness; they cannot take on a Messianic role, nor seek redemption in art. Even where the artist is set up as a Promethean figure, as is the case in *The Interpreters*, he is ultimately overshadowed by his social reality or images of his past. Sometimes, as with Solo in *Why Are We So Blest?*, the concept of the artist as redeemer is rejected as simply fallacious.

Loneliness and isolation:
The Beautyful Ones Are Not Yet Born

Armah's major achievement in his first novel is the establishment of a close, almost fatalistic relationship between his characters and their social and physical contexts. Characters and the landscape tend to exist in an antagonistic relationship, built up by symbols and images of rot and decrepitude, which functions as a commentary on contemporary Ghana. In the first few paragraphs of the novel the bus, itself a symbol of the country as a whole, is choked by rust and rattles along the road in a confused manner, as if it has lost its sense of direction; the driver's matches have been spent and he is resigned to his state; the passengers lower themselves from the bus almost unwillingly. This initial image of waste and decrepitude is sustained throughout *The Beautyful Ones Are Not Yet Born*. The idea of Passion Week sums up both the character of the landscape and the people's attitude towards it: at this time of the month, the world looms over the characters with a permanence and hostility which they are not equipped to deal with. The central conflicts in the novel arise when the characters try to understand, or deal with, a world which is beyond their powers. In these first pages, the characters are defined by their impotence and vulnerability: they are described as 'still bodies walking in their sleep'[9] or dwarfs walking in their sleep. Many of these characters — and the conductor is an appropriate example here — adopt the illusion of power and wealth to cover up their weaknesses and poverty. In most cases, this adoption of illusions to counter harsh realities leads to the kind of confusion and psychological imbalance we find in the conductor as he confronts the cedi note, a physical symbol of the power that corrupts characters. The smell of the cedi is described as 'a very old smell, very strong, and so very rotten that the stench itself of it came with a curious satisfying pleasure' (p. 3).

As we will try to show in the course of this section, Armah has tried to develop a narrative technique that exposes the contradictions of the world of power and corruption which constitutes the background of his novel, while showing us how such contradictions affect the inner lives of his characters. In the example above, the conductor's reaction to the cedi reflects both a confusion of values (power expresses itself through rottenness), and the character's inability to stand above these confused values. And as the case of the man and Teacher illustrates, those characters who question these inverted social norms enter into a violent relationship with their social and physical environment. On another level, Armah wants to expose the fallacy of those characters who have sought security in rot, while dramatizing the psychological pressures those who resist the rot must undergo to preserve their purity. This duality is effected through a consistent contrast between those characters who represent the ideals of beauty, love and life (the man and Teacher), and those who deliberately transgress such values (the conductor and Koomson).

The cedi note gives the conductor a sense of power and security, but when the sleeping man threatens to expose him through his presence, during a simulated act of acquisition, the hero of the gleam is turned into an object of self-pity. The conductor's state of psychological instability is further exposed by his hostile treatment of the man once he discovers that the latter 'was no watcher after all, only a sleeper' (p. 5). The man has to bear the full brunt of the conductor's 'savage indignation' because of his innocence; if he had been actually watching the conductor, he might have been offered part of the loot. Throughout the novel, the innocent suffer while the guilty are venerated. We find the man's mute acceptance of his suffering disconcerting; we admire his refusal to play the hero, but are left uneasy by his passive attitude. The reader's first and most lasting impression of the man is that of a human being condemned to apologize for his clean existence. As an agent of the narrative, he is not an active or assertive character. He rarely responds to his world in any self-supporting way, and the fact that he suffers because the world is corrupt is not always convincing; the man is simply overwhelmed by his situation. Even anger comes to the man as a delayed effect which is never activated. When the bus conductor spits a blob of phlegm on the man's face, the latter looks back 'in the anger of the moment, only to see the driver unrepentantly preparing his throat and mouth for one more effort' (p. 7), and he quickens his pace to get away. A few paces later, the man is nearly knocked down by a taxi; trapped by the 'brightness' which defines the forces working against the ideals he represents, the protagonist is not sure of his reaction.

But the man is not a protagonist in the strict sense of the word. The reader is made to assume that Armah's character is in conflict, both physically and psychologically, with his landscape, but this is a one-sided conflict. The man prefers withdrawal to reaction, and this is what makes him such a modernist character. He is introduced to the reader as a fallen man, and the author is not inviting us to witness his rise or further fall — the status of the man rarely changes in the course of the narrative — but to understand the causes and consequences of his present situation. The modernist character, as David Caute has observed, is rarely defined in terms of his social or personal history. He is thrown into a world which is depicted as a permanent, unchangeable entity. Development of character in this type of narrative does not, therefore, imply a growth of awareness, but 'the gradual revelation of an unalterable condition, a sequence of tenuously related experiential fragments'.[10]

As I will try to show here, the man does not really change in the course of the narrative, nor does his social context; only possibilities of change are suggested towards the end of the novel. There are well-considered aspects of his personal and social history in the novel, but these are segments from a drama which seems to have been going on for a long time. In other words, the narrative does not trace his genesis, but provides impressions of his life in particular or generalized historical moments. He is put in the middle of a volatile social situation, alone, without a name or individualized history. Pitted against the man is 'the world', which in spite of numerous claims of change and historical movement has remained the same since the man was thrown into it. The sense of permanence which we find in most of the institutions which the man confronts or comes across in the novel (family, school, government, place of work) poses an interesting question to which Teacher tries to address himself in Chapter 6 — Is change worthwhile?

The kinds of change the man and Teacher see around them tend to reinforce the feeling of permanence that looms over their lives. The coating of paint at the massive railway building where the man works is analogous with cosmetic changes in Ghana: it is 'just another inevitable accretion in a continuing story whose beginnings were now lost and whose end no one was likely to bother about' (p. 11). Reflecting on the cycle of decay in which the staircase is trapped, the man concludes that the wood will always win. There is, however, a Hegelian sense of irony in this conclusion: the final decay of the wood is a kind of triumph because it is restored to its original, organic nature, but it is also its ultimate defeat, since it loses its identity as wood. These kinds of paradoxical situation are common in *The Beautyful Ones Are Not Yet Born.*

There is, indeed, a major paradox in the man's relationship with the accreting world around him. Despite his passivity towards the seemingly permanent landscape, he tries to stand above it and its corrosive powers. There will be temptations for the man to dip into the muck and bring happiness to his loved ones, but his character is fixed so much that the reader is almost certain that the good man will not give in to Mammon. Here again we have Armah's ironic presentation of his character at its best: the man preserves himself by withdrawing from situations he cannot handle, while more ambitious characters such as his wife are prepared to take the risk. Society is an entity which the man seems to have given up as lost, but he is aware of the pressures it brings to bear on him and on people close to him and he cannot therefore ignore it. His colleague, the night clerk, is terrified by loneliness, especially when it bears down on him against the background of 'bands on the hill creating happiness for those able to pay money at all times of the month' (p. 15). The man sympathizes with the clerk's terror and his struggle against oppressive labour, but perceives solitude as a redeeming quality. We often find him retreating into himself, searching for 'the futile freedom of a thing connected to nothing else' (p. 17).

The man's retreat into his subjective self is an attempt to escape from the kind of connections and relationships which characters in Armah's latest narratives seek. The assumption here is that such connections only draw the character deeper and deeper into the corrosive landscape. The latter is often painted in sharp, sustained, but derogatory images, which are intended to justify the man's creed of withdrawal. Take his office, for example: like the bus, it is a microcosm of society and is part of a pattern of jagged relationships, waste and decay, which is common in the novel. The fan moves in 'tired slowness', and, placed in the same room with the Morse machine, it creates 'a sense of confusion', and the salt from the sea water eats into the walls to create 'a sticky mess'. This physical state of decrepitude is reflected in the inner selves of the characters; they sweat profusely 'from some kind of inner struggle that was always going on' (p. 20). The result is a vivid picture of physical and psychological decay, alienation and despair, reinforced by the narrative tone:

> So the sea salt and the sweat together and the fan above made this stewy atmosphere in which the suffering sleepers came and worked and went dumbly back afterwards to the homes they had fled. There was really no doubt that it was like that in their homes, everywhere save for those who had found in themselves the hardness for the upward climb. And he was not one of those. (p. 20)

The Subjective Narrative

The tone here is a mixture of disdain and self-pity: the silent sufferers are indirectly indicted for succumbing to a routine of which the consequences they fully understand, and yet they are pitied for having no other choice given their lack of 'hardness'. Most of the railwaymen understand their predicament on an intuitive level. But when they develop the same kind of consciousness as the man and see their unmitigated tragedy in its full scope, then their situations can only be tragic. The man stands above the rest not merely because he knows and understand the 'hardness' of the 'upward climb', but also by the knowledge he has about his own 'softness'. He cannot live under the illusion that things will improve, and this breeds a measure of cynicism.

The man is both the insightful observer and victim of a society in which ordinary people are so much in despair 'that there was nothing worse to fear' (p. 22). Such people lead a way of life which is referred to as 'living death', an awareness of which prompts the man to opt for escape: his movements are always away from the living dead and the corrupt, towards clear vision and taste. To satisfy his starved vision, however, he has to make his way through 'unconquerable filth', but when he comes across a clean pool of water which, like himself, has defied the muck, he does not feel triumphant. He gains a far deeper understanding of the struggle he is up against: he is satisfied that such a place of 'peace and purity' can exist amidst all the filth, but the power of the rot makes him melancholy. He understands the transient nature of his moments of escape, and when he returns to the office, 'the darkness of the place itself misted over the sharpness of everything he saw' (p. 24).

Symbols of cleanness serve two important functions in the novel. First, they are illuminatory in the man's quest for self-understanding, for the question that plagues him for most of the novel is why he has failed in spite of doing all the good things. Second, they present one of the leitmotifs in Armah's *oeuvre*: what is the justification of virtue and ideals in a universe that has lost its sense of values? After all, what is *The Beautyful Ones Are Not Yet Born* but the story of a small, honest, ordinary man hounded like a criminal by corrupt men in a world propelled by crude materialistic principles? And yet we are frightened by the honest man not because of what he is or does — it is easier to sympathize with his actions because they are positive and guided by the purest ideals — but by his affirmation of the helplessness of those who stand for life, love and beauty. We are particularly disconcerted by his assertion that nothing can happen to change a society that has learnt to drive so fast, for a number of reasons. The man uses a matter-of-fact tone which is not only absolute — he cannot contemplate any change for the better — but is not contradicted by an authorial intervention; it is thus easier for the reader to construe that the anti-hero represents the position of the real or implied author. But surface realities seem to reinforce the destructive character of this society and, by implication, the need to change it. 'Why do we agree to go on like this?' a co-worker asks the man on the Morse machine, posing a question which the reader is invited to raise throughout the novel. The fact that the man prefers to suffer rather than act is therefore an indirect form of criticism. He is angered by suggestions that it is possible for the oppressed to react against their situation, since words such as rejecting, acting and reacting demand withdrawal from his inner self. Because he is convinced that things cannot change (and 'nothing much would happen' [p. 25]), the man finds the idea of action absurd. Why?

The possibility of action may in fact threaten the man's own illusion that by withdrawing into himself he can preserve his purity in the midst of the rot that characterizes his world. His firm belief is that he is only nominally attached to his landscape; he has thus turned his loneliness into a virtue and, more practically, an instrument for self-preservation and justification. But, as the timber trader, who embodies the temptation of evil (or what is referred to as 'the gift of death') reminds him, 'a man is a man'. The man cannot preserve his purity without committing the kind of social suicide which his friend Teacher has embraced. And yet the man's creed of semi-detachment seems justified for a number of reasons. The world outside is presented as an aggregate of decay and waste, while the man's inner mind is a sanctuary, a self-contained entity which he controls. He guards this sanctuary jealously.

The man's subjective world is most vulnerable when it is confronted with its past history or images which remind it about the promises that the world it has rejected once offered. The man finds the cheerfulness and optimism of the new clerk dangerous because it reminds him of his youth (and also the possibilities of being happy in an uncontaminated situation). Characters such as the young clerk challenge the man's creed at its roots: they are romantic in the sense that they are still keen to establish relationships (even when the man knows how devastating these can be); they also move in the light because they have yet to discover how blinding it can be. In contrast, the man sees himself as the victim of relationships which were supposed to enhance his life:

> Outside, the sight of the street itself raised thoughts of the reproach of loved ones, coming in silent sounds that ate into the mind in wiry spirals and stayed there circling in tightening rings, never letting go. There was no hurry. At the other end there was only home, the land of the loved ones, and there it was only the heroes of the gleam who did not feel that they were strangers. (p. 35)

The man's fear of the 'outside' impresses himself mostly on his mind. In reality, he fares much better when he confronts his family than when he thinks of how he has failed them.

The terms 'outside' and 'inside' do not mean much in the man's relationship with his landscape. He moves from one depressing situation (the office) to another equally alienating one (the home). In between is a landscape which is defined by misery and despair. The observer merges long, broad shots of the physical landscape with close, intense portraits of its victims, ranging from the man himself to the prostitute who tries to solicit him, and the woman who sells bread to Komsoon. The larger social miasma draws the man's thoughts to his own personal failures — his inability to provide his family with the promises of the gleam — and he contents himself with the hope that his family has merely misunderstood him. Such a hope is, however, illusory, for there is an in-built destructive element in the 'place and time' which reminds him about the futility of his attempts to escape. The place reminds him 'that there was too much of the unnatural in any man who imagines he could escape the inevitable decay of life and not accept the decline into final destruction' (p. 48). In a situation where corruption has been instituted, extreme attempts to escape from the rot can lead to self-destruction. Rama Krishna's case is an illustration of this: he dies trying to escape corruption.

Time and morality are tyrannical; even when the singers preach stoicism (p. 50). For Teacher, the sad tone of the song raises thoughts 'of the lonely figure finding it more and more difficult to justify his own honesty' (p. 51). Comparing himself to a non-drinker caught among masquerading drunkards, he is forced to conclude that 'honesty could only be a social vice, for the one who chooses to indulge in it nothing but a very hostile form of selfishness, a very pervasive selfishness' (pp. 51–52). Herein lies the man's real crisis: he is forced to live in a perpetual state of psychological instability because his awareness of, and commitment to, what is right and just has cut him off from his beloved ones. He has to suffer for not doing what 'everybody is doing' (p. 54). Teacher concurs with the man's wife that the latter is a *chichidodo* in the sense that he wants to reject the values of his society, yet strives to relate to the same through individual relationships and established institutions. In short, the man cannot have his cake and eat it too; but Teacher is the first to admit that cutting oneself off from society entirely — the act of being completely naked — is not a guarantee of inner peace:

> I have not stopped wanting to meet the loved ones and to touch them and be touched by them. But you know that the loved ones are dead even when they walk around the earth like the living, and you know that all they want is that you throw away the thing in your mind that

makes you think you are still alive, and their embrace will be a welcome unto death. (pp. 55–56)

Teacher cannot relinquish the autonomy of his mind for social relationships, but when the man suggests that he has chosen the life of nakedness which he leads, the former responds with probably the most pessimistic statement in the novel. 'It is not a choice between life and death, but what kind of death we can bear, in the end,' the naked man says. 'Have you not seen there is no salvation anywhere?' (p. 56).

Both the man and his mentor have the kind of knowledge — of the beginning and end of the 'upward climb' — which 'normal' society considers dangerous because it debunks the illusion of power and wealth which the sleepwalkers live in. But whereas the man believes in the possibility of some form of human contact with his family, Teacher is a victim of his own majestic hopelessness. He has a totally pessimistic vision which alerts him to the end of things even before they are initiated. Chapter 6 is a confessional narrative — a dramatization of the process which led Teacher to despair. What impresses itself on both the reader, narrator and listener in this section of *The Beautyful Ones Are Not Yet Born* is Teacher's awareness of his modernity, his consciousness of living in a time and place defined by its sense of dissolution. The narrator's concern with the process of historical continuity and disruption, deprivation and inheritance, is symptomatic of Armah's modernist temper. In terms of narrative form, Teacher withdraws into his mind and thoughtstream to try to establish a pattern that will explain his particular mode of revolt in larger social and historical terms.

It is important to realize that Teacher begins his discourse by disestablishing the norms by which we judge social realities and how we relate to them. To the extent that each social movement develops its own character and individualized parameters of judgement, the terms 'traditional' and 'natural' — strong elements in establishing the bottom lines of human action — are superfluous. Teacher is fascinated by the discrepancies between historical time and the moods, impressions and characteristics they produce; unlike the traditional narrator, Teacher does not seek to establish a pattern linking cause and effect. The purpose of his discourse is 'the disestablishing of communal reality and conventional notions of causality.'[11] For me, the main achievement of this chapter lies in the narrator's ability to turn historical realities into subjective fictions which trace, even justify, Teacher's descent into despair.

Teacher straddles the historical period covered in the novel in a way the man is not capable of, having moved from one extreme (total hope) to another (abject despair) without losing his consciousness of either moment. As a man who has witnessed the birth of his nation and then seen its hasty decay (hence the apt image of the man-child), Teacher refuses to be enticed by the myths of the past, or to yield to the dreams of better times carried over from the days of heady nationalism. 'I will not be entranced by the voice [of false hope], even if it should swell as it did in the days of hope,' he affirms. 'I will not be entranced, since I have seen the destruction of the promises it made' (p. 63). His main target is the immediate past: his mind goes back to the period after the so-called Second World War, and his boyhood memories, filtered through the consciousness of the adult mind, bring out the images of the destruction of human souls. Even in those days of hope, he contends, his young eyes could see what he calls 'the truth' — that the land 'had become a place messy with destroyed souls and lost bodies' (p. 65). But observations of what was happening, however keen they might have been, did not amount to a full understanding of 'the approach of something much like death itself':

> The thing that would have killed us was that there was nothing to explain all this, nothing outside ourselves and those near us or those even weaker than ourselves that we could attack. There was no way out visible to us, and out on the hills the white men's gleaming bungalows were so far away, so unreachably far that people did not even think of them in their suffering (p. 66)

Teacher brings the People's suffering in those bitter times to the man, fully aware that in spite of the passage of time 'still there is no sweetness here' (p. 67). He speaks with an authoritative voice whose pessimism is not countered by either the man or the author.

In both the past and present, the two characters have striven for a conscious understanding of their place and time, for in spite of its isolation, the subjective vision cannot have meaning except in relation to historical realities. In his assessment of the naked man (pp. 78–80), the man struggles to come to grips with the realities that turned his mentor into 'a human being hiding from other human beings' (p. 78). Although he still questions Teacher's total loss of hope, the man seems to understand the reasons for this act of despair. An important technique in this part of the narrative is the relationship of Teacher's and the man's minds, and their linkage to larger historical and social events. Historical events and the characters' different reactions to them determine their visions in the present. For Teacher who has lived through, and participated in, various nationalist movements which once offered hope, only to be betrayed in the end, there can be no definite break from the cycle of decay. This cycle, asserts the naked man, is eternal, and the question he poses at the end of the discourse is whether we should be committed to change which, in his view, eventually leads to decay. In a world caught up in an incessant cycle of decay, yearning for rejuvenation is too much to ask for.

But the man cannot accept Teacher's pessimistic vision in its absoluteness. He considers his links with the corrupt society, however nominal they might be, central to the growth of his mind and the maintenance of psychological stability. But his longing for a less problematic relationship with his family and friends is posited to be as dangerous as the naked man's total isolation; as Teacher would put it, it is an invitation to death. This is exemplified by the man's entertainment of the Koomsons: he plays the game to satisfy his wife, and in 'the foolishness of the moment' feels happy for performing 'the heroic things that were expected all the time' (p. 115). But confronted by the true hero of the gleam, he realizes the heavy price one has to pay to play the game:

> In such situations he felt like a stranger from a country that was very far away, seeing everyone and himself also involved in a slow, sad game that would never end. It was awful, was it not, that the rich should have this effect on the poor, making them sacrifice future necessities just so that they could make a brief show of the wealth they could never hope to have (p. 131)

More than any other character in the novel, Koomson enhances the man's sense of alienation from his beloved: he is the perfect example of total corruption, yet benefits from the admiration of those people who are only too eager to spite clean men. It is not by accident that Koomson introduces the man to his wife as 'a stranger'; nor does Estella's response ('I didn't see anybody') surprise us. The man is both a stranger in his community and a nobody to his family.

The man desires all the material things that make the life of the heroes of the gleam so pleasant: 'It was not the things themselves, but the way to arrive at them which brought so much confusion to the soul' (p. 144). If the sweetness of life can only be acquired through the 'rotten way', then 'What monstrous fruit was it that could find the end of its life in the struggle against the sweetness and corruption?' (p. 145). This is a question which the man never resolves in his mind. His alienation is exacerbated by his family's betrayal by Koomson, but this is counterbalanced by his wife's readiness to accept his 'failures' for what they are after this betrayal. In general, it is difficult to argue that the man is a different person at the end of the novel from what he was at the beginning. There is a sense in which we see him moving closer to the naked man's vision of total despair. 'A man would just have to make up his mind that there was never going to be anything but despair,' he concludes towards the end of the twelfth chapter, 'and there would be no way of escaping it, except one' (p. 154). Despair or die; these are not options, and the man does not make up his mind about either. At the beginning of the following chapter, however, he suggests that one can preserve one's inner sanctuary by substituting surface realities with an inner, imagined, subjective world: 'It was not difficult so to forget the self and the world against which it had to live' (p. 155).

The man manages to escape from his world into his job, oblivious to movements outside his bare, blank sanctuary. Nothing seems to matter to him very much — not even the *coup* that causes so much excitement in the country. He concedes that meaningful change is feasible in the distant future, but he is neutral toward both Koomson (the epitome of the old corrupt régime) and the soldiers (agents of the new oligarchy). Towards the end of the narrative, the man stands above his corrupt universe, solitary, and like the flower painted on the bus, 'unexplainable, and very beautiful, but ineffective'. He has only succeeded in keeping his distance from the rot; he has no chances of triumphing over it.

Illusion and experience in *Fragments*

Fragments belongs to the same period as *The Beautyful Ones Are Not Yet Born* and exhibits the same modernist traits as Armah's first novel. But in Armah's second major prose work, we are struck by the way society, as a real and historical entity, is minimized, sometimes negated entirely, in preference to the characters' inner subjective world. In this novel, as in *Why Are We So Blest?* which follows it, characters do not struggle against a realistically depicted social universe which is both corrupt in its intent and oblivious to the ideals these characters hold dear, but are at war against an abstract principle of evil. The novelist's primary intention is not the delineation of a tangible context within which these characters can test their ideals; in the few moments when society is the subject of the narrator's reflections, it has simply been raised to be condemned. The inward turn of the narrative is thus a means by which the characters can withdraw from a society in which they were too involved at one time in their lives. This mode of narrative, and the characters in it, represent most graphically what Armah calls the 'crude Manicheanism of the colonial relationship'.[12]

The structure of *Fragments* is circular: the narrative opens and ends with Naana's attempt to come to terms with the values of a modern age which has not only overtaken her but has also destroyed her grandson, who should have been better equipped to deal with it. The novel's end is also its beginning, a formal feature which enhances the concept of the cycle of decay first developed in *The Beautyful Ones*. But there is an important difference in the circular movement in the two novels: the cycle of decay in *The Beautyful Ones* consumes itself, those trapped in it and those (like Rama Krishna) who have tried to escape from it; in *Fragments*, Naana's cycle is redemptive in the sense that her death is a transition from a destructive social realm to one that fulfils her dream of being reunited with her ancestors. As the old woman asserts at the opening of the novel, '[e]verything that goes away returns and nothing is lost'.[13] She is disillusioned with modern life, and her elegiac tone bemoans the loss of the values she cherished in earlier times, but Naana does not share Teacher's extreme sense of despair. The world she lives in blindly is one in which people and things have changed, and yet the essence of life — what she calls the 'changing circle of the world' — remains constant. Her 'constant life' principle is symbolized by the sun, which moves across the sky irrespective of the changing historical circumstances.

Naana is the constant factor in *Fragments.* She is important in the novel because she underscores the novelist's belief in a more redemptive set of social values, thereby balancing the pessimism which pervades Armah's first novel; she is also a counterfoil to Baako's tormented personality. As I will argue in the course of this discussion, Baako's sense of psychological imbalance results from his inability to confront the contradictions of his family and society fully and realistically. In contrast, Naana, who has been rendered ineffective by her blindness, is gifted with a penetrating moral and social vision which sees events before they occur. It is possible to argue that Naana and Baako are opposite sides of the same character, with the grandmother representing the stability of the past, and the grandson symbolizing the turbulence of his present, but Armah does not invite his readers to make this kind of comparison. It is only important that we keep in mind the close affinity between the two characters and ask ourselves what sets them apart from the other members of the family.

In formal terms, Naana is important in another respect: she sets the tone of the novel, establishing the principle of calm and certainty in a narrative dealing with disintegration and uncertainty. She also functions as a social seer; she not only predicts Baako's inevitable disintegration, but also foresees the incompatibility of the been-to's illusions, and the real-life experiences he must undergo to grow up. Even when other members of the family have lost hope of Baako's return, the old woman affirms her belief in the completion of the boy's cycle; while others see Baako as the hero who will facilitate their material wellbeing, he remains a child to his grandmother. Naana knows that the Baako who returns to his family is changed; her main concern is with his ability to cope with the psychological demands the rest of the family makes on him. For the old woman, Baako is the one charged with continuing the circle of tradition which his uncle Foli — who worries Naana because of his greed and insensitivity to the values of the past — celebrates before the boy's departure for the United States. The novel is prefaced by Naana's celebration of the very values the absence of which leads to Baako's psychological fragmentation.

There is, however, a sense in which Naana echoes, indeed affirms, her grandson's anxieties about the values that inform modern Ghanaian society. She functions as a stranger in a modern world whose *raison d'être* she does not really understand. Her dream image of Baako expresses her own apprehension about the future as much as it captures the been-to's plight:

> I closed my eyes against the night that had disappeared outside, and I saw Baako roaming in unknown, forbidden places, just born there again after a departure and a death somewhere. He had arrived from beneath the horizon and standing in a large place that was open and filled with many winds, he was lonely. (p. 15)

Baako's experience in the United States is a form of departure in the sense that it tears him away from the roots of his tradition; it is a death because he returns a different person, antithetical to the values of the cargo cult which his family associates with America. If Naana is Baako's traditional past clinging to its roots with desperation, Juana is his Afro-American contemporary, the creation of the new world. She is the product of what Naana calls 'an overturned world in which all human flesh was white' (p. 15).

We meet Juana in a catch-22 situation. She thought she had left her alienating and dehumanizing environment behind her when she left America, only to find herself in 'another defeated and defeating place' (p. 17). In this novel, as in *The Beautyful Ones*, the physical landscape is the manifestation of the sense of alienation which Armah's characters find almost overbearing, and their most consistent motions are modes of escape from places and situations which hightlight their sense of defeat. For Juana, the 'aborted town' represents a hierarchy of social values built around the worship of money and status which she finds more frightening in Ghana than in the United States because she did not expect it to be happening in the world of her dreams. She lives in fear of being overwhelmed by what she calls 'external things', so she tries to detach herself from such things even when, as with the man in *The Beautyful Ones*, she strives to establish union and communion with tangible things and persons. Her dilemma is typical of the character of virtue in Armah's fiction: she must keep away from ordinary life, which is contaminating (in her view at least), and yet she cannot find full fulfilment outside those situations.

More than Baako and Naana, Juana is able to explore the meaning of defeat and the kind of alienation that comes over the modernist character when he/she discovers the gap between the ideals he/she stands for, and the strength of the forces working against such ideals. She is particularly endowed for this exploratory role because she is a foreigner in Ghana, and hence brings a fresh perspective to bear on the situation; she is also, significantly, a psychiatrist, a doctor of alienated souls. In fact, Juana is marked out in the novel by her sensitiveness towards her world and her keen awareness of the wide gap between her inner desires and the demands of the external world. Her moments of escape — exemplified by her 'purposeless' drive in the countryside — are motions of self-search:

> Juana had come this way for the drive out before, several times, when after long days spent closed in, in the town and the hospital itself, all the boredom and the loneliness and a disgust she could not hold under in spite of all the power of her will, all this created inside her a feeling of attraction, a certain love for being out on the road. Several times, driving along it, letting herself go and pushing the little car to go faster and faster, she could reach back to a feeling that perhaps there would be some meaning waiting for her at the end of a long and aimless drive, that it was not true that every important thing that was worthwhile had run slowly out of her life. (p. 21)

But the drive is also a ritualized form of escape: Juana is fully aware of her helplessness in the face of all the mental wrecks that surround her in the psychiatric hospital (itself a symbol of Ghanaian society as a whole), and this makes her angry. But she knows that her anger, like her knowledge of the problems underlying society, is incapacitating. Her drive out is thus a short-lived easing-off of psychological pressures.

The mood of *Fragments* is taut: one of the important organizational principles in the narrative is the characters' awareness of an abstract evil principle which is underscored through some shrilling ritual actions, such as the killing of the mad dog. Watching this scene over Juana's shoulder, as it were, the reader is shaken not so much by the slaughter of the dog, but by the emotions that accompany it. We find the people's need to kill, the drive of evil that makes the act a moment of triumph, and the fatalism of the boy who helplessly watches his best friend being killed, almost incomprehensible. The ritual is presented as a miniature psychodrama which hurls us straight into the killer's warped minds and Juana's repugnant state almost simultaneously. There is an extent to which the act is incomprehensible because the killers are not totally responsible for their actions. Juana sees them as acting in their sleep: the crowd tightens around the dying dog and shifts in an 'unconscious' circle; the man with a scrotal sac has a manic shine which convinces the spectator that he 'needed something like the first killing of a dog for reasons that lay within and were far more powerful than the mere outside glory open to the hunter with his kill' (p. 27). The man with a scrotal sac is liberated by the ritual killing of the dog, but the impression the crowd leaves behind is that of total brutality provoked by despair. But there are also moments of tenderness against this bleak backdrop. A truck driver abuses the mother of a child he has almost run over, but the woman does not seem to mind; instead she yields to the intense emotions within her and 'her own silent crying' (p. 33).

The juxtaposing of such a gross act as the killing of the dog with the mother's flood of emotions shows how Armah subtly contrasts modes of symbolism and symbolic action to enhance the gap between the inner and outer worlds of his characters. The killers' inner desire to slaughter the dog and their insensitivity to the boy's pleas are an indictment of their social condition. As Juana aptly observes, they live in such a desperate and futile situation that they need 'outer toughening' to bear the stringencies of living in a 'messed-up town' (p. 21). The two modes of action enhance Juana's uncertainty. The killers seem to justify the kind of anger she has been directing at herself of late and her feeling of helplessness. In contrast, the mother's fear of death and her love of life bring out the characters' fear of 'the immensity of the long hazard ahead' (p. 33) in their search for more humane social values. 'So long as I have his little life, insult me,' the grateful mother tells the truck driver. 'There is hope.' (p. 33). She prompts Juana to contrast our innate desire for life with the external forces that stifle this life. But once she tries to face the realities that make her struggle hazardous, the psychiatrist is not sure that any individual is capable of rectifying the damage. The 'small saving attempts' she is capable of appear almost insignificant compared to the magnitude of what she calls 'immediate needs' (p. 34).

Juana is ultimately the victim of her own knowledge. This is what makes her experiences parallel and reinforce Baako's more tragic experiences. At this junction, it is appropriate to observe the interrelationships of experiences and personal histories in *Fragments*. Armah constructs his narrative in such a way that individual histories ultimately fall into a pattern to present a profound portrait of group and personal alienation. And yet differences in such portraits are as important as the broad similarities shared by Naana, Juana and Baako. Naana, for example, is able to bear her alienation from the world of the moderns because of her historical and mythical links to a world which celebrated values that were less demeaning and destructive than those she sees at work in contemporary Ghanaian society. She therefore awaits her moment of death with some anticipation: it is her path of return to her ancestors. Her self-assured manner makes Baako's and Juana's sense of fragmentation, and their fear of death, that much more vivid.

Juana is different from Baako in a fundamental way: the knowledge that makes her suffer so much has helped her dissipate some of her illusions, not least the belief that her 'small saving attempts' amount to much. Like Teacher in *The Beautyful Ones*, she takes her loss of hope as the turning point in her struggle to find some meaning in her life. But her acceptance of failure creates an inner turbulence which differs from Baako's disintegration only in the sense that it is not clinical. As the following passage shows, she has to keep on struggling with the tensions generated by lingering hope and her new sense of realism:

> What a curse it was to have the constant remembrance of a time when youth was not something one had lived through, not just a defeated thought, but the hope of constant regeneration, the daring to reach out towards a new world. Life then had taken its color from the brilliance of an always imminent apocalypse, and if the beautiful colors were mixed with the red of blood and the sulfurous yellow of flames, that was in no way a reason to run from the drama. (p. 45)

Up to a point, then, this passage establishes the psychological state which Juana and Baako share. They are both caught up in situations where youthful hope is frustrated not only by a harsh, uncompromising, utilitarian environment, but also the knowledge of their inability to change their society — what Juana calls 'defeated thoughts'. The crucial difference in the two characters' reaction to their apocalyptic world has more to do with the range of their experiences than with basic philosphical attitudes. Juana has gone through her baptism with fire — she has learnt the meaning of defeat. Baako, on the other hand, begins his journey into the landscape of chaos from a point of innocence, unaware of the deathly nature of the apocalypse.

Juana's importance as a consciousness and narrative agent in *Fragments* is not always appreciated, although most of the key sections in the novel are reflected through her mind. Equally important is her function as the judge (or psychoanalyst, appropriately) of Baako's experiences. In this respect, Juana shares a basic function with Teacher in *The Beautyful Ones* and Solo in *Why Are We So Blest?*: she is both the mirror of Baako's illusions and the lamp of his experiences. But whereas Teacher and Solo are non-problematic characters in the sense that they have accepted their defeat totally, Juana's interrelationship with other characters suspends her fate almost perpetually. She develops internal mechanisms to cope with her stultification, but this does not guarantee her peace of mind; not even flight can kill the 'disturbing sensation' within her.

'Disturbance' is of course what defines Baako. In this respect, he is the archetypal Armah anti-hero whose sense of psychological failure arises from the discovery of the wide gap between illusions and experiences. Baako suffers from the uniformity of the life he finds in Ghana;

the continuity of values which Naana celebrates at the opening of the novel is a tyranny the consequences of which he is not equipped to bear. The tone of the narrative — set, as we have already observed, by Naana — suggests that this is an allegory of a soul that must suffer. His development points only to the kind of dissolution which Juana knows only too well. And if Baako is not keen to return to Ghana, it is because his instincts point out the same kind of psychological death which he dies in America; his encounter with Brempong on the flight back home confirms his worst fears — the cargo cult has become a shrine. He does not fail to interpret Brempong's clear signals — naïvety is not one of Baako's weaknesses — but his personality revolts against the kind of philosophy that guarantees a been-to honour and glory. 'It is no use . . . going back with nothing' (p. 76), Brempong warns the young man, and yet Baako dares to confront the naked, uncouth ambitions and wild expectations of his family armed with nothing but the sense of being right.

The image of death and dissolution which we associate with Baako's return has already been pre-empted by Naana, who compares the been-to's mother to a cat prepared to devour its own kind. This devouring gesture is pinpointed by other smaller but telling signals: Brempong's friends 'bared' their teeth at the airport in a 'preparatory welcome gesture', and his sister throws herself at him with 'demonic energy'; the entire episode is summed up as 'some disease that has descended upon us' (p. 85). This showbiz only adds to Baako's growing sense of isolation.

Baako is, of course, innocent of the real-life experiences which he must undergo to find his moral centre, but his expectations are lower than Juana's. If he is a fallen man — at least in the spiritual sense, expecting nothing to redeem him, hence returning to accept his gift of death, as Teacher would put it — Baako is only so in an instinctive and rudimentary way. His encounter with Ghana does not affect his personality in any marked sense, but it adds to his knowledge of what defeat means. For most of the narrative, Baako struggles to define himself against a backdrop of 'troubling thoughts' and situations, not simply to understand himself in context, but also to force his feelings into modes of thought he can grasp. Such feelings are like a 'very strong impulse that gained in the potency of its beat with the awareness of every new event and every new thing that has passed outside' (p. 87). Forcing feelings into thoughts is, first and foremost, a connecting act, the linkage of small gestures and events to larger social maladies. Baako discovers, for example, that Brempong is not involved in 'a mere game', and is thus able to understand the meaning of the cargo cult; a logical understanding of the cult leads to the conviction that he cannot survive in Brempong's happy world. Predictably, the recognition of the wall between him and Brempong makes Baako yearn for an inner subjective reality outside the world of external things; he wishes to retreat into himself to preserve his sanity in 'ambiguous comfort' — 'savoring this sense of being so alone back home, connected for the moment to no one, with no one save himself knowing where he was' (pp. 92–93).

But as we have already observed in respect of *The Beautyful Ones*, the world of external things has different ways of forcing itself on Armah's internal exile. Baako's family asks him to cease being himself and play, not one, but many roles — 'impotent sometimes, growing, sometimes strong, confused , often weak, changing, many things by turns' (p. 93). For Baako, art is a way of rejecting all these roles, an instrument of making life 'mean something more'. In Ocran's view, however, this is a fallacy, since even the artist has been forced into a situation where nothing works, nothing has meaning. To be effective, contends Ocran, one must walk alone, rejecting all social roles, confronting the world without illusions, and, if possible, transcending it; the horrible alternative is the character's acceptance of the saviour role imposed on him by his family and community.

Unlike some of the characters in Armah's later works, Baako does not suffer from a limited understanding of his situation, but from what is referred to as 'an expanding consciousness'. He is too much aware of the unattainability of his ideals, of the discrepancy between his own sensibilities and what Juana calls the 'general current'. And, unlike Juana, Baako does not utilize the weapon of escape effectively; he seems to play up to those situations that oppress his inner being. For instance, he insists on taking up a job at the television station, although people who should know have warned him not to expect anything useful to happen there; he agrees to be the master of ceremonies at the premature outing of his sister's baby, even when he abhors the motive behind it. It is as if he confronts the most naked aspects of the oppressive culture to convince himself that he has indeed failed. In this respect, Baako, the man (*The Beautyful Ones*) and Modin (*Why Are We So Blest?*) constitute a peculiar pattern in Armah's *ouevre*. Their inner need — expressed though their sexuality in most instances — is the yearning for salvation even after they have convinced themselves that this is no longer possible. These characters seem to wear a mask which does not take them very far from their illusions; they try to convince themselves that they no longer care about salvation, be it personal or social, and that they are no longer concerned with the world of external things. Juana offers us some useful insights into the function of this mask:

She had had to admit she was concerned with salvation still, though she permitted herself the veil of other names. Too much of her lay outside of herself, that was the trouble. Like some forest woman whose gods were in all the trees and hills and people around her, the meaning of her life remained in her defeated attempts to purify her environment, right down to the final, futile decision to try to salvage discrete individuals in the general carnage. (p. 177)

Sexual contact is one way of dealing with the mask: it is a means by which these characters can reach out for external things (i.e. reinforce their physical being) without compromising themselves. But this kind of contact is itself illusory — the real world exists outside the narrow universe of the lovers.

Sometimes what promises to be a liberating experience in *Fragments* turns out to be a mirage. Baako resigns his job, hoping to work out a more meaningful relationship with his world, but when the moment of resignation arrives, it fills his mind with 'a whirling torture' as he tries 'in vain to grasp some substance out of the blighted year behind' (p. 186). What he seems to learn at the end of the narrative is something which he has known all along — 'You can't win' (p. 271). This is a bitter conclusion; not even Naana's optimism can ameliorate the sense of futility which overwhelms Baako. In her epilogue, the old woman concedes that she does not understand the sounds of the world she lives in — 'I myself an lost here,' she says, 'a stranger unable to find a home in a town of strangers so huge it has finished sending me helpless the long way back to all the ignorance of childhood' (p. 282) — but foresees a time when the impasse will be broken and her end will become her beginning. But Baako and Juana are still strangers in a universe where hopes and dreams are crushed under the weight of what the old woman calls 'the mass of things here and of this time' (p. 282).

The consciousness of failure: *Why Are We So Blest?*

The tone of Armah's most pessimistic novel is set by Solo in a cry characteristic of the fallen man in modernist fiction: 'Even before my death I have become a ghost, wandering about the face of the earth, moving with a freedom I have not chosen, something whose unsettling abundance I am impotent to use.'[14] Solo knows only too well what it means to be a living dead and to operate in a social void against one's will. Unlike Juana and Baako, he has no illusions or false hopes of regeneration; he does not reach out for any tangible matter, for he is not sure where he stands in relation to 'external things'. Solo's despair is deeper than that of Teacher because, unlike the latter, he has no memories to seek solace in; remembrance of things past only accentuates the sense of death which he carries around his neck like an albatross.

The Subjective Narrative

Why Are We So Blest? is constructed in such a way that its pessimism, and the Manichean vision that underlies it, are set in the foreground against the characters' attempt to understand their own impotence in the face of overwhelming social forces. First, most of the narrative is mediated through Solo's tortured mind, which structures images and symbols. Second, the novel is built around a set of philosophical principles which make broad generalizations on the human condition in a wide and, sometimes vague, manner; the novel does not explicate any particular themes, and any attempts to treat it as anything but one single unit cannot yield much in terms of value and meaning. We will examine these two propositions in turn.

Solo's lack of belief in anything but the inevitability of his death is significant to the overall design of the novel because he is not only the narrative's informing consciousness, but a key narrative agent in himself. He reiterates the futility of belief in the modernist landscape he lives in, and simultaneously tries to kill the illusion of belief. In Solo's vision, to be subjective is to recognize one's significance in relation to natural and human elements, for 'our personalities are battlefields on which our subjective demands meet the harsher demands of life and time' (p. 14). And the world — that harsh, often unredeeming entity which the prototype Armah character struggles against — is dismissed as a hideous place which is not worth any major act of will. And yet Solo's awareness of the ugliness of his world elicits a feeling of guilt. 'I am surrounded by this ugliness, insistent and grim, and yet the only occupation I desire is with beautiful truths,' Solo says of his divided consciousness. 'When I have had a day's fill of looking at what goes on, I wonder if anything exists that is at the same time both beautiful and true' (p. 15). Solo rejects his world because what is beautiful in it has no essential truths. In other words, social realities do not correlate to his deepest ideals.

There is, however, some inconsistency in Solo's conception of 'world' which is largely due to the absence of a tangible context which he can relate to, or react against. The psychiatric hospital is a symbolic context which coincides with Solo's view of the world outside, but it does not hold up any possibilities of redemption, renewal, or change in the characters' situation. The setting of the novel is merely an existential canvas. But the absence of a tangible setting in Solo's present situation is essential to the design of the novel, for it enhances the sense of mental disintegration which is an important aspect of narrative organization (or disorganization) in the novel. The narrative is carried by the characters' fragmented thought processes; it moves from past to present action and hence provides a situation in which past hopes merge with present despair. At the same time, the level of action in the novel moves from the lowest ebb of the characters' moral state (in the present) towards the highest points of their dreams (in the past), before plunging deeply into the inner recesses of the fallen man's mind. If there is a central theme in the novel, it is the pointlessness of movement, and this cyclic structure carries it very well.

In *Why Are We So Blest?*, action leads to death; ideals also lead to the degeneration of character. As the Congherian veteran reminds Solo, society is moved by idealists committed to specific modes of action, but 'they are destroyed in the process' (p. 27). Modin goes to study in America, ostensibly to help his people 'develop', but what is supposed to be a process of uplifting becomes his spiritual death. He becomes the victim of a social structure which is anti-African in its design, yet pays him to become a willing victim in a cycle of self-annihilation. The central irony in the novel is the transformation of aspiration into self-annihilation: characters aspire to ideals which are in themselves humane, but have to go through a process of spiritual death to attain what, they discover in the end, is unattainable. Later in life, when he is able to pattern his past experiences, Modin realizes that his invitation to America was a call to a spiritual disintegration far beyond the merely social disintegration Africa has suffered 'since how many centuries?' (p. 159). He sees his life in retrospect as a cycle of moments of dissipation which move him to his final dissolution. He has a keen awareness of his death:

> The more I think of what has happened, the harder I find it to escape the same conclusion: I am fated to undergo some form of death. There is no sanctuary. I have known periods of spiritual death when I have shut myself up away from this world. There is a loneliness that is a kind of death. But the solution that is available, involvement with these people, is itself a deeper form of death. (p. 159)

And yet his involvement with the Congherian revolution, which he hoped would help him break from the hold of death, leads him to a form of spiritual dissolution which hurts him much more because it is built around the illusion of hope. The above quotation is important in another respect: it illustrates how the novel is built around a subtle linkage of social, psychological and metaphysical suppositions and how these determine the shaping of Armah's characters. Modin's reflections on what is happening to Africa lead him to an understanding of what he calls his fate, and places his spiritual death in a real context.

The relationship between Solo and Modin has some interesting thematic and formal implications, too. The critical misunderstanding which seems to arise from any discussion of the two characters' functions in the novel — most of which lead to the conclusion that Solo has usurped Modin's role — arises from a negation of the latter as a centre of consciousness. And yet, we cannot treat Modin and Solo as equal agents of narrative movement (or non-movement) in the same way we treat Juana and Baako. True, Modin is the character who is destroyed before the reader's eyes and his dissolution evokes a measure of pathos similar to the one evoked by Baako's mental disintegration in *Fragments*, but whereas Juana can only comment on Baako's state of mind from her own immediate diagnosis of the character, Solo, whose dissipation takes place outside the novel, is able to subject Modin's experiences to his knowledge of what it means to die spiritually, and hence offers a stage-by-stage commentary on the process by which great expectations lead to self-annihilation. When we meet Solo at the beginning of the novel, he is just beginning to escape from the consciousness of 'external' things which has led to his despair; in contrast, Modin is introduced to us at the moment when he is about to explore the last frontiers of hope. If there is an element of inevitability in Modin's discovery that all his efforts are bound to failure, it is because Solo offers a parallel example of what happens to a soul that aspires to an ideal state where beauty and truth coalesce.

But Modin is not merely a passive character in relation to Solo: he probes into the latter's state of mind. When the two meet in Laccryville, for example, Solo is oblivious to the outside world: 'The only thing I was aware of these days was despair, and it was not a thing I wanted to sit and talk about, not in this place', (p. 55). Modin and Aimee challenge Solo's assumption that he has, like the Nietzschean hero, undergone his 'tragic act', that his descent into despair and spiritual dissolution is his liberation from physical forms. They are mirror images of his past and the idealism that fired him then; they remind him, at least momentarily, of the existence of love and aspiration:

> Images of desire filled my mind, and this time even the frustration I felt at being unable to satisfy these desires did not seem immediately painful. In fact it gave my longing a faintly pleasant sourness, the kind that comes with the mild forms of self-pity. (p. 61)

Love — later condemned as the gift of death — draws attention to Solo's human essence and, for a limited time, becomes his illusion.

There is another sense in which Solo and Modin probe into each other's personalities. Looking back on that period of his life when Modin looked up to him for some guidance, Solo mourns his inability to save the quester; and yet he is dubious about his abilities to save anyone, since he does not foresee any possibility of breaking through the Armahian circle of decay. Our disease, he observes, is 'ordained', and we have embarked on a journey without meaning. Characters like

Modin thus find their terminus in a context which does not provide avenues for further development: 'Here is physical space to wander in, space not for life's movement, space in which to turn in circles, again, again, again.' (p. 84).

To develop a consciousness of his failure — an important reinforcement of characters in a situation of complete despair — Solo has to keep on reminding himself of his self-annihilation. In spite of claims to the contrary, his consciousness is divided between that love of life, beauty and truth which he thinks he can never achieve, and a deep feeling that life is 'the tyranny of things'. He echoes a sense of despair which is familiar in Armah's early works — 'The meanness I hoped to move beyond stretches before me — an infinity' (p. 114). When he tries to look beyond his immediate situation, Solo sees only death.

The reality of spiritual death is one which Modin had to confront during his journey in America. He had to reject the honorary white status offered to him by Mr Oppenhardt (the representative of the American ruling class) because this would have forced him to live contrary to himself, maybe driven him to the frigidness he encounters in Aimee. But if he rejects his honorary white status to escape from spiritual and sensual death, Modin's efforts are destined to fail: by taking Aimee with him on his quest for liberation, he has carried the seeds of his destruction with him. He dies because of his sexual relationship with Aimee in a scene that recalls a Jim Crow lynching; when Aimee calls him 'nigger' towards the end of the novel, she is reaffirming her rights as the daughter of the American Revolution. 'He had found his own dissolution and he called it love,' observes Solo, who has been condemned to bear the burden of Modin's fate. In the former's fatalistic vision, the young African has merely relived his destiny, that 'ordained destruction' which we have inherited from the West.

Solo finds the idea of redemption deceptive; he only hopes to live out his littleness, his emptiness. Adopting the Ishmaelian role of the man who survives the tragedy to tell the tale, Solo sneers at Modin's belief that he could escape 'his destiny': 'he did not know his death was multiform, waiting for him whichever way he choose to turn' (p. 232). As a would-be artist, Solo knows that he cannot escape into the modernist illusion of a pure art form that liberates the artist from the realities of history. 'In my people's world, revolution would be the only art, revolutionaries the only creators,' Solo concludes. 'All else is part of Africa's destruction' (p. 231). Solo does not act out this role of the artist as revolutionary, but, as we saw in our first chapter, it is a key theme in Armah's later works.

Prometheus unbound: *The Interpreters*

The artist figure is central to the form and meaning of Soyinka's first novel, but whether he is the embodiment of the communal consciousness, or a detached critic of his society, he is a cause of disagreement among critics of African literature. For Abiola Irele, the myth of the artist in Soyinka's works 'rests on an idea of his role as the mediator of the inner truths that sustain the collective life, and on his function in renewing the fundamental values that govern it'.[15] The artist's relationship with his community is, however, more problematic, partly because he exists on the fringe of his community, yet claims to represent some of its key values, pure and unadulterated. In *The Interpreters*, the artist is a Promethean figure who stands up against Zeus's authority with culture, intelligence, and justice, but beyond this function, real or imagined, the Soyinkan character is a modernist creature struggling against both conflicting impulses within him and the demands of his socio-historical situation. In this respect, questions of choice and apostasy are central to the dénouement of such a character: he believes, against existing evidence, that he has chosen to lead the life of an apostate; but society, the corrupting factor, thwarts the protagonist's quest for wholeness and his illusion of free choice.

'Life is the dome of continuity,' stutters the spiritual Sekoni in *The Interpreters*, introducing one of the key themes in the novel — the relation between past and present.[16] The bridge of time joins the past and present, but the movement of this bridge is ill-defined, and the characters must swim with the tide, so to speak, to find their bearings. Sekoni's philosophizing is of course the signal that initiates Egbo's mental propulsion to his past and his attempts to return to his traditional community and leave the modern city behind. On the surface, Egbo has every reason to accept his role as the future leader of his clan — compared to his boring civil service job, this is a more invigorating role — but the closer he comes to the creek, the more he doubts the wisdom of the choice he is about to make. He is attracted by the silent world of the dead, but he does not think he is well equipped for the role he has been asked to play — that of the 'enlightened ruler'. Nor is Egbo sure of the past's claims to moral superiority: he has every reason to get away from an alienating present ('he knew and despised the age which sought to mutilate his beginnings' [p.11]), but he is not convinced that there is any real difference between 'the ugly mudskippers of this creek and the raucous toads of our sewage-ridden ports' (p. 14). Both live on ill-gotten gains. By refusing to make a conscious choice, preferring instead to flow with the tide, Egbo abandons his claims to free will.

The tide brings Egbo and his fellow interpreters back to the city. The corporate image of the group is that of an alienated bunch plunged into eternal despair. Trapped in the alienating metropolis, they can only fall back on memories of that moment when they nearly returned to the past, but they know that their experiences at the creek amounted to nothing more than 'an interlude from reality' (p. 10). While the past can provide momentary escape, it also adds to the characters' depression because it reminds them of their failures to consummate the ideals that brought them home from overseas. The interpreters have entered into a dialectical opposition with their realities — itself a vague concept in the novel — but they differ from Armah's internal exiles in the sense that they would like to change their society if it were possible. Finding themselves in a situation where 'reality' engenders forces which they cannot deal with adequately, Soyinka's characters are forced to recreate the world of their dreams in their own minds. Egbo's portrait of the 'awolebi' dancer in the night-club scene is a purified model of the original: he has seen her not as she is, but as he should like her to be, and thereby expresses his disillusionment with things as they are; reality, then, becomes a hallucination, dreams are presented as realities. And as we will see in reference to Kola's pantheon, works of art and mental images express the interpreter's yearning for a perfect, probably romantic, image of life. Those with the power to create works of art masquerade as deities. 'I cannot draw,' moans Egbo, dejected about the unattainability of his perfect 'awolebi' dancer. But he still yearns for what he cannot have: 'I would put my head between her breasts and smother my ears in them' (p. 25). The use of the auxiliary verb suggests Egbo's awareness of his inability to achieve what he dreams of; at this stage in his life, he does not have the energies to pull himself out of the state of lethargy we find him in.

Although there are some lurid portraits of the social scene in *The Interpreters*, society in the novel exists as the backdrop against which Soyinka's characters act out their own sense of frustration. The interpreters are keen observers of the social scene, but they do not react to their context in any significant way: having detached themselves from the goings-on of what they perceive as an unjust and corrupt society, these characters do not grow or degenerate in the present; the causes of their growth, and the motives for their actions, all lie in the past. Memory is the instrument by which the interpreters fashion their past lives and give the semblance of pattern to a novel that is fragmented by a complicated use of flashbacks. Such memories are intricately tied to the characters' aspirations in the past, their frustrations in the present and their uncertainty about the future. Sekoni, the engineer, returns to Nigeria yearning to tame nature, but his dreams are constructed outside a context that takes realities into consideration, and his failure is thus predictable. The poetry and music of Sekoni's dream cannot blur its unreality; he casts himself in the role of a god or a prophet and dreams of harnessing the powers of nature to human use:

> So he opened his palm to the gurgle of power from the charging prisoner, shafts of power nudged the monolith along the fissures, little gasps of ecstasy and paths were opened, and the brooding matriarchs surrendered at their strength, lay in neat geometric patterns at his feet. Sekoni shuffled them like cards and they reshaped to magic formulae in sweeping harbours. (p. 26).

And like a house of cards, Sekoni's sweet dream is brought tumbling down as soon as he confronts harsh reality. The omniscient narrator is of course having fun at the expense of his character, who has been condemned even before he has started.

In general, the satire in Soyinka's novel arises from the narrator's awareness of the gap between his characters' illusions and the realities they ignore in their sweet dreams. There is a strong suggestion in the novel that the characters' lives are controlled by some malignant fate which is quick to frustrate their efforts: witness the speed with which Sekoni's dreams are destroyed, or the destination of the tide to which Egbo trusts himself. The cynical Egbo even presents his seduction of Simi as his 'first act of singlemindedness, and my last' (p. 53); in contrast, Sagoe does not even commit himself to any recognizable mode of action; he advocates an absurd belief in nothingness as a *raison d'être*. In Sagoe's view, contemporary Nigerian society is defined by irrationality, and those who try to explain this society in any rational terms end up on 'the pyre'.

And yet Sekoni, the character who tries to act decisively, is the focus of the interpreters' life, both as an example of what they had all wanted to be but couldn't, and the object of their pathos. Part Two of the novel lacks a sense of cohesion largely because of the absence of a human centre around which the other characters and their disparate thoughts can revolve. It is as if Sekoni's death has broken the 'dome of continuity' which brings the interpreters together in spite of their different temperaments. Sekoni's death does in fact have a devastating effect on the other characters:

> It helped Egbo not at all that he fled to the rocks by the bridge until the funeral was over where unseen he shed his bitter angry tears, or Sagoe locked in beer and vomit for a week and Dehinwa despairing of his temperature, battling to keep quiet while he bawled you're wetting me all over with your goddamn tears. (p. 155).

This is the last time the interpreters have Sekoni as the object of their sympathy. After this, the narrative shifts to Joe Golder, Lazarus and

The Subjective Narrative

Noah, who do not galvanize its different strands in the same way as Sekoni's pathetic figure. In spite of this failure, it is not true that 'the quasi-religious antics' of Lazarus and Noah, to use Lewis Nkosi's term, 'illustrate very little in the novel'.[17] For the interpreters, they provide a different mode of escape from a depressing and alienating social situation.

The quest motif is central to the form and meaning of *The Interpreters*. We cannot be sure whether the interpreters conceive any viable means of putting some of their dreams into action — except of course through the painless medium of art — but they are all involved in a personal quest which will enhance their sense of being. In the first part of the novel, the quest takes a more personalized form, distinct from the evangelical quest of Noah and Lazarus in the second part: Egbo, as we have already observed, is a romantic quester for his traditional roots against the backdrop of contemporary Nigerian political and social realities; before his hasty fall, Sekone tries to harness nature for human use, while Sagoe's quest is for the meaning of meaninglessness. All these three projected modes of self-fulfilment involve a measure of withdrawal from society and all its realities into a self-gratifying, isolated world of the self. After the failure of their various quests, the interpreters turn to art as a medium of recreating the world that has frustrated their desires in more acceptabe terms. For Sekoni, whose frustration is most vividly dramatized in the novel, art becomes nothing less than a lever against encroaching insanity, so that whereas he could not have the opportunity, or be allowed to harness nature before, he can now turn a block of wood into 'a magic locked in energy' (p. 100). In art, Sekoni finds his true vocation; the artistic medium releases him, at least in his mind, from the hold of society. But art is more than a liberating medium for the failed engineer: it is the pathway to his godhead. Among the more flamboyant characters, such as Egbo, Sekoni is 'the most non-existent person in the world' (p. 121), but he is the most reflective, determined to reach for the centre of existence where life and death are contained in a 'single d-d-dome' (122).

Even Egbo, the man who wants to stamp life with his presence, searches for the meaning of existence outside the world of people and things. Reflecting on the choice he fails to make (his inability to relate to the past of his ancestors, his inherited materialism), Egbo conceives the claims of the community as a kind of tyranny. The choice he was supposed to make when he was borne by the tide, he insists, was not a real choice but 'a measure of tyranny'. He notes that a 'man's gift of life should be separate, an unrelated thing. All choice must come from within him, not from the promptings of his past' (p. 120). Returning from a silent grove, from what he calls a 'place of pilgrimage', Egbo discovers what he believes will be the weapon of his quest, or as Soyinka puts it in a classy way, 'a divine boon': 'Knowledge he called it, a power for beauty often, an awareness that led him dangerously towards a rocksalt psyche, a predator on Nature' (p. 127). As in the case of Armah's modernist man, the gifts the interpreters discovers inside themselves (not least knowledge and the love of beauty) are often the source of their discontent and inability to come to terms with their social and natural landscape.

As a journey away from exteriority, the interpreters' quest must inevitably define their relationship with their context. Their goal is to stand above the corrosive powers of society, ministering to it without being a part of its corruption. Kola, the least discussed of the interpreters and the one with little substance as a persona, illustrates the form of élitism that puts the artist above his community. He is a near angel, stands above everything else and is only perceived through intuition. No wonder he drives the down-to-earth pedant Lasunwon mad with his superior demeanour:

> What is he anyway that he goes round giving himself some special status in the universe? And I don't mean just him, it's the whole tribe of them. Everyday somewhere in the papers they are shooting off their mouths about culture and art and imagination. And their attitude is so superior, as if they are talking to the common illiterate barbarians of society. (p. 163).

Lasunwon is of course riled by what he believes is his own insignificance, but he nonetheless offers us an apt indictment of the élitism of the interpreters as artistic figures. This élitism is founded on a common modernist notion: the belief that power (the energy of society as a socio-political body) corrupts, and that the duty of the artist is to stand above this corruption, save himself as it were, and preserve the eternal human values which bourgeois art is supposed to embody.

But art is not posited as mere powerlessness in *The Interpreters*. Those who deride social and political power also seek a strange Promethean energy to activate their ideals. Take Kola as he stands before his pantheon, as an example:

> Fitfully, far too fitfully for definite realisation of the meaning, he had felt this sense of power, the knowledge of power within his hands, of the will to transform; and he understood then that medium was of little importance, that the act, on canvas or on human material was the process of living and brought him the intense fear of fulfilment. (p. 218)

For the modernist character in search of his identity, art is not merely a medium of self-signature, but also an expression of the artist's ahistorical energies. In a situation where nature and society are seen as monstrous encroachments on human life, art becomes an instrument of struggle against history; under Kantian idealism, the world of the artistic imagination comes to being when the raw data of experience is organized by the mind into something new, through the creative powers of the sensibility. In the case of Kola, the quest for self-fulfilment reaches its apex when the artistic imagination gets hold of the world (empirical reality) and remodels it in mythical terms.

A different, more theological, quest is illustrated by the Lazarus/ Noah sub-plot. Lazarus's real significance in the novel lies in the way he demands the total submission of his would-be disciples, expressing his determination not only to expose his world, but also to convert it to his singular faith. The sinner, argues Lazarus, must be cleansed to receive 'the holy spirit of God' (p. 177); but what is the sinner after the cleansing? As the case of the petty thief Noah illustrates, the convert is deprived of his vitality, prompting Egbo to question the logic of modes of social salvation, like the ones the interpreters had dreamt of in their more idealistic days, which emasculate the subject. 'To cleanse . . . to really cleanse a human being,' reflects Egbo, 'you must leave him like Noah, dead, devitalised, with no character of any sort, a blank white sheet for accidental scribbles' (p. 231).

And yet there are those for whom the quest for self-identity in a 'circle of emptiness' (p. 244) has become a form of morality in itself. Such is the case of the American Joe Golder, described as 'an archaic figure disowned by a family album':

> Joe Golder sought the world in hope, the faceless, unfathomed world, a total blank for man whose every note tore him outward, Joe Golder bared his soul, mangled, spun in murky fountains of grief which cradled him, the long-lost child, but would not fling him clear . . . (p. 245)

The interpreters are endowed with the knowledge that Golder's quest for home is bound to fail. Towards the end of the novel, they have sought refuge in art, and yet their sense of dissociation from a meaningful context never ceases to torment them. It is this sense of alienation that strikes Kola as he watches Bandele (the symbol of Prometheus' power in the pantheon) change from 'a protagonist in pilgrim's robes' into a 'total stranger, and becoming increasingly inscrutable' (p. 244). Again, the interpreters' dilemma arises from their need to be meaningful in a context they have signified as meaningless. Here is Kola again:

> . . . if only we were, if only we were and we felt nothing of the enslaving cords, to drop from impersonal holes in the void and owe neither dead nor living nothing of our selves, and we should grow

toward this, neither acknowledging nor weakening our will by understanding, so that when the present breaks over our heads we quickly find a new law for living. Like Egbo always and now, Bandele. (pp. 244–45)

But Egbo and Bandele have found their real reasons for being in neither the past nor in the future, and the challenge facing the modernist character in Soyinka's works is that of coming to terms with the present.

Being and understanding: *Season of Anomy*

It is appropriate that we end this essay with a brief examination of Soyinka's second novel, for *Season of Anomy* modifies some of the key modernist assumptions in the novels we have been discussing so far, represents a conscious determination to break away from the ideology of modernism and pre-empts the literature of social praxis in Africa. *Season of Anomy* is the only novel, in the category we have designated as the subjective narrative, in which the landscape functions as an active character (instead of a fixed, deterministic universe) which changes its nature and meaning in the course of the narrative. The changes in the landscape reflect not so much the characters' growth to consciousness, but the historical degeneration of the society in which the novel is set. This is one of the few novels in the modernist tradition in African fiction in which the memories and reminiscences of the characters are not as important as episodes and set dramatic scenes. Instead of the characters simply reflecting on their context, we have them engaged actively with both their socio-historical context and other characters. Hence there is actual development of character in this novel, not a mere restatement of the initial situation of despair and degradation.

The narrative opens in the most ideal social situation. In a country dominated by the cartel, held under terror by the gun and the purse, Aiyero is Utopia: an organic community whose values seem to grow directly from nature, untouched by the creed of Mammonism that afflicts the rest of the landscape. Before its 'discovery' during a census, Aiyero relates to the rest of the country on its own terms; external events have never determined the development of the community's political culture in any decisive way, so that her sons go to work in the city (the most glaring and infamous symbol of modernism in the African novel) but still return with their primeval values intact. In Aiyero, then, Soyinka offers us a concrete, communalistic, liberative myth (similar to the myths in the works of the later Armah). How such a communal entity can exist in the midst of a modernist world is the riddle Ofeyi tries to unravel.

The Subjective Narrative

Ofeyi is himself a developed portrait of the artistic figure in the African modernist novel: he is an interesting fusion of the pilgrim and the protagonist, a character who strives to understand his context and to change it too. His energies grow out of an idealistic desire to turn the modernist wasteland into a productive garden against all the odds, and the movement of the narrative is created by the tension between his ideals and harsh historical reality. If Ofeyi does not succeed in his initial attempt to decipher the codes that make Aiyero humane, it is because of his sense of superiority; he believes he can give this community a pep talk on humanistic ideals, and what Aiyero teaches him, in turn, is to be humble. In reality, there is no antagonism between the young quester and Aiyero because both speak the same language, so that in the end the community influences the quester as much as he influences it.

Ofeyi changes the character of Aiyero in a number of significant ways. He argues for the extension of the community's values beyond its boundaries, and goes on to become an agent of this extension, thereby bringing Aiyero into a direct confrontation with the cartel state; at the same time, he pushes the community beyond its complacency and hence prepares it for the inevitable struggle with the forces of modernism. As he tells Ahime, the waters of Aiyero 'need to burst their banks' and the grain 'must find new seminal grounds or it will atrophy and die'.[18] In the same vein, Aiyero forces Ofeyi to play out his ideals against realities in a way he would not have done if he had remained a mere dreamer in the service of the cartel: it 'promised much, tantalizing him with answers, potencies. It had to yield something to his search' (p. 7). He sees the transformative hand of Aiyero in the transfiguration of Iriyise, who is brought into contact with 'this earth of ours which you take so much for granted' by Ahime and emerges from the experience complete, a symbol of a brave, new, fruitful world.

To criticize Soyinka for creating a too upright and balanced image of a community in Aiyero is to miss the functioning of the protean myth in his work, for the Utopian community is not important for any sense of verisimilitude (or its absence), but as a probable social reality. The major flaw in the novel is not the incredibility of Aiyero, but its development in relation to the cartel state; it is only late in the novel that the two entities relate to each other in any significant way, and we are not really convinced that the youth of the commune could have spent much time in the domain of the cartel without picking up some of the corrupting influences of the modern state. Part of the problem has to do with the location of the commune on the time-scale, since it is unusual for a protean community in African fiction to be situated in the present; the values such communities embody are often in the form of a past memory or a longed-for vision.

The Subjective Narrative

What defines Aiyero, though, is its consciousness of being modern; as modern as the cartel and, significantly, still humane. The characters in *Season of Anomy*, unlike their counterparts in *The Interpreters*, do not live under the tyranny of the past; as Ahime puts it bluntly, the people of Aiyero have rejected the 'shackles of memory':

> We are here, we prosper and we know harmony. It suffices. It is the first principle we teach our children, they grow up despising dead knowledge whose nature is the nature of what is gone, dead, rotten. This is not to say that we keep things hidden. All our people know from where we came, and they know that we founded Aiyero to seek truth, a better life, all the things which men run after. They also believe that we found it. That is why our children always come back. (p. 9)

Aiyero was founded by people who broke away from the modernist state to search for a better ideal of life; Ofeyi comes from the 'outer cesspits of the land' to teach this community communalistic ideals borrowed from European social philosophers only to discover that such ideals are practised in real life in his adopted landscape. He thus becomes an apprentice, bent on learning the social implications of his ideas, the rationale for praxis.

But Ofeyi, the would-be communal activist, is also a modernist in a critical way. As we have already suggested, he is distinguished from the interpreters by his activism, not least the will to put his ideas into practice, and foresees ways of retrieving his occupation 'from its shallow world of shingles and the greater debasement of exploitation by the cartel' (p. 19). His modernist tendencies are reflected in his almost naïve trust in the powers of his mind which, ironically, lives under the fear of what modernism really means, and is, therefore, haunted by doubts. Witness his refusal to become a custodian of the grain: his reasons for refusing the most significant role in Aiyero are an acknowledgement of the shackling of the mind to the sensibility (and reality) of being modern. Hence his cry: 'I came to Aiyero wallowing in the filth and compromises of Ilosa' (p. 23).

Ofeyi struggles with the status of being marginal, both in Aiyero and Ilosa, until he comes across the Dentist, a man who has overcome his existential condition and is about to play his role to its logical conclusion. The Dentist's clarity of vision, in particular his ability to justify the use of violence without any lingering doubts, disconcerts Ofeyi, and he returns to Ahime in desperation. 'I believe in Aiyero,' he tells Ahime, trying to justify his passiveness; he has to undergo an experience that will show him how ideas fare when they come face to face with experience. By borrowing some of Ahime's men to form a revolutionary cadre that will spread the ideals of Aiyero in the cartel state,

The Subjective Narrative

Ofeyi again reinforces his faith in the power of the mind (and ideas) as an instrument of social change, one which will hopefully pre-empt the Dentist's more drastic, surgical measures. In failure, he learns the deficiency of his method in the same way the Dentist recognizes the full implications of his unmediated acts through success.

Ofeyi's decision to join the war against the cartel at the end of the second book is his first decisive movement away from mere contemplation and is questioning of the effectiveness of the weapon of theory. But the modernist man in him still struggles with doubts: when the agents of the cartel hit at the 'moral thorn in the complacent skin of the national body' (p. 82) and the defeat of the Aiyero vanguard appears imminent, Ofeyi is seized by such a deep crisis of doubts that Ahime is compelled to wonder whether the young man still believes in his own words any more. What Ofeyi has discovered in his struggle with the cartel is the cycle of decay (or historical determinism) which we discussed in respect to Armah's novels. Ofeyi, who saw in the new dam at Shage a symbol of a 'marriage of the physical and the ideal', believes that its destruction by the forces of the cartel is a physical expression of failure. 'Failure,' Ofeyi reflects. 'Was this the smell, the colour, the phantasma of failure?' (p. 85). Doubts about the viability of his plans are merged with an almost pathological fear of failure, the same kind of failure which extreme modernist characters such as Solo in *Why Are We So Blest?* see as an affirmation of their suspicion that there can never be meaningful change in the wasteland. The temptation to take the history of the land as one vicious cycle of plunder, death and destruction, propelled by innate forces that defy change, becomes great as Ofeyi struggles with his 'doubts upon doubts' (p. 85). But to accept the determinism of history is to abnegate his ability to function as an agent of social transformation:

> The refutation of change brought moments of despair. Behind the canoe, even the lake conspired to breed spores of this paralysis, closing up the scar of passage, blotting out the challenge of the voyager, substituting a statement of immutability even for this simple rite of passage. Ofeyi muttered, Camouflage! The regenerative powers were only jealously contained within the pool, hidden but attainable, awaiting only the rightful challenger. It awaited only the precise trigger to arouse it to its function within convulsive, rock-blasting, honing tides. (p. 87)

Unlike the archetypal modernist character who tries to affirm himself by justifying the need to despair, Ofeyi tries to overcome his doubts by asserting the vincibility of the enemy. At the same time, however, he is forced to reconsider his methods in the face of the cartel's violent drive against even its most passive critics, and to reappraise, almost against his inclinations, the Dentist's position.

Even without going into the ethics of the Dentist's violent methods, it is not difficult for Ofeyi to see why the man scores so many points with his 'unassailable logic of extraction before infection' (p. 88). The cartel has wreaked havoc on the land with a ritualistic, murderous drive which does not seem to have any logical explanation. For the Dentist, however, every act of violence demands an equal and similar response: 'Beyond the elimination of men I know to be destructively evil, I envisage nothing,' he tells Ofeyi, 'What happens after that is up to people like you' (p. 108). His assumption that nothing good can come out of the cartel is justified by what we see on the landscape, including curfew town, the cocoa company's own creation:

> City of the New Era, Future Cosmopolis, its spotless ultra-modernity was a symbol of the progressive and unblemished character of the men of Jekú. It was the planned city, it proved that Jekú had a plan. An old, crumbling village, primitive, clannish and locked in decadent rituals of vengeance had been transformed into a clinical exhibition city of factories, colleges and civic contentment. (p. 126)

The town expresses the cartel's understanding of modernity: artificiality and strict control, exploitation and repression. Against this background, Ofeyi struggles to reconcile his desire to heal the wounds that have been inflicted on the land by the company and its native agent class, and his own inability to act decisively.

But dealing with the cartel's artificial and murderous reality is not gamesmanship. Making another journey through the wasteland after a second spate of slaughter, Ofeyi is almost overwhelmed by the power and relentless drive of the cartel's repressive machine which has turned the Shage project into 'the netherworld' (p. 170). He tries to substitute this harsh reality with 'the Anubis-headed multitudes of his dream': 'They poured into the abyss from all sides, swarmed over the rim and raced downwards towards a promised feast, a coalescence of that feast whose seated aftermath he had just witnessed at the dam (pp. 170–171). But dreams cannot substitute Utopia for the netherworld, and this is a lesson Ofeyi learns quickly.

The relentless image of horror and death in *Season of Anomy* does not merely exist as perceived by Ofeyi; it is dramatized on its own. Although the use of set scenes in the novel is not very successful when they are either overdone or are not related to the characters' perspective, they often evoke the kind of fear and repulsion of the cartel which Soyinka intended them to have: Chapter XI is a forceful mural of death and decay which brings out the kind of fusion of landcape and character which I think is the hallmark of this novel. The chapter opens with an eerie evocation of the people waiting for death with 'a stare of resigned preparation for just that final unexpected blow' (p. 187); we then follow Ofeyi and his entourage into what is aptly described as 'the territory of hell' (p. 187). The landscape is defined by terror, organized carnage, putrefaction and general miasma, delivered with an ironic tinge:

> It took no energy to kill or maim. It took much to bury the dead. The wells and inland waters proved receptive, insatiable. When the streets were piled high and the vultures proved too tardy scavengers, glutted beyond their airborne dreams in this mostly barren landscape, then the trucks moved in, gathered up the gruesome debris and tipped them into the reservoir. (p. 188)

These graphic images of death remind Ofeyi how futile dreams and ideals can be when pitted against brutal force. Such thoughts push him further and further towards the Dentist's equally violent creed, raising doubts in his mind about what is right and wrong:

> It is not real, Ofeyi murmured, and inwardly cursed his growing incapacity for immersing himself even in pauses of relief. The feeling persisted and grew that there could be no natural entitlement to this, that the moment's normality was doomed to be revealed a mere mockery, a sham of a dream. (p. 238)

But every movement Ofeyi makes reminds him of the reality of this nightmare, so that by the time he finds himself in the catacombs, he cannot continue deceiving himself. It is easier to explain this violence in metaphysical and pseudo-psychological terms, but, as the Dentist would say, there is a logical explanation for everything; the mind that struggles to free itself from the consciousness of modernism must first release itself from the notion that failure, despair and inaction are the index that defines the African experience. As he struggles to release Iriyise from the mental asylum, Ofeyi strives to shrug off the temptation to rationalize or explain what he has been through in purely metaphysical terms. In the meantime, the Dentist has followed his rational choice to its logical conclusion, and the African novel has, in both form and meaning, shifted from a heuristic mode to one that recognizes the function of the novel as praxis.

Notes

1 'Tradition and Continuity in African Literature' in *Exile and Tradition: Studies in African and Caribbean Literature*, ed. Rowland Smith (London: Longman, 1976), p. 166.
2 'Post-independence Disillusionment in Three African Novels' in *Neo-African Literature and Culture*, eds Bernth Lindfors and Ulla Schild (Wiesbaden: Heymann, 1976), p. 166.
3 'The Notion of Modernity in African Creative Writing', *East African Journal* 8 (October, 1971), p. 31.
4 See *The Dehumanization of Art and Notes on the Novel*, trs. Helene Weyl (Princeton: Princeton University Press, 1948), p. 6.
5 Cited in *The Modern Tradition: Backgrounds of Modern Literature*, eds Richard Ellman and Charles Fiedelson Jr. (New York: Oxford University Press, 1965), pp. 740–41.
6 *Symbolism: The Manichean Vision* (Lincoln: University of Nebraska Press, 1975), p. 4.
7 'The Introverted Novel' in *Modernism 1890–1930*, eds Malcolm Bradbury and James McFarlane (Sussex: Harvester Press, 1978), p. 401.
8 *Ibid.*, pp. 404–405.
9 *The Beautyful Ones Are Not Yet Born* (London: Heinemann, 1969), p. 2. Further references to this edition will be made in the text.
10 *The Illusion* (London: Panther Books, 1972), p. 113.
11 See Malcolm Bradbury and James McFarlane, 'The Name and Nature of Modernism' in *Modernism 1890–1930*,
12 'African Socialism: Utopian or Scientific?' *Presence Africaine* 64(1967), p. 20.
13 *Fragments* (London: Heinemann, 1974), p. 1. Further references to this edition will be made in the text.
14 *Why Are We So Blest?* (London: Heinemann, 1974), p. 11. Further references to this edition will be made in the text.
15 *The African Experience in Literature and Ideology* (London: Heinemann, 1981), p. 192.
16 *The Interpreters* (London: Heinemann, 1970), p. 9. Further references to this edition will be made in the text.
17 *Tasks and Masks: Themes and Styles of African Literature* (London: Longman, 1981), p. 70.
18 *Season of Anomy* (London Rex Collings. 1980), p. 6. Further references to this edition are made in the text.

4
The Political Novel

Community, Character and Consciousness in
Sembene Ousmane's *God's Bits of Wood*,
Alex La Guma's *In the Fog of the Season's End*
and Ngugi's *Petals of Blood*

From our discussion of the African novel so far, we can safely conclude
that the subject of this mode of narrative, indeed its necessity, is politics. The novels we have been examining in the preceding chapters are
invariably concerned with the political realities of contemporary
Africa in a time context. These novels try to establish a historical link
between a mythical past in which African communities were more
united and organized around a set of humane principles (as in *Two
Thousand Seasons*), through the more immediate past of violent con-
tract with the colonizers (*Houseboy*), to a post-independence wasteland (*Season of Anomy*). That 'seasons' constitute a major emblem of
temporality in these novels is not accidental: the African novelist has,
on his own admission, sought to place his people on a specific time
scale, to understand the meaning and dimension of history. But to
acknowledge the centrality of politics in African fiction is not to
resolve the problems of genre and interpretation which we have tried to
confront in this study, for the body politic manifests itself in different
ways, most of which have a firm theoretical foundation. These ways
range from Armah's mythical-historical dramatization of an earlier
period of the African experience in his later works, to the use of ideology as an instrument of explicating social reality in some of the works
we are going to examine in this chapter. In the 'psychological' novels of
Beti and Oyono, on the other hand, characters are presented in more
minute situations in which they are used as agents for exploring the
effects of colonialism on the African culture and psyche. This steady
process of individualizing reality — presenting it in terms of perception and mediation through a mind that exists uneasily in its

context — reaches a peak in what we have loosely labelled the modernist novels of Armah and Soyinka. We can then submit that Ousmane, Ngugi and La Guma see themselves as revisionists of the modernists and write from the assumption that in spite of presenting our sense of betrayal and failure accurately and dramatically, and placing the blame squarely on the shoulders of the neo-colonial ruling class, the modernist novel has failed to encapsulate the totality of the African experience.

The modernist novel is a fiction of crisis; the modernist novelist is not overtly concerned with specific social modes; he is concerned more with the symptoms rather than the socio-historical dynamics of our experience; the reality of his novels is thus limited to the perception of a character who lives on the periphery of a society he would like to negate in its entirety. There is a sense in which the central characters of the modernist narrative is not presented as a creation of easily explicable socio-economic formations; they exist, instead, in the reality of art, since the universe in which we seek meaning is the one the artist figure in these novels has created to counter historical reality. The ideology of modernism, as George Kateb has observed, is based on an absence, a gap in meaning and understanding, a hint of something to come, but barely an assertion.[1]

The novelist who wants to represent society as a totality and make concrete political assertions about community, character and consciousness in his narrative must come to terms with the nature and meaning of ideology in fiction. Soyinka reflects an angry attempt to hedge the whole question of ideology in art. In his foreword to *Opera Wonyosi*, he declares his preference for 'reflective and expositional' modes of writing in contrast to what he terms 'explanation and analysis'; *angst* is adopted as an expression of the artist's social activism, driving him to expose, 'indeed magnify the decadent, rotted underbelly of a society that has lost its direction, jettisoned all sense of values and is careering down a precipice as fast as the latest artificial boom can take it'.[2] In trying to draw a distinction between social and literary ideology, Soyinka insists that he is primarily interested in literature as an immediate-effect medium, but not as an 'anodyne of "correct" class analysis'.[3] Yet Soyinka has developed an elaborate literary ideology in his own works; a ritual archetypal system of ideas which his detractors have labelled 'ogunism'. His opposition does not appear to be to literary ideology as such, but to the meaning and implications of the concept itself.

The problem of ideology in literature has been created through a misconception, nurtured by both 'vulgar' Marxists and their ideological sparring partners, that art can be reduced to specific political and philosophical forms of consciousness; hence ideology tends to be taken as dogma, a set of definite laws which function as reductive agents that bring art to the level of the socio-economic structure. But as Terry Eagleton has noted, ideology is more than a set of doctrines: it is a mode of perception that 'signifies the way men live out their roles in class society, the values, ideas and images which tie them to their social functions and so prevent them from a true knowledge of society as a whole'.[4] Ideology as an instrument of total understanding becomes particularly urgent in a modernist, fragmented world, because the writer's sense of alienation arises initially from his inability to understand his social context fully. For this reason, the writer (and his characters) feels that he is not the creator of his world, and can barely influence events in it; hence he works from, and with, small situations which he can control and explain. The anti-modernist writer, on the other hand, tries to overcome his existential status, to become a master of his world, hopefully triumph over what we have already referred to as the landscape of chaos.

In the latter case, ideology is many things to the artist. It is an instrument of understanding creations of culture and of relating these creations to their specific social and historical structures; it is a mode of consciousness that helps the artist analyse patterns in the experiences he is writing about and accord them some meaning. Ideology is also what Gramsci would call the ruling class's justification of its economic, political and cultural practices: an agent of hegemony. In this case, the artistic ideology in the narrative is one way in which the writer can counter the hegemonic culture, reaching beyond apparent reality to a deeper, more significant reality that lies hidden beneath the ideologically determined superstructure which the text inherits from social reality. Finally, a literary ideology enables the novelist to shape and rationalize the world in his novels; it functions as a philosophical referent, what Karl Mannheim calls 'the ultimate and fundamental interpreter of the flux in the contemporary world'.[5] We can thus argue that the limitation of the modernist novel as an interpretation of contemporary reality is the author's assumption that he can represent a fragmented world without ideological mediation.

The political novel strives to represent a reality beyond the merely representational. This is a genre which goes beyond reality towards an anticipation of life and society beyond present reification; unlike the modernist novel, the literature of praxis is informed by a belief that 'structure', or 'history', or the 'mechanics of society' provide man with referents which can enable him to know himself and the world.[6] This is the kind of novel which, as Georg Lukacs argued in *The Theory of the Novel*, tries to capture human life as a totality in spite of contemporary alienation, and grows out of the premise that art is an instrument to counter fragmentation by establishing the link between the inner world of men and their outer reality.[7] Or, as Lukacs insisted in his dispute over abstraction with Ernst Bloch, the goal of the realist novel is 'to penetrate the laws governing objective reality and to uncover the deeper, hidden, mediated, not immediately, perceptible network of relationships that go to make up society'.[8]

In this essay, we are concerned with three novels which confront the body politic during three historical phases in the development of modern African society. Sembene Ousmane's pioneering political novel, *God's Bits of Wood*, deals with one important episode in the anti-colonial struggle on the continent, the strike on the Bamako-Dakar railway in 1947; La Guma's *In the Fog of the Season's End* reaches for the nerves and threads of the struggle against apartheid in South Africa, while Ngugi's *Petals of Blood* is a structuring of the dynamics of neo-colonialism in Kenya. All three works are political novels in the sense that political ideas and ideology are not merely aspects of 'local colour', but function as determinants of form and content; they have a distinctive ideological principle underlying them, and in Irving Howe's terms, they are always 'in a state of internal warfare, always on the verge of becoming something other than [themselves]'.[9]

The making of a community: *God's Bits of Wood*

At a time when the artistic persona-cum-intellectual has become a central figure in the growth of the African novel, Sembene Ousmane's concern with the evolution of a whole community in *God's Bit of Wood* is unique. Unencumbered by that intellectual bent which is the bane of the so-called francophone novelist, Ousmane has never conceived alienation as the fate of the modern African. He has, like the traditional griot on whom he has fashioned himself, stayed close to the 'listening tree', observing and recording the lives of his community, determined 'to remain as close as possible to reality and to the people'.[10] Reality and people: these are the two words which best sum up Ousmane's understanding of the role of the literature of praxis. For this novelist, 'reality' is conceptualized by the word 'politique' (the affairs of the city), which unifies the actions of men and the context they have created by their deeds and acts. He does not conceive his art outside its social, economic and religious context: as he asserted in a telling quarrel with the francophone cultural élite, 'Every form of culture, especially literature, has its own ideology, so the problem is a political one'.[11] Unlike other political novelists, such as Ngugi and La Guma, Sembene Ousmane does not present the artist as the receptacle for a specially-endowed consciousness. He sees writing as 'a social necessity, like the jobs of the mason, the carpenter, or the iron-worker'.[12]

Predictably, the primary reality in *God's Bits of Wood* is the place and the people; they are presented plainly, without authorial intrusion and manipulation. If we take the opening scene of the novel as an opening shot in a movie, we cannot but appreciate Ousmane's sensitivity towards the landscape and its engaging technicolor quality: 'The last rays of the sun filtered through a shredded lacework of clouds. To the west, waves of mist spun slowly away, and at the very center of the vast mauve and indigo arch of the sky the great crimson orb grew steadily larger.'[13] The cinematic quality of the first few lines of the novel is reinforced with sharp, vivid, descriptive phrases: the sun is described as a 'celestial projector' focusing on significant features on the landscape; the governor's house is 'poised like a sugar castle on the heights that bore its name' (p. 1). Ousmane's real skill as an artist is evident in the way he comments on the scenery through the subtle positioning of visual details in the documentary tradition. The mud-walled houses of the workers who feature prominently in the evolution of the colonial community are viewed from the governor's residence. From this broad sweep across the landscape, the author's camera eye focuses on Bakayoko's house, and we are introduced to Niakoro. Once more the positioning and contrast of characters constitute a form of silent commentary: Niakoro is a figure from a past which was firm and stable, with what is called a 'framework'; in contrast, her son Bakayoko represents the present state of turbulence and uncertainty in the colonial state. Little Ad'jibid'ji advances the historical frame a stage further: she is both a product of the strike that is dramatized in the novel and Ousmane's hope for the future. Her 'maturity,' 'quickness' and 'intelligence' are inherited from the past and present of the anti- colonial struggle; she combines Niakoro's thoughtfulness with Bakayoko's desire to be free.

In spite of its casualness, Ousmane's narrative is peopled by characters whose significance lies in their ordinariness: these characters are not elevated or typified to represent anything more than themselves, and the reader is not nudged to read more than is necessary into them. And yet we cannot fail to see a motive of significance behind such characters, so that they become, in hindsight, important ingredients in a well-patterned narrative. Even in microcosmic situations, we can see the author's sense of pattern manifesting itself in a number of ways. First, we have the linkage of characters such as Niakoro, Bakayoko and Ad'jibid'ji, which also constitutes a link between past, present and future time, Second, these characters are always presented as members of a community, or in relation to a social group that holds certain distinctive values, so that their growth as individuals indicates significant changes in the nature of this society. Sometimes, of course, the author presents the community directly, either through overt descriptions of some of its key institutions, such as the union building or the market place, or by giving prominence to family and social units. The union building is situated, symbolically, near a prison: one represents the gathering of the railway men's energies; the other is an instrument of arresting these powers when they challenge the hegemony of the colonial authority.

Nothing illustrates Ousmane's sense of a community which is always in motion better than the regular gathering of the workers; he is concerned both with the latter's perception of their role within the colonial context and their potential for changing their historical situation. The accent here is naturally on the workers' active and militant character, and their nascent unity: on the day of the crucial meeting called to discussed the impending strike, the union building is described as a 'beehive of activity, with workers from all of the locals arriving or departing' (p. 6); the gathering mass becomes a human barricade against the soldiers and militia standing guard outside, and a symbolic meeting of souls is represented in the men's devotion to their union, and their adoption of Ad'jibid'ji as their daughter. But the present crisis is not the sole source of the men's fraternity; they are linked together by a history of struggle against the colonial regime which is embedded in Mamadou Keita's memory: 'the epidemics . . . famines . . . and . . . the seizure of tribal lands by the [rail] company'.

The fusion of individuals into masses appeals to the novelist's camera eye. The narrator has positioned himself on the wall, like a fly, and from this vantage point he can watch the people losing their individuality and metamorphosing into the mass character that plays such a significant role in the novel. There are cases where the authorial point of view is merged with that of a key character to explore the scene from within, as it were: Ad'jibid'ji, for example, initially sees the crowd in the union hall as a 'collection of bodies and heads, of shaven skulls and wooly ones, of rags blackened by axle grease' without any trace of personality (p. 7). But the statement that amplifies her first observation is certainly endowed with authorial authority: 'As if some giant eraser had rubbed out their individual traits they had taken on a common mask, the anonymous mask of a crowd' (p. 7). As we will try to show in the course of this section, *God's Bits of Wood* is the kind of narrataive which uses conventional terms that the novelist must however define and redefine with every episode and situation. In this particular case, the narrator is redefining the words 'mask' and 'crowd' even as he uses them. Through insinuations and selected images, Ousmane shows individual workers (often characterized as 'hands' or 'work objects' by employers of labour), coalescing into one common human body which is the source of energy and struggle in the drama that ensues. He shows how this mass is made up of individuals who have different traits and opinions: old Mamadou Keita is a symbol of the past, he is more cautious and urges the workers to tread carefully in their dealing with their adversaries; Tiemoko is his antithesis, a young, rash worker yearning for confrontation. In this and other cases, the narrator adopts the role of a synthesizer, bringing out the disparate points of view, pinpointing the differences and similarities in the mass.

A similar pattern is discernible in the presentation of places. Thies, at one end of the railway line, is a rallying point for the workers and has features which are not very different from those at Bamako at the other end. The workers in Thies are, however, in a more advanced stage of alienation and dehumanization, and Ousmane uses short, sharp, sentences to evoke a situation which is defined by the almost total disengagement of people and things; these are backed up by what appears to be a catalogue of woes:

> Hovels. A few rickety shacks, some upturned tombs, walls of bamboo or millet stacks, iron barbs and rotting fences. Thies: a vast, uncertain plain where the rot of the city has gathered — stakes and crossties, locomotive wheels, rusty shafts, knocked-in jerricans, old mattress springs, bruised and lacerated sheets of steel. And then, a little farther on, on the goat path that leads to the Bambara quarter, piles of old tin cans, heaps of excrement, little mountains of broken pottery and cooking tools, dismantled railway cars, skeletons of motors buried in the dust, and the tiny remains of cats, of rats, of chickens, disputed by the birds. Thies: in the midst of this corruption, a few meager bushes — wild tomato, dwarf peppers and okra — whose pitiful fruits were harvested by the women. Bald-sided goats and sheep, clotted with filth, came here to graze — to graze on what? — the air? Constantly hungry, naked children, with sunken chests and swollen bellies, argued with the vultures. Thies: a place where everyone — man, woman and child — had a face the color of the earth. (p. 13)

Again, we have a merging of people and things which coalesce to form an image of fragmentation which also serves as a mode of social commentary. Where another novelist might be inclined to make an overt authorial observation, Ousmane skilfully positions objects and subjects in such a way that the reader's response to either cannot be neutral. The rhetorical question — 'to graze on what?' — demands some emotive response from the reader, as do the various descriptions of people who have been thrown into this social junk. Such descriptions are important for both the degree of social realism they bring to the narrative and the way they parallel other situations, creating the kind of social pattern which is central to the making of the community in *God's Bits of Wood.*

Although microcosmic and set scenes in the novel have a pattern which is largely similar, none is an exact fascmile of the other. The description of Thies advances that of Bamako in a number of interesting ways; the most salient of these is the merging of time and action. We are introduced to the workers at Thies just when the workers at Bamako have decided to go on strike. The decision to go on strike hence becomes a kind of thread that establishes the common nature of the workers' problems, while bringing out both the sense of joy that comes with the ability to act, and also the fear that is occasioned by the contemplation of an uncertain future. These group sentiments are once more underscored by the presentation of the individual responses to the general situation; the authorial periscope moves from outer reality into the minds of the characters, enabling the reader to establish some personalized relationship with them. In this respect, the conflict between Bachirou and Samba N'Doulougou is not merely a reflection of different class interests, but is caused by both characters' fear of a decision they have been a party to, and a recognition that from this moment on they must bear the consequences of their actions. A common notion in this, and other individual or group conflicts in the novel, is the centrality of the strike in the making of the worker's community, for the strike highlights the precarious position of the people as dependants of the railway company and their potential for liberation as workers.

The relationship between dependancy and potential requires a neat balancing act on the part of the narrator; it is presented largely through characters in a period of crisis, characters who catch our attention through their individual traits, yet acquire their significance only as 'God's bits of wood'. In many instances, as we will see in an examination of some characters below, the qualities that define a character also contain the potential for his or her downfall. The important point, though, is that the function of these characters is various. Some exist as portraits that add colour to Ousmane's landscape: casual examples include proud Dieynaba 'puffing calmly at her pipe, wreathed in a cloud of smoke' (p. 16), or blind Maimouna 'the prisoner of her infirnity, queen of her shadowy realm' (p. 20). Such characters are human units who bring out the richness of Ousmane's community in failure and triumph. But there are also characters designed to represent the authorial perspective or ideology.

There is always a degree of authorial manipulation in any narrative, but Lewis Nkosi seems to overstate the point when he says that Ousmane forces his characters 'to carry out an illustrative programme especially designed by the author'.[14] Some of the characters we are going to discuss in detail are certainly designed to illustrate and dramatize an overt authorial perspective and are woven into the narrative with that particular function in mind; their growth is really their coming around to the novelist's point of view. Characters and situations are inevitably functional only within the author's ideological framework. And yet we never feel that Ousmane is presenting a situation which is clearly settled in his mind, hence the dynamism of his narrative. The case of Bakary the fireman is a good example of the author's invitation to the reader to question assumptions which are made from a first reading of the text, so to speak. Bakary, we are informed, was tuberculous, 'and no one who saw him could have failed to know it. The years behind the firebox of the trains had turned the skin of his face to gray and covered it with a tough film, like callus' (p. 17). Since we have seen Bakary and identified with him emotionally, we cannot question the author's view of the reasons why the fireman has been reduced to his present state. Ousmane takes this trust still further when he uses Bakary as the worker's spokesman in their struggle to acquire pensions from their employers, but he does not indicate, overtly, why this character is suited for the role. Authorial manipulation of characters is not as singular as Nkosi would like us to believe.

The same can be said of the narrator's manipulation of symbols in the novel. To the extent that he is keen to go beyond the immediate and surface reality envisaged by his characters, Ousmane cannot but use symbols as pointers to the inner laws governing the workers' traumatic experiences. The basic unit of the community is the family, which is symbolized by the 'motherhouse of Ramatoulaye,' centred around 'a big, shed-like structure, painted the color of earth and standing on the foundations of bricks' (p. 50). The brick foundation suggests strong grounding in history and tradition; the earth, on the other hand, is a symbol of the community's primeval character, which has been disrupted and changed by the machine. Indeed, all human activities in the novel take place against a background of the earth and the sky, two stable frames for an otherwise dislocated universe; in certain key instances, the earth and the sky reflect the unstable state in which the characters have been plunged by recent events. After the vote to go on strike has been taken in Bamako, for example, night falls on the earth like 'the closing of the lid on a kettle' (p. 10); it closes in the heat of the day (which is also the heat generated by this historic moment), and the people's anxieties are played out by drums being beaten in the night: 'In the darkness that enclosed the city the deep-toned drumming seemed now to come from everywhere at once, twisting and turning through the heads of those to whom sleep would not come' (p. 12).

The idea of 'home' conjures up a culture which has managed to retain its essential unity despite colonial alienation. Characters like N'deye Touti who try to move away from the hearth by adopting the culture of the colonizer are presented as prisoners 'in the place that should have been her home' (p. 58). In turn, the community spites those who try to exist outside its fold, since they are seen as the agents of the people's cultural death. As old Niakoro notes, those who prefer the white man's tongue ('a language of savages' [p. 5]) are accomplices in the death of the Bambara language. As the case of Sounkare illustrates clearly, being alone in Ousmane's community is a self-inflicted death sentence, since the fate of every person is tied up with the destiny of the mass; or as Diara the scab discovers, to be excluded from this society and then be humiliated in public is a wound that 'would never heal' (p. 96).

Ousmane's celebration of his people's communal values is presented without being mediated through a predetermined ideological perspective, and the key themes in the novel seem to develop almost spontaneously from the actions of the workers on strike. The movement of the workers is from one common concern (the need for better working conditions) to another desired goal (freedom and independence). The narrative strand in the novel is, in social 'realistic' terms, the motion of people, first in defeat ('The station looked like the camp of a conquered army, carrying with it its plunder, its wounded, its dead and its limitless vermin' [p. 82]), and then in triumph. However, the affirmation of the workers' sense of community as the source of their energy in their struggle with the directors of the railway company does not exclude conflicts among the strikers. The African community in the novel is presented as both a stable entity and as part of a historical period which is defined by change and crisis. In real and symbolic terms, the strike functions as a forum and act for resolving the crisis of change in later colonialism. As Nicole Medjigbodo has noted, Ousmane conceives change as a process of dialectical struggle, 'an antagonistic movement in nature and society, whose resolution leads to the attainment of a necessarily superior level of development'.[15]

The most obvious conflict in the novel is that between fear and hope, which we have already commented on. There are cases when this conflict is evoked as an antagonism between the characters' inner life and a socio-historical context in a state of transmutation; it is also the conflict between the will of the collective and any individual who feels vulnerable and unsure of himself. Balancing these levels of conflict is a noticeable aspect of Ousmane's narrative method. Often, it is the individual character who functions as a conduit to the inner levels of the more perceivable physical conflict in the novel. After the first physical conflict between the workers and the forces of coercion, for example, what lives vividly in the reader's mind is the image of a blind, lonely woman who no longer knows where she is (because the world she had learnt to know has changed almost overnight), returning home 'as though she had been the solitary victim of the battle' (p. 27). The other women share Maimouna's sense of loss and solitariness, because her loss of one child signifies their loss of a part of their past lives.

The Political Novel

Another source of conflict in the novel has to do with the characters' perception of a world which, being in a state of flux, demands new tools of explication. Doudou, the secretary of the strike committee, who carries with him memories of a past strike which was crushed ruthlessly by the owners of the railway; often wonders whether the justification for the strike is enough to meet the power and might of the company's directors. But once he thinks about the condition of the workers waiting outside the union building, he realizes that old fears cannot be the basis of present actions. Individual emotions are thus suppressed in the face of a more pressing reality.

There is, however, a mode of social conflict which cannot be suppressed merely by an act of individual will — the conflict of entrenched economic interests and the new awakening of the workers. As a work of art committed to both the interpretation and change of existing social reality in Africa, *God's Bits of Wood* is essentially a novel about changes in positions which were initially perceived as firm and unchangeable. The strike serves as a link between the purpose and activities of the various antagonistic groups in Ousmane's colonial situation, and as a springboard for the world of the future:

> An unlimited strike, which, for many, along the whole length of the railroad, was a time for suffering, but for many was also a time for thought. When the smoke from the trains no longer drifted above the savanna, they realized that an age had ended — an age their elders had told them about, when all Africa was just a garden for food. Now the machine ruled over their lands, and when they forced every machine within a thousand miles to halt they became conscious of their strength, but conscious also of their dependence. They began to understand that the machine was making of them a new breed of men. It did not belong to them; it was they who belonged to it. When it stopped, it taught them a lesson. (p. 32).

It is in the course of the strike that the workers are forced to ask themselves questions about their status as a colonized people; as Tiemoko observes later, the strike is 'like a school, for all of us' (p. 85). To the extent that they have invested their future, honour and worthiness as workers in their ability to sustain the strike as long as possible and necessary, the stoppage crystallizes the past and present values of the community. More significantly, the strike is the *locus* of confrontation between the two sides in the conflict, raising questions that are important to the survival of each group. To the workers, the strike is 'a formless thing' which causes 'furtive astonishment at the forces they had set in motion, and an uncertainty as to how they should be nourished — with hope, or with resignation' (p. 33). For the employers of labour the question is rather simple: 'How could such a small minority feel safe in the midst of these sullen masses?' (p. 33). The search for an answer to this, and other questions, is a process which involves nothing less than the transformation of the colonial situation.

To bear the brunt of a present which causes as much uncertainty as it raises expectations, then, the workers fall back on tradition and authority. But they soon realize that the past cannot be recovered wholly, and they must learn to live with the machine. In Bakayoko's words, '[t]he kind of man we were is dead, and our only hope for a new life lies in the machine, which knows neither a language nor a race' (p. 76). The demands of tradition and authority conflict with the needs of the machine in Diara's trial:

> Subconsciously they were torn between the feeling of brotherhood that each of them had for the others — including the accused — and a vague memory of what was meant by the law, which they knew only from fragments of stories they had heard. Because of this conflict of emotions, they had a curious feeling of having been removed from their natural element, but the very newness of being forced to make a decision of this kind for themselves had sharpened their interest and their curiosity. There were some of them who real- ized that, for the first time, they were being called upon to play the role of a man — of their own man. (pp. 78–9)

The whole question of what it means to be new men responsible for their own actions is raised in the trial. As Tiemoko observes, if he asks why he should judge his uncle and participate in his humiliation, then he must ask ' "why" to the whole question of the strike, and the white men, and the machines' (p. 114). On another level, the trial marks the workers' first attempt to regulate their lives and set up a superstructure outside the colonial framework; they set out to convince themselves that they can organize their lives in the age of the machine without imitating what Fa Keita calls 'hierlings and barbarians' (p. 95).

To ask questions about the meaning of the present is to challenge the assumptions of the past, and of tradition. Cast against the workers' world of fear and uncertainty, old Niakoro's universe is stable and patterned; but this stability is not a synonym for justice. In this 'ancient' world, the perfect wife is 'docile, submissive and hard-working' (p. 106). For Ousmane the greatest transmutation in the strikers' community is in the status of women, whom he sees as the real pre- servers of African culture.[16] Ramatoulaye is the mother figure in the Bakayoko household, but she is hardly visible until the strike thrusts women to the forefront of the struggle against the company. The strike places greater responsibilities on her as the oldest woman in a large household; her anxieties are compared to the ease of her brother, El Hadji Mabigue, who prefers the privileges of collaboration to the birth throes of the anti-colonial struggle. Ramatoulaye's gestures and acts — she rushes at her brother's goat 'like an avenging fury' when it eats her family's grain — exemplify her duty to the family and community. The women have been forced to bear a heavy burden by the strike, she says, but they carry 'the life and spirit of others', hence the need for fortitude: 'In the cruel times we are living through we must find our own strength, somehow, and force ourselves to be hard' (p. 69). In a passage which expresses Ousmane's ability to comment on, and judge, his characters' actions using third persons, the other women marvel at Ramatoulaye's strength, noting the changes she has gone through in the course of the strike:

> She had always been quiet and unassuming and gentle with the children; at the street fountain she never took part in the arguments, and she never spoke badly of her neighbors. Where, then, had this violence been born? What was the source of this energy so suddenly unleashed? (p. 74)

The omniscient narrator knows the answer to the last question, has in fact created in Ramatoulaye the kind of character who can dramatize these energies, but he prefers to let third-person narrators probe into the forces that move other characters:

> It was not the war; Ramatoulaye was not a man and knew nothing about the rancors that went well up in soldiers on the march. It was not the factory; she had never been subjected to the inhuman dictatorship of machines. It was not even in the too frequent association of men; she had only those of her own family. Where, then? The answer was as simple as the woman herself. It had been born beside a cold fireplace, in an empty kitchen. (p. 74)

Being in a situation which is not different from Ramatoulaye's, the other women can readily confirm authorial suspicions: they too have learnt from hard experiences.

N'deye Touti is a character we cannot but compare to the indefatigable Ramatoulaye, for whereas the latter is the 'walking encyclopedia of every family in the district', the school girl knows very little about her people. She goes to a colonial school where she is taught 'everything about life', but apparently nothing about her country. She lives in a world, and is taught about a universe, 'in which her own people had no place, and by the same token she no longer had a place in theirs' (p. 57); her life is like a long dream 'that was constantly filled with the image of some Prince Charming from her books' (p. 57). The kind of education system she goes through has been designed to evoke a dream world of Europe and America as the 'civilized' entities of the universe;

by the same token, her people are depicted as savages, beggars and cripples. Of all the women characters in the novel, then, N'deye Touti has the most to learn from the strike, and one of the key ironies in her growth as a character is the way her dreams are exposed by the colonials who were supposed to be her 'natural' allies.

N'deye Touti has yielded to the hegemonic colonial culture: she disapproves of the other women's actions against the colonial machine because she believes in the sanctity of established laws whose validity she has not been taught to question. In a very telling scene, the other women mourn the burning of their ancenstral homes, but for the school girl, this erasure of a past she never wanted to be a part of is cause for celebration:

The memory was as sharp as the pain of an open wound, and she was almost ready to bless the fire which had destroyed the witnesses to her childhood and her shame. She had a vision of houses painted in clear, fresh colors, of gardens filled with flowers, and children in European clothes playing in tidy courtyards. (p. 115)

Her real shame comes when a couple of colonials refer to her as another 'savage', effectively killing the illusion that she is closer to them than to her people. When Bakayoko later refuses to marry her, N'deye Touti is forced to question her previous assumption that her colonial education has made her a better type of person.

Like N'deye Touti, Penda has also retreated from her community and withdrawn into an unreal world of film stars, pop singers and 'drawings of white women from fashion magazines'. But she finds a role in the strike and emerges as one of the most formidable leaders of the workers' movement in the novel; the strike restores her honour as a woman and her belief in her own worth, so that the discovery of vocation becomes a liberating act of faith. Those characters, like Sankoure, the watchman, who do not join hands with others, preferring instead to retreat into their 'absolute solitude', become easy victims for the machine and its 'temple' of metal. In other words, those people who learn from their experiences or from the examples of others are elevated into cultural heroes, even when, as in the case of Penda, they die serving their people. On the other hand, characters who prefer to serve their own needs are destroyed by the very forces they do not want to confront.

Bakayoko is an example of this moral pattern, but he is conspicuous in the novel for his absence and distant influence. In trying to explain the functioning of this absence, Nkosi has noted that characters in *God's Bits of Wood* have a 'collective rather than an individual hold upon our imagination which is intended to emphasize the strength of their shared responsibility and, equally, to diminish the moral significance of any single character'.[17] Soyinka also argues that Bakayoko calls attention to himself through his absence; he is a Promethean figure, remote, enigmatic, 'sculpted out of pure intellect and omniscience'.[18] Ousmane must have had this function in mind, too, for although his cultural hero does not enter the narrative until much later, he is the brains behind the strike: 'His words and his ideas were everywhere, and even his name filled the air like an echo' (p. 64).

There may not be a main character in *God's Bits of Wood*, but it is fallacious to argue that Ousmane's narrative has no hero(es); the acts and demeanour of most of the characters we have mentioned in this section are heroic enough; Bakayoko is simply idolized. In the chapter called 'The Return of Bakayoko', for example, this cultural hero makes his entry against a golden haze which seems to signify a change in the seasons and, by implication, the workers' fortunes:

> The stars were strewn across the sky like some golden seed sown by the wind. The earth cooled beneath the touch of a night breeze from the north, heralding a change in the season. The insects and the birds of the tropics sang their nocturnal hymns. (p. 170)

The man himself is completely married to the earth and seems to move to the rhythms of nature: 'He was whistling a cheerful little tune and stopped from time to time to listen to the mewing of a cat or the sonorous snoring from a nearby house' (p. 170). Bakayoko encapsulates the old and new values of his people, but to the extent that he is not rooted in what Soyinka has called 'a realistic location among the flesh and blood of an embattled humanity',[19] he is the least convincing and memorable character in the novel.

As a political novel, *God's Bits of Wood* is remarkable for authorial restraint: Ousmane does not intrude into the narrative unnecessarily, and his work has none of the tendentiousness which often plagues this genre. But authorial absence in any novel is a double-edged weapon. The major shortcoming of Ousmane's narrative is the absence of a central consciousness, individual or collective, which can be used to cast light on objective reality. That the author prefers to dramatize the coming of a people towards full consciousness is apparent from our discussion so far, and yet what Lucien Goldmann called a 'world vision' can never come into being until the collective group or class develops consciousness of their new consciousness. In Goldmann's terms, a world vision — 'a convenient term for the whole complex of ideas, aspirations and feelings which links together the members of a social group' — is the product of a 'collective group consciousness which reaches its highest expression in the mind of a poet or a thinker'.[20] As a griot who observes and presents only what he sees and understands, Ousmane seems to have a lot of faith in the ability of objective reality to yield a consciousness of its own (and of its own will); this consciousness, he assumes, can then affect the reader's way of seeing the dramatized reality (and reading the text). His narrative certainly points a new way for both his characters and readers, but rarely are the latter invited to share the fate of the former. It is possible for the reader of *God's Bits of Wood* to exhibit the kind of aloofness which the authorial narrator maintains for most of the novel.

Beauty, Patches and the Beast: *In the Fog of the Seasons' End*

A political reading of novels and an ideological interpretation of literary texts is not 'the absolute horizon of all reading and all interpretation,' as Frederic Jameson has suggested,[21] but there is always an incompleteness in any apolitical reading of an explicitly political novel such as Alex La Guma's *In the Fog of the Seasons' End*. This kind of reading often assumes that the novelist's priorities are the same as those of the critic and sees the gap between the intentions of the writer and those of his reader as a formal weakness. In a recent criticism of *In the Fog of the Seasons' End*, for instance, David Rabkin is uneasy with what he perceives to be the novel's departure from the genre's 'heuristic functions', its 'consistent departure from typical procedures of the novel form', being concerned rather to illuminate the moral character of South African society, than to portray the personal and moral development of individual characters'.[22] The critic's attempt to posit society and individuals as oppositions, and to suggest that the novel as a genre is essentially concerned with moral character, is old-fashioned and erroneous. Any meaningful reading of a political novel must start from the assumption that the novel is a genre grounded in a tradition the conventions of which it always seeks to revise as it reflects or 'reads' its immediate context. In considering the question of art as representation, as Lukacs and others have noted, the novelist works with one proposition in mind: What is the nature of the reality his novels are supposed to recreate in a fictional universe? For Alex La Guma, the realities of South Africa — the reality of eighty per cent of the people living below the breadline, over seventy thousand political prisoners, and the attempt by capitalist racism to destroy the culture of the African people — have provided a ready answer to this central question.[23] This is a reality in which human morality has no meaning except within the larger social set of mores and the social-economic structures that underly them; the artist is not concerned with any historical movement which does not fuse him with ordinary people, for he sees the struggle for culture as the struggle for the nation and national consciousness. 'Deprived of the right to live according to their own values, our peoples are engaged in a struggle that will lead them to full expression in terms of their own history and culture.'[24] The meaning of *In the Fog of the Seasons' End* cannot be sought outside the context of this struggle.

Although the overwhelming, some might say naturalistic, evocation of the landscape which critics have long admired in La Guma's first major work, *A Walk in the Night*, is never duplicated in his later works, the novelist still exhibits an unusual sensitivity towards the landscape in *In the Fog of the Seasons' End*. In fact the political and social landscape is more functional in the latter novel because it is integrated into the development of characters, of the community, and is worked into the ideological principles that inform the novel, not to mention its narrative methods. Unlike the landscape in *A Walk in the Night* where physical images often seem to have a life of their own, existing outside and above the characters in a strong deterministic way, the physical world in *In the Fog* is organized and controlled by the author's immediate ideological needs; nothing appears gratuitous in this work; even the oppressive system, complete with its sense of claustophobia, has a logic of its own. This patterning of the landscape is evidence of the novelist's attempt to transcend the disintegration brought on his people by the oppressive structures of apartheid and to reach for the essence and the mode of belief that unites them in their struggle against racism.

The dramatic movement in the novel is provided by the constant struggle between the forces of apartheid on the one hand, and the national liberation movement on the other hand. This contrast is brought out most vividly in the opening of the novel which, as we will see later, is also a kind of ending and beginning. A grim, violent confrontation of the victim and the victimizer, the prologue is intended to assault all our sensibilities in an attempt to force us to re-evaluate our notions about the reality the novelist is portraying. The prison cell, La Guma's singular prototype of the police state, finds its way into his other novels under various guises; it is in this novel, however, that it is presented in its most violent and relentless character, by sharp, brutal images which point to the larger dimensions of Elias Tekwane's personal tragedy.

It is not difficult to see how nature and the physical landscape is etched into Tekwane's universe, already blunted by his captors. On the night he is arrested, for example, 'a thin mist frosted the stars like a veil flung over the spangles of a bride',[25] but the bridal image (an ironic allusion to a beginning) is perfunctory; it is built up with symbols of decay and termination. The car carrying the prisoner goes past 'the suburb slum, past ramshackle houses' as 'the haze of the ending summer's night' lifts off the landscape; in the city proper, parking meters point out the grotesque character of this world: they are described as 'regiments of armless robots' (p. 2). The prisoner is thus presented with the face of the system in its worst form, and he does not really know what is going to befall him. His challenge, then, is to read his landscape anew, to probe into the inner laws that move it:

> Behind the ugly mask of the regime was an even uglier face which he had not yet looked on. You went through the police charges in the squares, the flailing clubs, the arrogant rejection of all pleas and petitions, blood dried on the streets like spilled paint where a shot body had lain, but here, behind the polished windows, the gratings and the government paintwork, was another dimension of terror. (p. 3)

The regime's mask is a sign which the narrator, and his character, must penetrate in order to represent the system's reign of terror in its profundity. The long-shot image of the cell is, therefore, enhanced by short but sharp images of the men who man the system: the major is described as a robot which is 'constructed of a series of pink ovals'; his hands are 'pink and plump and oval' (p. 3). In short, he is an epitome of the blank and insensitive character of the system. In this, as in other cases in which the regime wears an impenetrable mask, eyes provide us with clues to the real nature of its supporters. Hence the major's eyes are appropriately described as 'small and round and shiny, like two glass beads, small, bright, conscienceless eyes' (p. 3).

In the Fog is a novel about perception, and the eyes are indicators of how the regime perceives the people it has brutalized and turned into 'things'. The major sees Tekwane as an object and scans him with eyes which are compared to 'the points of surgical flashlights, bright and without expression' (p. 5). To remind the prisoner of his objectification, or reification, is to deny him his innate power to act and react, and Tekwane, who understands this psychology of intimidation better than most characters in the novel because he has been its victim since birth, must vocally reassert his humanities:

> You are going to torture me, maybe kill me. But that is the only way you and your people can rule us. You shoot and kill and torture because you cannot rule in any other way a people who rejects you. You are reaching the end of the road and going downhill towards a great darkness, so you are selfish and greedy and afraid of the coming darkness . . . (p. 6)

Through this speech-act, the prisoner reasserts his moral superiority over his oppressor and manages to transcend his captive status: 'He was afraid, but clung to his pride and sense of injustice' (p. 6). What

Tekwane must preserve at all costs is that area of himself — his pride and consciousness — which the regime tries to destroy at all costs.

Throughout the novel, La Guma tries to balance the prisoner's awareness of his vulnerability with the deep sense of injustice which drives him to revolt. Much later in the novel, when the omniscient narrator has placed Tekwane's revolt in context, the latter's concern is not so much his individual fate, but the destiny of the movement that has given meaning to his life. He does not therefore see his inevitable death as the termination of the historical movement (as the modernist characters sometimes tend to do), for every act has a reaction, and every motion is but a tributary to the larger stream of history. Tekwane's mind recedes into his past to seek connections between his personal fate and the fate of others who have adopted a similar cause. The author's primary concern here is the fusion of characters, the landscape and historical events, which is central in his patterning of the experiences he is writing about. For young Tekwane this linkage is important to full understanding; for example, the labour camp with its 'bleak rows and . . . shabby fabricated huts' and 'makeshift tents flapping like broken wings' (p. 156) parallels the kind of destruction and disintegration which he witnessed in his village as a boy. The transformation of his people into 'efflux' is vividly illustrated by old Tatsu, who collapses and dies on a heap of rubble 'like a bundle of discarded old clothes', and is buried in a common grave which is 'like a place where the crumbs of humanity were brushed away under a carpet of stony earth' (p. 156).

In a situation where the past seems to be replayed in the present, Tekwane's death is inevitable: the regime insists that he betray not only his friends in the movement, but also his ideals and beliefs, a price which he is not prepared to pay. He is not in a position to avert his death, but he, nevertheless, strives to give his context some meaning in the hope that an understanding of how the past became the present can provide a way out of this cycle of decay in the future. His battered body hangs on 'a framework of pain' sustained only by his understanding of the inhumanity of his oppressors ('rags from which all the water of humanity had been squeezed' [pp. 170 . 71]); he has been tortured into a 'badly-manipulated puppet' (p. 173), but this has only reinforced his belief in the need for his people to continue a struggle whose roots can be traced to the beginning of colonialism:

> His silence, his resolve, now seemed to take on the form of a force within him: the amalgam of pain and brutality atomized slowly into the gathering ghosts of his many ancestors which seemed to insulate him from pain. Pain was there, yes, but somehow something apart, a satellite revolving the planet of his being, his mind, which was full

of the faraway ululations, the rattle of spears on shields, the tramp of thousands of feet. (p. 172).

But the death of the individual, the annihilation of the self is only the end of the textualized experience; for La Guma the historical movement that promises the survivors fulfilment and completion is barely beginning. As Beuke observes at the end of the novel, as he watches some of his friends go to war againts the regime, 'what we see now is only the tip of an iceberg of resentment against an ignoble regime, the tortured victims of hatred and humiliation' (p. 180).

In spite of the ideological anticipation of the future which we find at the end of *In the Fog*, authorial control in La Guma's novel is measured and the narratorial agent hardly intervenes to bend the story against its natural grain. The informing vision has an equivocalness — not least the fact that the end of the novel is also its beginning — which allows characters to develop their own individual personalities and to respond to their context variously. La Guma's image of the police state is not singular; he employs numerous images of contrast which enhance the hopes of his characters, their dreams and ideals, interrelating with the harsh realities of apartheid. Towards the end of the prologue, for example, the image we are left with is that of Tekwane 'experiencing an awful sensation of asphyxiation and horrifying doom' (p. 7), an image which is directly undercut by the description of the municipal park in the first few pages of the chapter that follows, and 'the golden-haired and healthy' infant under Beattie Adam's charge. And yet, this image of tranquility in a violent sea is largely unreal, hence the narrator's subtle, ironic exposure of Beattie's complacency about her 'home':

> Home was a room in the servants' quarters off the backyard of a big, pink and white house near the park. It was comfortable enough: a single bed with a candlewick cover, some store furniture — discarded when the missus had purchased a new suite — a picture of her mother in a cheap frame and another of a country scene, bottles of lotion on the dresser, and a motley collection of paraphernalia which all went into making life liveable. (p. 10)

Beattie (like Tommy, the musician) is not entirely innocent, for the reality of apartheid is such that it controls every aspect of the character's life; she has consciously decided to accept her status, to be oblivious to politics, because to be political is to acknowledge the conflict between the oppressor and the oppressed and to activate this cognizance in a way that demands involvement in the struggle for national consciousness. 'But what can us people do?' Beattie asks Beukes, when the latter challenges her simplistic view of life; this is a 'guilty'

The Political Novel

question which denotes her awareness of the need for acts which she is
not capable of; similarly, Tommy has withdrawn into 'a world of
sugary saxophones' because he 'found it easier to live under the regime
than to oppose it' (p. 53).

To mediate the realities of apartheid, and to concretize one's knowledge into a programme of action, is the major process of transformation which La Guma's characters must undergo to come closer to the
dream of the future foreshadowed at the end of his novels. The processes of gnosis(knowing) and praxis(doing) are closely linked in *In the
Fog*, and it is the ability to establish this link consciously that distinguishes characters who have knowingly made their choices (Beukes
and Tekwane) and those who prefer not know, because knowledge
demands some kind of action (Beattie and Tommy). Knowing is not in
itself a passive act, because it denotes an understanding of what one
must do to break out of the cycle of decay and repression which
Tekwane rejects at the opening of the novel. Beuke's understanding
of what lies behind the regime's outward image of peace, and his
ideological exposition of what really constitutes the oppressor's
mask — 'the picture of normality, the cobwebs and grime of a spider
reality' (p. 25) — bring him into an inevitable confrontation with the
oppressive machine. It is out of this confrontation that he seeks his new
self. Although the only alternative to this confrontation is an acceptance of one's self-annihilation, it is not a choice that characters in the
novel make too easily, partly because of their awareness of the logi-
cally violent consequences of their choice. In his attempt to make his
choice, we find Beukes withdrawing into memories of his past, or
hanging on to certain beautiful, abeit isolated, moments in his present
situation. But in both cases his mind brings him back to the startling
realities of apartheid: in the first case, his mind takes him back to his
first confrontation with segregation during a visit to a circus; in the
latter case, he realizes that his love affair with Frances is illusory within
a context that denies people the opportunity to express their essential
human qualities. Frances might be Beuke's idea of absolute beauty, but
she has been roughened by her factory job and lives in a block of flats
that resembles a prison. There can be no real beauty in a represive
situation, Beukes realizes.

But as we have already observed, the repressive reality in La
Guma's novel is not singular. There is, first, a superficial reality, an
icon of peace like the picture of the band-leader in Tommy's room.
Then there is the actual reality of political terror which Beukes and
Tekwane have discovered and must hence suffer. The minds of those
who have seen through the mask of apartheid must, like those of the
workers in *God's Bits of Wood*, vacillate between the two forms of
reality in a constant process of doubt and self-questioning. In this

respect, knowledge or consciousness is a double-edged weapon that opens the minds of the characters to the possibilities of the life and beauty which the regime has denied them, but also exposes them to the violent tentacles of the police state.

Tekwane's fate illustrates how gnosis must eventually yield to praxis if the characters in the political novel are to be complete. The author distances this particular character's gruesome fate from the 'postcard' memories of his rural childhood, but the reader can still see how his murder is the culmination of a long process of reification. So significant is Tekwane's initial objectification, as he is processed for the regime's labour gangs, that La Guma adopts an uncharacteristically didactic tone and a mixture of bitterness and parody to call attention to it. If young Tekwane does not follow the rules designed to proscribe his life, the official issuing the pass reminds him, then he will be imprisoned, his permits will be cancelled and he will 'cease to exist':

> You will be nothing, nobody, in fact you will be decreated. You will not be able to go anywhere on the face of this earth, no man will be able to give you work, nowhere will you be able to be recognized; you will not eat or drink; you will be nothing, perhaps even less than nothing. (p. 82)

Tekwane is being asked to live a life whose limits have already been set, and, once he understands the logic behind this enclosure, then he sets out to destroy the structures that fence him in.

La Guma uses set scenes to place his characters in their historical context and to transcend one of the major problems which the political novel, as a genre that seeks to represent reality, must confront sooner or later: how to reflect the world as a totality, to fuse the self with its universe, without resorting to overt political discourse. There are, however, set scenes which function as explicit instruments of what one critic of the novel has called 'social mechanization'.[26] This problem is most apparent in La Guma's dramatization of Sharpeville: the Washerwoman, the Bicycle Messenger, the Child et al are typical victims of the massacre, but insofar as the reader cannot enter into an immediate emotive relationship with them, they remain remote symbols of oppressed peoples, not social beings. There is no vital relationship between these facets of external reality and the lives and experiences of those characters who constitute the 'intrinsic or immanent subtext'[27] of La Guma's novel. In contrast, the set scene in which Tekwane's 'permitting' is ritually performed is directly related to his growth and development as a victim and opponent of apartheid; it is portrayed as both his first moment of humiliation and an example of what 'the white people have done to this land' (p. 125). The success of this piece lies in the fusion of what Aristotle calls the 'universal' (*kathalou*) and the 'particular' (*hath hekaston*). Even when Tekwane recalls this scene, he sees it as a gauge of his psychological distance from acceptance to rebellion.

Set scenes are, however, only a limited part of La Guma's portrait of the realities of apartheid: spread across the novel are patches of what has already been referred to as 'the spider reality of cobwebs', etched out in images and symbols of fragmentation and abandonment. The landscape is often presented as something incomplete, hidden from ordinary eyes, or a 'terrain of empty squares and isolated buildings'; the regime's celebrated cities are like 'ghost towns' which are inhabited by the 'survivors of a holocaust' (p. 26). Individual objects seem to have the same characteristic, to yield a similar meaning: a woman who has been thrown out of her house (Chapter Two) sits on a worn-out chair which signifies her desolation; the chair's canvas has been patched and stitched all over and the threads hang 'in dirty streamers, like dehydrated entrails' (p. 28). This initial image of abandonment and weariness is reinforced by a succession of similar images: the old perambulator epitomizes ragged township life, while the rubbish bin is a symbol of a worn out landscape populated by 'efflux'. The latter are usually tired, anonymous figures who move like 'drab phantoms and tawdry spectres of saints among the ruins of abandoned cathedrals, like characters in some obscurely metaphysical play' (p. 61). Torn clothes are common symbols of shattered life in the novel: people who have been arrested for pass violations are held behind a meshed wire fence like 'shabby bundles of second-hand clothing ready for transport to a sale' (p. 63). Clothes appeal to Beuke's sense of what the regime has done to his people. He waits for Abdulla, his union contact, in the middle of a floor 'scatterd with offcuts and pieces of thread', which remind him of his first date with Frances when he had to climb 'the inscribed stairway' to her flat, 'past the wash lines and the flat vista of grass worn in patches like the coat of an old dog, the rows of single-storey council cottages like frayed uniforms' (p. 92). Beuke's consciousness of fragmentation is thus the link between his past and present, confirming his belief that nothing has really changed, that a new world must be sought outside the dress of apartheid.

La Guma's characters strive to transcend their sense of fragmentation, to move beyond their past and present towards the future of struggle; they are forced to make rational choices once they have understood how the regime stifles any search for that beauty which they see in isolated situations. And although it is through those characters that we see and perceive this landscape, none of them constitutes a single centre of consciousness in the novel. They may share the author's ideological inclinations, but they cannot overtly be identified with him. Put together, these characters constitute one unified consciousness that runs through the book. The replacement of central characters with a central consciousness is prompted by the political novelist's desire to move beyond the habituating role of character, to go beyond the limitations of an individual mind, in an attempt to extricate that vital force that moves his people to something new from surface reality.[28] But to the extent that this kind of novel mediates reality to the reader, consciousness does not draw the reader into the world of the novel; it yields knowledge of the fictive world without demanding any measure of involvement. The major weakness of *In the Fog of the Seasons' End* is precisely this inability, or refusal, to drag us intensely into the belly of the beast and force us to live there; while Michael Adonis (*A Walk in the Night*) pulls us along to this violent fate, Beukes and Tekwane must yield us to those 'who have gone to war in the name of a suffering people' (p. 180), characters whose actions and achievements have yet to be written about.

Character and consciousness in *Petals of Blood*

Politics and ideology are key concepts in the triangular relationship between author, character and reader in the works of Ngugi wa Thiong'o, a novelist who is conscious of the potential conflict between the artist and the ideologue, 'the eternal problem involving the delicate transmutation of not just a political idea but a political programme into art'.[29] To surmount this problem, Ngugi tries to strike a balance between consciousness and characters as modes of mediating reality, and to fuse the mimetic function of the novel with its symbolic one. In this regard, the novelist seeks to be both the mirror and lamp of his society: to reflect and illuminate its 'economic structure, its class formation, its conflicts and contradictions; its class power, its political and cultural struggles; its structure of values — the conflict and tensions arising from the antagonism between those which are dying and those which are pointing to the future'.[30]

But there are certain formal problems inherent in any attempt to reflect society in its most comprehensive and panoramic character, because reality as a whole is beyond one man's vision, and the use of social mechanization does not always bring the reader into a vital relationship with the world of the novel. What the political novelist strives for, then, is the unity of feelings and thoughts evoked in his characters by their experience of reality, and the author's own ideological mediation of the same reality; the result is what Brecht would call a *Kausalnexus*. The political novelist thus seeks a medium which can express his point of view without resorting to mere sloganizing; the challenge is to create a fictional world which is an accurate depiction of the real world in the course of which the authorial vision will emerge as a logical development of the interaction of characters and their situations. In *Petals of Blood* character is the key to Ngugi's world view and narrative perspective.

The most salient feature of characterization in *Petals of Blood* is no doubt Ngugi's use of a group of characters from different social backgrounds who are, nevertheless, consciously presented as agents of authorial views and thus function as instruments of mediating the character of the neo-colonial state in modern Africa. In the opening paragraphs of the novel, this world is seen, almost simultaneously, through the eyes of the four characters whose lives form the core of the narrative. This is the point when the reader must evaluate the reliability of each persona, since our eventual judgement of the world of Ngugi's novel depends on the extent to which we trust one character's version of events more than that of the other characters. And yet the omniscient narrator implicitly determines the way we trust one character more than the other; he alone has made some characters more reliable than their counterparts. Munira's vision of the events that led him to jail, for example, is of necessity limited: he has detached himself from the material world, declared himself the predictor of its doom. Hence he cannot see his world as anything more than a wasteland. Abdulla, on the other hand, does not contemplate his fate outside the real, material world, but his view of the events that have led to arrest and imprisonment is clouded by a resurgence of 'old anger and new bitterness'.[32] In the same vein, Wanja, whom Ngugi originally intended to make the central consciousness of the novel and the major victim of the historical forces it dramatizes, is in a state of 'shock and hallucination' which has blurred her vision. As the character with the clearest vision and most developed consciousness at the end of the novel, Karega is the natural choice as a central perspective. But Ngugi does not want to put him and his activities in the foreground because his strength as a leader of the workers' movement lies in his ability to eschew élitism and remain one of them. Karega is also introduced late in the novel and does not have roots which are as deep as those of Munira or Abdulla in the history of Ilmorog. The author tries to surmount Karega's obvious limitation by having Munira tell most of the story, with the help of the other characters, with the leader of the workers functioning primarily as a consciousness that crystallizes some of the key ideological views in the novel.

Because the story-tellers in *Petals of Blood* tell their stories from a perspective which is far from disinterested, their view of things is constantly subjected to authorial censure or qualifications; the reader is often urged to be on his guard. Chapter Two, for instance, opens with a traditional third-person narrative describing Munira's discovery of Ilmorog; this is fused with the villagers' collective view of the teacher, and the teacher's own subjective view of the villagers and his spontaneous reaction to the wasteland. As a close examination of any minimal units of discourse in the novel will show, this multiplicity of views is the real mark of Ngugi's perfect craftsmanship. Sometimes we have a total fusion of omniscient narrator and character: Munira first enters Ilmorog and crashes 'through into a room full of dead spiders and the wings of flies on cobwebs on all the walls, up to the eaves' (p. 5); later, the same narrator adopts the voice of the collective: 'Munira stayed on, and after a month we were all whispering — was he a little crazed — and he not so old' (p. 6).

In general, Munira's view of reality is juxtaposed with the narratorial perspective and the community's conception of itself. He sees Ilmorog not so much for what it is, since he is rarely able to confront vital reality, an act which demands that he establish a causal connection between the things that happen around him; he sees this world solely as a reflection of his own dreams and expectations. His idealism, which is referred to as 'missionary posture and fervour' (p. 10), is often in conflict with 'this world', including Old and New Ilmorog, and a past dominated by his father and an overriding sense of failure. Munira's consciousness of sin and guilt, itself a foreshadowing of his apocalyptic vision at the end, has its roots in his childhood and youth: Siriana was for him the promise of heaven, and he sees his expulsion from the élite school as 'a big break in the continuity of his life and memories' (p. 15). Unlike Karega's late pilgrimage to Ilmorog, which parallels the teacher's in many significant ways, Munira comes to the wasteland to escape, is therefore not eager to understand this community and its place in the neo-colonial system of exploitation; he is content to be treated with reverence as the bearer of knowledge in the hope that this will prove that his dreams of a new age, first hatched in Siriana, were not in vain.

Standing above Ilmorog 'with an aloof understanding and benign indifference' (p. 16), Munira's understanding of reality is confined to what he sees and perceives. As a narrative agent, he does not take the reader beyond the superficial aspect of his world, an existential state dominated by his 'sense of being without involvement' (p. 20). And since the political novel seeks to portray a vital reality beyond this existential state, a world of potential and possibilities, Munira's way of seeing is constantly qualified by a second-person narrative voice which calls attention to his inadequacies as a representer of complex experiences. When the villagers discuss colonialism and the ways it has affected their culture, Munira is spotted by the second-person narrative voice trying to distance himself from their 'involvement with both the land and what they called "things of blood" ' (p. 18). Endowed with the powers of the omniscient narrator, this voice is able to explain

Munira's state of mind and to establish causal relationships where the teacher can detect none:

> Any talk about colonialism made him uneasy. He would suddenly become conscious of never having done or willed anything to happen, that he seemed doomed to roam this world, a stranger. And yet, yet, why this ready acceptance of undeserved homage, why this secret pleasure at the illusion of being of them? (p. 18)

The second-person narrative voice acts as the scribe for Munira and the other characters; it traces their process of self-questioning and their relationship with the context in which they seek their identity. In most cases, as the example above illustrates, the amanuensis stands above the character, pointing to the gap between his ideals and the reality in which they function. But this relationship is not always detached and critical, for there are cases when Munira's glimpses into his past, itself an important part of Kenya's history, bring out details which the amanuensis cannot but concur with. An important example in this regard is Munira's testimony on the emergence of Chui as a hero of neo-colonialism and the function of Siriana as a training ground for the neo-colonial élite.

Munira is also an important instrument of confession in the novel. Although his statements to the police at the beginning of the narrative are subjective and largely discredited by the rest of the novel, they are important as ironic commentaries on the rise and fall of Ilmorog. Each interrogative in the police station revolves around a problem: What was the source of unrest in the country? The clue to the meaning — 'the signs, the evil web' — being woven in Ilmorog by the revolting workers? These questions do not get a full answer until the whole story is told, but we can already see a conflict between author and character in their search for answers, which provide us with very useful hints. If Ngugi is seeking the inner laws that were at work in the transformation of Ilmorog, Munira's sole reason for reconstructing his past is to show 'the operation of God's law'. Sustaining the conflict between author and character is crucial to the undermining of Munira's version of events and his rationalization of his creed of withdrawal, the corollary to which is the enhancement of authorial perspective and authority. But Ngugi pushes the case a bit too far when he forces Munira to echo his own views. The problem here is simple: How does the author of a political novel make an important ideological point through a character with a limited, or opposed, consciousness? Ngugi's solution, it seems, is to usurp Munira's narrative voice, to draw a sharp image of underdevelopment. 'Our erstwhile masters had left us a very unevenly cultivated land,' Munira says in an uncharacteristic tone,' the centre was swollen with fruit and water sucked from the rest, while the outer posts were progressively weaker and scraggier as one moved away from the centre' (p. 49). The conflict between tone and *telos* here is obvious: we have already been told, in very clear terms, that Munira is not interested in 'things of blood', has never wanted to be his brother's keeper; why then does he concern himself with issues he is supposed to know little about? This apparent conflict between what Wayne Booth calls 'showing and telling'[32] is, in Lukacsian terms, a larger conflict between the inner reality of the novel and social reality on the one hand, and on the other the character's individualized view of the world the novel represents and the author's more objective and self-conscious mediation of life and experience.[33]

Since Karega's perspective is closer to that of the author/narrator, his importance as a character and centre of consciousness is *Petals of Blood* lies in his ability to mediate between the inner reality of the novel and the author's ontology. While Munira is always portrayed moving away from peoples and things, ultimately finding 'spiritual satisfaction' in solitary confinement, Karega seeks his identity in 'things of blood' and his involvement in the historical process, as it were; he is the character most associated with the mass movement in the novel and the workers waking 'to their own strength' (p. 4). And yet, Karega is portrayed largely through Munira's subjective mind until much later in the narrative. There are two possible explanations for this apparent paradox: if he dramatized Karega (the representative of authorial consciousness) too early in the novel, Ngugi might suggest a rather simplistic answer to Munira's creed of 'being without involvement', which is the source of the personal conflicts in the narrative. Second, by placing Karega at the end of the narrative when the people of Ilmorog are moving away from Munira's gospel of acceptance to the notion of struggle, which the young man articulates so well, Ngugi gives his narrative a balance of paradigms. The reader has to contrast the characters as the narrative nears its climax in order to come to grips with the author's ideological inclinations.

Karega's relationship with Ilmorog is active: he relates to the town and its people in such a way that they shape his vision and understanding of the neo-colonial situation; in the same vein, he influences and shapes the community's sense of itself and its ironic fate. Fate is an important term here. When he returns to Ilmorog for a second time after a life of humiliation spent on the tourist circuit, Karega sees his return as a 'covenant with fate' foreshadowing his destiny and that of Ilmorog. Unlike Munira, Karega does not dismiss objective reality as 'the ways of the world', but as an important piece in a larger historical pattern in which Ilmorog is linked to the rest of Kenya and the continent of Africa in a relationship of exploitation and struggle. More significantly, Karega cannot conceive Ilmorog detached from his own experiences and consciousness,

> For to confront Ilmorog, this poverty- and drought-stricken, depopulated wasteland; to confront the expectant eyes of those who tomorrow would run away to the cities whose cruelty he had experienced and where they would face a future which held the hope of a thousand mirages, was at once to confront himself in a way more profound and painful because the problem and the questions raised went beyond mere personal safety and salvation. It seemed to him, looking at the drought, at the tiny faces, at the lack of any development in the area — where, he wondered, were the benefits of modern science? — a collective fate to which they were all condemned. (p. 110)

This passage underscores the relationship between character and consciousness in the political novel: Karega confronts his objective reality in all its multiplicity and with all its contradictions; he relates these to his own experiences, including his past and present knowledge of what it means to be underdeveloped; finally, he asks himself questions about the identity of his self and its world. His ability to establish all these connections between cause and effect mark him out as a character of praxis; he is able to develop an ontology out of his world and to use this as an instrument of mediating the same world. At the same time, he penetrates the surface reality of Ilmorog, capturing its rhythms of nature, its complexity and its sheer simplicity. He moves beyond Nyakinyua's communal memory of times of grandeur and struggle and confronts this community as a creation of 'the twin cruelties of unprepared-for vulgarities of nature and the uncontrollable actions of men' (p. 116). But there is a degree to which, in order to know Ilmorog, Karega must transcend his own mere, naked understanding of what the town really is and establish a definite link between his past and present as a prelude for the future he envisages. In other words, he must effect the patterning of his reality.

The first major step in Karega's patterning of his experiential and historical reality involves the linkage of the world of 'authority' and 'power', symbolized by the city, with the immediate reality of exploitation represented by Ilmorog. Looking back on his failed epic journey to the city, he sees himself as an idealist who was being pushed by what Munira later calls 'lost innocence and hope' to fight forces he did not fully comprehend. The failure of the 'epic' journey underlines the limits of Karega's understanding and range of action. At this juncture, meaning and form in the novel interrelate in a full of insight way, for while Karega's post-journey narrative is on the betrayal of the 'African dream', his mind, and the minds of his listeners, is concerned more with the future than the present. As the narrator notes, 'there was a slightly pathetic note in Karega's narration, something between despair and dumb incomprehension' (p. 173). There is an interesting parallel, too, between the character's thoughts and experiences and those of the community in which he is cast: the story of Nderi was Riera and his false promises is Ilmorog's version of the betrayal of 'the African dream'. Both Chui, Karega's nemesis, and Nderi, Ilmorog's betrayer, embody the dream of independence which has since been betrayed.

As the consciousness of *Petals of Blood*, Karega must constantly make and remake himself in order to transcend the limits imposed by his understanding of new situations which often seem insurmountable; unlike the hero of the modernist novel, he cannot yield his consciousness to his reality. His experiences in the city after the failure of the 'epic' journey threaten to overwhelm him, and he desperately turns to the progressive lawyer for 'a vision of the future rooted in a critical awareness of the past' (p. 199). At this stage, the lawyer becomes the surrogate mediator of Karega's reality as the youth's stream of consciousness moves towards its final revelation. On another, less successful level, the lawyer is an authorial puppet. He is a thinly disguised instrument of authorial consciousness whose failure as a fictional persona has serious implications on character and consciousness in the political novel.

There is an extent to which the lawyer's existence in the novel is imperative: he is Ngugi's unproblematic consciousness, a character who has transcended the limits of his objective reality and his own class contradictions; Karega, in fact, sees him as the epitome of total knowledge. But as a character or persona, the lawyer is not very convincing; he has yielded too much of himself to the authorial ideology. We hear the voice behind the man and adore his idealism, but we are never invited to relate to him as a man with a vital link to a problematic context. The scene in which he entertains Karega and the peasants of Ilmorog in his house is one of the weakest in the novel, for in both scenic presentation and development of character the author is not really sure how to bring the lawyer's ideology to life without sacrificing his personality. In other words, he is presented in a context which reflects the author's preconceived idea of how a progressive lawyer lives and relates to people: when he talks to the peasants, the lawyer is not effecting any communication with them, for he does not pay heed to the listeners' level of understanding, but is holding a dialogue with 'an inner self' (p. 163). When he is told of Wanja's humiliation at the hands of Kimeria as the degradation of a woman he knows (first and foremost), the lawyer moves fast to turn it into a social case study. And when he finally tells the villagers about his personal life, he does not merely relate experiences which have had meaning to him as a character (again, first and foremost); he tells a parable in which every word, gesture and episode are shaped to respond to one important question which the lawyer himself raises — What was the cause of the betrayal that dominates the characters' consciousness so much; 'What happened?' (p. 164).

The lawyer is an example of Ngugi's unnecessary intrusion into the narrative: whereas Karega is a successful fusion of character and consciousness, the former exists as pure consciousness developed through a formula extracted from objective reality. He is conceived outside the novel and imposed on the epistemology which is developed in the internal world of *Petals of Blood*; he is predetermined, implying a measure of distance between him and the interiority of the novel on the one hand, and the reader on the other. Because we are not able to enter into a personal dramatic relationship with the lawyer (or pure consciousness, for that matter), we are not drawn into the external reality whose facets he articulates so forcefully. What the lawyer offers the reader, in short, is what one critic of fiction has called 'the specification of reality which depends entirely on the author's vision'.[35]

And yet there is a sense in which all characters in any novel function, consciously or otherwise, as instruments of authorial perspective, and hence operate within a specified reality. The failure of the lawyer as a character cannot be blamed entirely on his predetermination as an explicit authorial agent; he fails to come to life, as it were, because he is not merged with the authentic reality of the novel; as we have already observed, he brings his own ontology into the inner world of Ngugi's narrative. There is, however, an extent to which the lawyer succeeds in conveying authorial intentionality precisely because of his failure to emerge as a credible character. He is the grown consciousness that has come to grips with its class contradictions, mastered its reality and found answers to Karega's pertinent question on what happened to national consciousness in Kenya. If Karega and the other characters mirror reality as they move towards total consciousness, then the lawyer is the lamp that illuminates the way to full understanding; he forces these characters to see their reality anew and establish causal relations between their individual and social experiences in a teleological context.

The relationship of characters and the juxtaposing of consciousnesses on different levels of growth is one of the means by which Ngugi presents contemporary experience in *Petals of Blood*. Characters are related with other characters, with diverse experiences, and are then subjected to a continuous process of doubt and self-questioning. These relationships take numerous forms. There are characters with natures which beg contrast: Wanja's outgoing nature and her total immersion in her experiences is starkly contrasted to Munira's creed of withdrawal. And yet, this contrast is the basis of their relationship, for she sees his withdrawn character as a reflection of her past, while he sees her active embrace of life as a portrait of what he would have wanted to be and is thus 'irresistibly drawn toward her' (p. 33). But a common past does not necessarily evoke parallel responses in Ngugi's characters: Munira and Karega are both products of Siriana, wedded together by the dominating personality of Chui, but their visions have developed along totally opposed paths. But neither character can be understood clearly without being contrasted to the other: Karega's 'apparent self-possession' (p. 47) irritates Munira because it suggests an alternative to self-withdrawal; as he puts it succinctly, it is 'another threat to my self-imposed peace in this land' (p. 54).

Munira would like to present his Ilmorog experiences retrospectively as 'a series of unconnected events', but the movement of the narrative contradicts this assertion, for characters are always being brought into significant relationships. For Wanja, the four main characters in the novel are 'maimed souls' looking for a cure in Ilmorog. This is an indirect comment on Ngugi's structural design of the narrative: he plots out the lives of four different characters who are forced to enter into a dynamic relationship with their history, either willingly or subconsciously, and are forced to change in the process. The novel opens with the process it dramatizes, but this does not suggest any circular movement in society, for, in Ngugi's world view, movement 'is inherent in nature and society . . . nature and society are in perpetual motion . . . nothing is really static, fixed, final'.[35] The contrary world vision is one that sees nature and society as predetermined, fixed, unchanging, where every movement is fated to lead to its beginning. These contrasting points of view are presented dramatically in the dénouement of Karega on his second return to Ilmorog, and the regressive movement of Wanja who abnegates her quest for full womanhood in the face of what she deems as overwhelming social forces.

The divergence of Wanja and Karega begins after their ill-fated journey to the city. While Karega is spurred by failure towards new levels of knowledge and understanding, Wanja's personal need for a child leads to a severance of the self from the context that originally gave it meaning. There are some interesting narratorial implications for this ideological parting of paths: Karega is the agent of the reader's involvement with Ngugi's social reality, drawing us more and more into the inner world of the novel, trying to establish the relationships between this interior universe and its historically-determined exteriority; he is the investigator of causes and consequences, probing the subterranean laws that have made Ilmorog what it is. In contrast, Wanja becomes an example of the social victim who has lost the will to transcend her historical limitations. There is, however, a degree to

which Wanja's enclosed world is important to our understanding of
Karega's larger context, hence Ngugi's use of authorial devices to question the assumptions underlying each character's quest. The most
important authorial device in *Petals of Blood* is the dramatization of
Ilmorog, the community, as a character with a life of its own.

Ilmorog is the fifth character in Ngugi's novel: it begins as a small
decrepit village subject to the ravages of a yet unconquered nature, and
develops in the course of the novel to become a domain of multi-
national corporations and international capitalism. Old Ilmorog is the
organic community symbolized by primeval tools such as iron and fire;
but it is the slave of a historical reality which looms above it like worms
which threaten a 'solitary bean flower' (p. 21), worms which later
metamorphose into cars and aeroplanes. Ilmorog has never been the
centre of any destructive forces per se, but events that take place outside its boundaries affect it in major, sometimes unforeseen, ways. The
'epic' journey to the city typifies this kind of influence.

For Munira, the would-be historian of modern Ilmorog, the journey
pushed him to a point where he could now see 'that man's estate is
rotten at heart' (p. 118). But Munira, as we have already noted, is not a
very reliable narrator and is contradicted by the omniscient narrator
who sees the journey as 'the exodus toward the kingdom of knowledge
. . .' (p. 118) — a quest for consciousness. The first part of the book
dealing with the journey begins by recapitulating what Ilmorog stands
for, in real and symbolic terms: the history of the community is the
history of Kenya from the Stone Age to the era of foreign occupation,
the struggle for national independence and betrayal. Nyakinyua is the
faithful witness to both Ilmorog's 'days of glory' and its present 'crisis';
in the same way Ndemi stands for 'the primeval man' and Munoru
symbolizes a new class of land-owning peasants.

The journey is central to the characters' process of self-
understanding: it appeals to Karega's idealism and accentuates his
search 'for the meaning of the riddle of the meeting-point of the ironies
of history, appearance and reality, expectations and actual achievement' (p. 127); it takes Wanja back to the city, her original place of
humiliation, mingling her consciousness of the hurt she has suffered in
the past with her awareness of the wasteland that surrounds her in the
present; the journey also reveals the real Abdulla, bringing out his
consciousness of a vision that was betrayed and memories of other
journeys undertaken in the name of a great dream. To the group as a
whole, the journey unravels the riddle epitomized by the question that
Karega asks the lawyer — 'What happened?'

What happened? That is the question that lingers long after the
journey is over and the earth has revealed itself in Wanja's 'wings of
expectation and numerous desires' (p. 196). Ilmorog's season of

drought is superseded by one of rain, but the 'rain spirit', like the spirit of 'development' that succeeds it, is a fluke; beneath the villagers' 'tranquil existence' is 'their consciousness of the journey and the experiences which spoke of another less sure, more troubled world which could, any time, descend upon them, breaking asunder their rain-filled sun-warmed calm' (p. 197). The journey marks the turning point in Ilmorog's development, launching the village from its secluded past into a present of corporate exploitation. Subconsciously, at least, the villagers know that 'things would never be the same'

> For the journey had presented each with a set of questions for which there were no ready answers; had, because of what they had seen and experienced, thrown up challenges that could neither be forgotten nor put on one side, for they touched on things deep in their psyche, in their separate conceptions of what it meant to be human, a man, alive and free. (p. 197)

But this knowledge is spontaneous and limited to only the experiences the villagers have been through and what they have seen. They do not have the conceptual ability to see a logical link between their past and present on one hand, and the future of 'Thengeta' which heralds their communal decay on the other hand. Only the authorial narrative voice has the kind of prophetic insight which makes him the major source of irony in the novel; not insignificant in this regard is the omniscient narrator's knowledge that 'Thengeta', the spirit that momentarily rejuvenates Ilmorog, is also an invitation to death.

In a novel where the author relies on a variety of narrative voices to establish the link between the self and its context, and present the perspectives that develop out of this linkage, the omniscient narrative voice is the ultimate ideological authority in the narrative. The influence of this kind of narrator, as Stanislaw Eile has noted, is manifested by his dual position as both an interpreter and judge of experience in the novel, 'these attributes being the essential privilege of omniscience':

> The author who uses an auctorial narrator assumes that in the created world of the novel, the choice between presentation 'from the outside' or 'from the inside', and the correlative range of the information made available to the reader, is secondary in importance to the potential claims of the narrator.[36]

The reference to the villagers as 'they' in *Petals of Blood* denotes some degree of detachment between Ngugi and his subject, a privilege which the authorial narrator uses to question both Munira's version of events and Ilmorog's self-deception in the season of rain. But it is the collective 'we' narrative voice, used sparingly in *A Grain of Wheat*, which is the basis of the greatest authorial authority in *Petals of Blood*.

To label the 'we' voice as simply collective is to simplify some of its narratorial and ideological ramifications, for the omniscient narrator can equally reflect the views of the collective without identifying himself as one of them. The 'we' voice does not, in fact, have a singular role. There are instances when it adopts the position of an observer, standing above characters and their experiences and judging their activities against certain communal norms which it embodies; it is the voice of history watching newcomers to Ilmorog come to 'our midst' (as in the case of Abdulla) and others (like Munira) who try to become 'one of us'. It is the voice that speaks for 'us' in terms which the more refined and ideologically sophisticated characters cannot use; it is a voice that can even articulate or represent 'our' naïvety, as it does when Wanja is brought back to Ilmorog by a taxi, or when a malfunctioning aircraft signals 'our' doom. The difference between the collective 'we' voice is often the difference between the authorial narrator's self-conscious cognizance of experience and the villagers' more spontaneous and immediate response to phenomena. The latter's welcome to Wanja on her permanent return to the village is a case in point:

> Nyakinyua broke into Gitiro, for which she had once been famous in Ilmorog and beyond: she sang in a low voice in praise of Ndemi and his wives long long ago. The other women chimed in at intervals with ululations. Soon we were all singing and dancing, children chasing one another in the shadows, the old men and women occasionally miming scenes from Ilmorog's great past. It was really a festival before harvest-time a few months away . . . (p. 32)

'We' have assumed our primeval innocence and submerged 'ourselves in the esctasy of the moment', unaware of the ironic play signified by the word 'festival'. This is the kind of identification which the authorial narrator cannot effect because he is not only the agent of this irony, but also has prior knowledge of how festivals herald the community's death. Hence he adopts the third-person narrative voice to place the villager's festivities in context:

> But their laughter concealed their new anxieties about a possible failure of the crops and the harvest. When a good crop was expected it was known through a rhythmic balanced alternation of rain and sunshine. A bad crop was preceded by sporadic rains or by a continuous heavy downpour which suddenly gave way to sunshine for the rest of the season. The latter was what had happened this year. (p. 32)

The last observation has the kind of authority that develops out of an interpretation which has been merged with a judgement. But in those cases where the authorial narrative voice conceives the 'we' as the reader (instead of Ilmorog's collective consciousness), then the results are not very successful, as this description of Munira's father clearly indicates:

> His father was an early convert to the Christian faith. We can imagine the fatal meeting between the native and the alien. The missionary had traversed the seas, the forests, armed with the desire for profit that was his faith and light and the gun that was his protection. He carried the bible; the soldier carried the gun; the administrator and the settler carried the coin. Christianity, Commerce, Civilization; the Bible, the Coin, the Gun; Holy Trinity. (p. 88)

Here, the author combines direct commentary with a parable and caricature, and uses the 'we' to camouflage and minimize the presence of the ideologue.

Ultimately, the major weakness of *Petals of Blood* is one of authorial intrusiveness, which manifests itself in three broad ways. First, as we saw in the lawyer's case, the author forces his characters to echo his thoughts as if they were expressing a perspective developed within the world of the novel. This situation either leads to incredible characters, or to an apparent conflict between author and character, which is also the conflict between the inner ontology of the novel and an extraneous authorial ideology. Second, the author's tendency to comment on scenes whose meaning is apparent leads to redundancy. Abdulla's killing of the antelopes to feed the hungry marchers is aptly described as 'a magic act in a dream', a judgement which the dramatization of the act supports; but the authorial narrator still thinks it is necessary to observe that the ex-freedom fighter had been transformed 'into a very extraordinary being whom (the people) had never really known' (p. 139). This kind of intrusiveness is even apparent in some of the characters' thoughts and words: a typical example is Karega's description of Wanja's abuse by Kimeria as 'a collective humiliation', which is stilted; or his moral conclusion that 'whenever any of us is degraded and humiliated, even the smallest child, we are all humiliated and degraded because it has to do with human beings' (p. 161), which is a naked ideological cliché. There are also cases when the novelist misuses his omniscient authority, becomes unequivocal and forces situations and characters to fit into a predetermined ideological position: the education of Joseph is a good example of this unequivocalness in a context which has become more problematic; the boy does not seem to grow with the doubts or struggle with the contradictions which have preoccupied the other characters in the novel.

The Political Novel

Towards the end of *Petals of Blood*, Ngugi's authorial perspective slides too easily beyond the world of conflict and contradictions which neo-colonialism engenders: Munira moves closer to his father, Abdulla and Wanja have a child, Karega awaits a tomorrow in which he will not be alone in the worker's struggle, and Joseph leaps towards full consciousness. This movement of characters and situations towards something else may strike the reader as simple and too linear, but it is as pronounced in the works we examined in the first essay as it is in the political novels of Ngugi, Sembene Ousmane and Alex La Guma. The assumption here, as in all the texts we have examined in this study, is that the novel's primary function is to interpret, judge and pattern the everchanging African reality.

Notes

1 'Politics and Modernity', *New Literary History* 3 (Autumn, 1971), pp. 93ff.
2 See Soyinka's foreword to *Opera Wonyosi* (London: Rex Colings, 1981), n.p.
3 *Ibid.*
4 *Marxism and Literary Criticism* (London: Methuen, 1976), pp. 16–17.
5 *Ideology and Utopia*, trs. Louis Wirth and Edward Shils (New York: Harcourt, 1936), p. 20.
6 See Michael Zeraffa, *Fictions: the Novel and Social Reality* (Harmondsworth: Penguin Books, 1976), p. 20.
7 *The Theory of the Novel*, trs. Anna Bostok (Cambridge, Mass.: MIT Press, 1971).
8 See 'Realism in the Balance' in *Aesthetics and Politics* (London: NLB, 1977), pp. 38–39.
9 *Politics and the Novel* (New York: Horizon Press, 1957), p. 22.
10 Quoted by Vere W.Knight, 'The Writer in the Post-Colonial Situation', *Black Images* 3(1974), p. 48.
11 'The Writers Speak' in *African Writers on African Writing*, ed. G.D. Killam (London: Heinemann, 1973), p. 149.
12 *Ibid.*, p. 150.
13 *God's Bits of Wood*, trs. Frances Price (London: Heinemann, 1970), p. 1. Further references to this edition are made in the text.
14 *Tasks and Masks: Themes and Styles of African Literature* (London: Longman, 1981), p. 41.
15 'Sembene Ousmane: Marxism and the Novel', paper presented to the Ibadan African Literature Conference, 1978, p. 40.

16 For a good discussion of Ousmane's heroines and their growth to consciousness, see Sonia Lee, 'The Awakening of the Self in the Heroines of Ousmane Sembene' in *Sturdy Black Bridges*, eds. Bettye J. Parker and Beverly Guy-Sheftall (New York: Doubleday, p. 52–60.

17 *Tasks and Masks*, p. 44.

18 *Myth, Literature and the African World* (Cambridge: Cambridge University Press, 1976), p. 117.

19 *Ibid.*, p. 117.

20 *The Hidden God*, trs. Philip Thody (London: Routledge and Kegan Paul, 1964), p. 17.

21 *The Political Unconscious* (Ithaca: Cornell University Press, 1981), p. 17.

22 'La Guma and Reality in South Africa', *Journal of Commonwealth Literature* 8(1973), p. 60.

23 La Guma in 'Discussion' in *The Writer in Modern Africa*, ed. Per Wastberg (Uppsala: Scandinavian Institute of African Studies, 1968), p. 24.

24 La Guma, 'Literature and Life', *Afro-Asian Writing* 1(January, 1970), p. 239.

25 *In the Fog of the Seasons' End* (London: Heinemann, 1972), p. 1. Further references to this edition are made in the text.

26 Michael Zeraffa, *Fictions*, p. 28.

27 The terms are used by Frederic Jameson in *The Political Unconscious*, p. 81.

28 For a good general discussion of character and consciousness, see John Bayley's 'Character and Consciousness', *New Literary History* 5(1974), p. 225.

29 Ime Ikiddeh, 'Ideology and Revolutionary Action in the Contemporary African Novel', unpublished paper, p. 23.

30 Ngugi wa Thiong'o, *Writers in Politics* (London: Heinemann, 1981), p. 72.

31 *Petals of Blood* (New York: Dutton, 1978), p. 3. Further references to this edition are made in the text.

32 *The Rhetoric of Fiction* (Chicago: University Press, 1961), pp. 3–16.

33 See *The Theory of the Novel*, especially Chapters 3 and 4.

34 'Character and Consciousness', p. 232.

35 *Barrel of a Pen* (Trenton, N.J.: African World Press, 1983), p. 60.

36 'The Novel as an Expression of the Writer's View of the World', *New Literary History* 9(1977), p. 188.

5
Rereading the African Novel

Myth, Language and Culture in Chinua Achebe's
Arrow of God and Elechi Amadi's *The Concubine.*

Rereading is here suggested at the outset, for it alone saves the text from
repetition (those who fail to reread are obliged to read the same story
everywhere). Roland Barthes, S/Z

If the literary critic's concern is the novel's apprehension of reality, then
there is no doubt in my mind that questions of myth, language and
culture are more important than has hitherto been assumed. These
questions have dominated literary theory in the last three decades, but
much criticism of the African novel suffers from an acute poverty of
theory, especially a theory of language. Undoubtedly, our critics have
written at length on the 'anthropological' dimension of the language of
African literature, especially in oral narratives, and there has been a
long debate on the sociological dimensions of language; but as to how
culture and language dominate all aspects of reality in general and the
novel in particular, both as formal and contextual concerns, there has
not been much research or criticism. My premise in this chapter is that
to confront the issue of language as both the form and content of
literature is to confront the larger questions of power and knowledge in
society. It is above all to confront the revolutionary character of the
novel as a representative mode. The kind of representation I am concerned with here is not that which goes under the vague term 'realism'
in which the novel is assumed to be a mere reproduction of reality, and
language a *tabula rasa* that expresses a one-to-one correspondence
between words and things. On the contrary, I want to posit representation as both a narrative process which opens up the conflicts that
inform society as they are represented in language. Indeed, language
becomes more than the outer shell of meaning; it is the primary subject

of the novel in the sense that all the key issues that concern society — power politics, class struggle, the status of women, culture and domination — are all reflected and promoted through language. Language in this sense is truly 'practical consciousness'.[1]

My second assumption is that nowhere is this overtly political dimension of language as marked as in the use of myths. I am not simply referring to traditional myths which have become de-historized over time and hence appear to be independent of ordinary experience, but also to contemporary myths which are promoted by the daily media: myths about leadership, education, culture. Of course, the study of myths is itself a contentious issue and is vulnerable to still greater mystification. This mystification takes two directions. The first tendency, which is most notorious in the study of Yoruba myths, is the privileging of myth (and ritual) as a special kind of insight, the key to a total understanding of the African world. Thus in his discussion of myth and ritual in *Myth, Literature and the African World*, Wole Soyinka posits myth as a 'primal phenomenon' and as an 'embodiment of nature and cosmic principles'.[2] But to write of myths as natural phenomena or to claim that certain myths represent the 'Yoruba point of view' is to ignore the fact that myths have actually been naturalized by the dominant culture or class to justify its hegemony. In other words, while myths are instituted to express a certain ideology and to protect a particular political and economic interest, they are, nevertheless, represented as a natural and universal phenomenon to coerce the dominated into an acceptance of their domination. Through myths and rituals the activities of the ruling class are recycled as the will of the gods.

There is still a further limited approach to myths, which is promoted by some schools of Marxists and materialists. In these schools, the argument is often made that a culture relies on myths because it lacks scientific knowledge about natural phenomena; that myths point to a gap of understanding, or consciousness in this culture; and that the culture manifests a fear of the unknown. And yet, as I will show in my discussion below, myth can also be a source of insight; in fact, there will be cultures in which the use of myth is a manifestation of a keen understanding of social and natural phenomena. We simply cannot isolate one aspect of myth and privilege it over another, for myth can be an expression of collective dreams, aesthetic play, or even ritual. It can be the medium through which a community expresses its deepest shared values or repressed feelings; it can be a mode of insight into phenomena, but it can also be 'false consciousness' which deludes people about their real interests.[3] But whatever the character a myth takes, it cannot exist outside language and narration. As Roland Barthes observed in an essay written in 1956, myth is a form of communication, and it is through an analysis of its language that we can grasp its essential cultural function.[4] It is this relationship of myth, language and culture which I want to examine as it is manifested in Chinua Achebe's *Arrow of God* and Elechi Amadi's *The Concubine*.

Culture and domination in *Arrow of God*

The initial problem posed by the analysis of myths is that the critic is often made to arbitrate between the spiritual and material realms which constitute the mythological universe. Some critics obviously prefer to underscore the spiritual, and find the material unsettling while others see the material and nothing else. Striking a balance between the two is rarely easy. Thus Wole Soyinka, whose theory of myth is contingent on the atemporal and cosmic character of the mythical, has this to say of the political dimension of myth in *Arrow of God*:

> The struggle among the gods has been placed squarely in the province of the political, and although the spiritual and the mysterious are never absent or invalidated — certainly the effective or responsive in the lives of the community is constantly used to reinforce this dimension of reality — yet the strongest argument in favour of a divine factor in the life of Umuaro is deliberately subverted by impure associations insinuated through the manipulations of language, contradicting situations, or the preponderant claims of a secular wisdom.[5]

Soyinka does not seem to approve of this encroachment of the secular on the spiritual, and yet there is a sense in which it is the primary theme of the novel. For what Achebe is dramatizing is a conflict in which various factions in Umuaro compete over the meaning of myth, the uses of language and the authority of the gods over men. For although the myths which express the authority of the priest of Ulu have become naturalized with time, we are constantly reminded that the god whom Ezeulu serves was created by men. Indeed, very early in the novel, we discover that myths and rituals are not eternal, but are a manifestation of individual or communal needs: they are what I will call the symbols of culture.

Such myths have no meaning in themselves in the sense that they have to be 'read' or interpreted to become accessible to the community. Thus while the moon may be just another natural phenomenon in some cultures, to the people of Umuaro it is a symbol, a sign from the gods. At the opening of the novel, Ezeulu, the priest of Ulu, is caught trying to read this sign: 'The moon he saw that day was as thin as an orphan fed grudgingly by a cruel foster-mother. He peered more closely to make sure he was not deceived by a feather of cloud.'⁶ The meaning of the gods is invested in the moon; as a medium between the dieties and men, Ezeulu's role is to interpret such meanings. Because the moon could either be a symbol of good fortune or bad fortune (p. 2), then Ezeulu's interpretation affects the way the community defines its relationship with Ulu. Thus in his invocation to Ulu after the sighting of the new moon, Ezeulu's prayer is for health and prosperity for both his family and the community he ministers over. Later, when his son Obika meets a spirit, it is up to the priest to interpret the designs of this god who has been sighted: 'You have seen Eru, the Magnificent, the One that gives wealth to those who find favour with him.' (p. 9).

Thus it can be said that the role of the priest is equivalent to that of the ideologue in contemporary society: he determines or maps a people's place in the universe of things. Furthermore, this universe is encapsulated in, and defined by, symbols: a man's life is signified by his household shrine, his *ikenga* his *ofo* and *okposi* (p. 6). Such symbols not only encapsulate a man's soul, they also signify his identification with the spiritual. In fact, it is also through symbols that the actions of men are consecrated and regulated, or negated. Ritual activities serve the former role: sacrifices are undertaken to cleanse people before the harvesting season, or when they have committed an abomination. At the 'Festival of the New Pumpkin Leaves', Ezeulu cleanses the six villages of their 'countless sins, before the planting season' (p. 60); the accompanying ritual is not merely a celebration of life, but also an acknowledgement of the gods' presence among people. Thus Ezeulu's ritual dance becomes both an embodiment of 'the unseen presences around him' and an enactment of 'the First Coming of Ulu and how each of the four Days put obstacles in his way' (p. 70). Ritual cleansing demands of the priest that he momentarily sacrifice himself for the sake of the community he serves — 'For who could trample the sins and abominations of all Umuaro into the dust and not bleed in the feet? Not even a priest as powerful as Ezeulu could hope to do that' (p. 87).

It is important to note that when we talk about Ezeulu's powers, we are really referring to his social function as an intermediary between Ulu and Umuaro. When he later sides with Ulu against the people, then his powers cease. More about this later. What I want to note here is that the intervention of the gods is not always benign: when they become involved in the follies of men, they can cause havoc. We see the punitive function of the deities in the conflict between Ebo and Akukalia in the second chapter. So long as the two men fight among themselves, their grim and bloody fight is accepted as normal, but once they have involved their personal gods, then they have invited the intervention and wrath of the gods: 'What happened next was the work of Ekwensu, the bringer of evil. Akukalia rushed after Ebo, went into the *obi*, took the *ikenga* from his shrine, rushed outside again, and while everyone stood aghast, split it into two.' (p. 24). The destruction of the *ikenga* is presented as a violation of its owner's soul. Without the symbol of his manhood, of his relationship with his ancestors, Ebo has been confronted with the destruction of his spiritual being; between him and the gods is only a yawning gap:

> At his shrine he knelt down to have a close look. Yes, the gap where his *ikenga*, the strength of his right arm, had stood stared back at him — an empty patch, without dust, on the wooden board. 'Nna doh!' he wept, calling his dead father to come to his aid. (p. 25)

If a man cannot exist at peace with himself without his personal god, the converse is also true: the gods cannot exist without the men whose wills and desires they symbolize. When men want to signify their autonomy over the gods, an autonomy which is rarely expressed directly, then they wear masks. One could argue that the mask represents a fetish, a god whose powers have increasingly become secularized. Ezeulu's chief rival, Nwaka, has such a fetish:

> He had a great Mask which he assumed on this and other important occasions. The Mask was called Ogalanya or Man of Riches, and at every Idemili festival crowds of people from all the villages and their neighbours came to the *ilo* of Umunneora to see this great Mask bedecked with mirrors and rich cloths of many colours. (p. 39)

It would be a mistake then, to see the conflicts in Umuaro as essentially between two rival gods, Ulu and Idemili. These conflicts are a struggle between two conflicting ideological interests and authorities: for instance, Ezeulu wants to maintain the authority of the gods and sustain the dominance of the spiritual over the secular. While the gods were instituted to maintain a subtle balance between the conflicting interests of the communities that came together to become Umuaro, Ezeulu has reached a point when he sees Ulu as solely spiritual and autonomous. On the other hand, Nwaka claims that he wants to maintain the old balance between the gods and men. However, there are indications in the novel that he would actually like to control the gods, to turn them into a personal mask. Towards this end, he has become the patron of Idemili: 'Nwaka's drummer and praise-singer was none other that the priest of Idemili, the personal deity of Umunneora. This Ezidemili was Nwaka's great friend and mentor. It was he who fortified Nwaka and sent him forward.' (p. 40). We will later see how this conflict is played out on the linguistic and symbolic levels.

Achebe's portrait of a community in the throes of change is made still more vivid by the modulations we see manifested in the people's attitude towards myths and rituals. For the colonial white culture has also introduced its own symbols which are subordinated to the task of cultural and political domination. Old standards are being questioned and new ones instituted in an arbitrary manner. Myths become instruments of domination when historical events are represented as manifestations of an ahistorical and natural order. Thus in the Lieutenant Governor's memorandum to Captain Winterbottom, the Igbo's system of government is either denied or denigrated: they are represented as lacking 'Natural Rulers' (p. 55). The memorandum does not even deal with the obvious point that the whole notion of natural rulers is absurd or even contested; it is taken for granted that there are rulers who have been appointed by God, and that the political system they represent provides a standard for the rest of the world. Thus not only is the myth of British cultural superiority represented as 'given', but the puported absence of a political system among the Igbo is posited as a justification for instituting the colonial machinery of government in the interests of 'a higher civilization' (pp. 55–56).

'Words, words, words', complains Winterbottom of this memorandum. The colonial functionary would like to see himself as a man of action, not words. And yet, it is through such words that the mythology of colonialism seeks to justify the new order. It is even through words that Winterbottom justifies his own personal involvement in the colonial 'mission': he sees himself as the man on 'the spot who knew his African and knew what he was talking about' (p. 56). On another level, colonialism peddles its own myths and fetishes in an attempt to win over new converts to its cause. Thus the battle for Umuaro's soul is fought as much in the real world as it is fought in the symbolic and mythical universe. Christianity, the cultural arm of colonialism, sees its primary function as the degradation of Umuaro's traditional symbols. Idemili's sacred symbol, the golden python, is represented by the Christians as a mere snake and attributed a negative function. As the evangelist, Goodcountry, tells his congregation: 'You must be ready to kill the python as the people of the rivers killed the iguana. You address the python as Father. It is nothing but a snake, the snake that deceived our first mother, Eve.' (p. 47).

The reason why symbols and myths are such appropriate tools for political and cultural domination is because they are so arbitrary and depend on a particular culture's willingness to accept them as the truth. As an object, the snake in itself is just a reptile. But elevated to being a symbol and myth, it becomes different things to different people: for the people of Umuaro it is a benign paternal figure which must be protected for the wellbeing of the people; for the Christians, it is an embodiment of the temptation, of evil, of man's fall from grace. The important point, though, is that the Christians can only succeed in controlling the minds and hearts of the people of Umuaro by degrading national symbols and denying them their mythical significance. By the same reason, Christian myths are narrated to provide new models of behaviour, of examples of heroic feats to be emulated and the promise of desires to be fulfilled. In the war of myths taking place in Achebe's novel, the god who will win is the one who will promise more material and spiritual objects than the other.

Moses Unachukwu is first confronted with the myth of the white man's invulnerability as a porter at the destruction of Abame: 'What he saw during that punitive expedition taught him that the white man was not a thing of fun' (p. 47). From this moment onwards, Unachukwu sees the way of the white God as his personal destiny; as a missionary, he seeks to plant the seeds of the new faith among his people and to justify his mission by citing the new mythology: 'He saw his sojourn in Onitsha as a parallel to that of the Moses of the Old Testament in Egypt' (p. 47). The new Moses may have his doubts about the zeal of his new brethren, since he still seems to have some sentimental attachment to the old mythologies, but he also knows that underlying such symbols are tangible political and economic benefits to be harvested. To benefit from both worlds, Moses tries to fuse the teachings of the Bible with 'the myths of Umuaro' (p. 48). Indeed, what has often been seen as cultural conflict in this novel is the struggle of some characters to deal with a very real paradox: on the one hand, Christianity and its values are a very recent phenomenon which has yet to penetrate into the psyche of the community; its myths have yet to be naturalized in the same way as traditional myths have become. But, on the other hand, as colonialism imposes its political hegemony on the land, it has become apparent to people with as diverse an outlook as Ezeulu and Moses, that the colonial authorities call the political and economical shots; that survival is dependent on some mode of compromise with the new order of things.

There are numerous attempts to deal with this paradox in *Arrow of God*. Ezeulu sends his son Oduche to the mission to be his 'eyes and ears' among the colonials, while Moses wants to protect the Idemili's python and still be a Christian. Similarly, young Oduche decides to kill a python to prove that he is a Christian, but when the moment of reckoning arrives, 'his heart lost some of its strength' (p. 50). Like many people caught between the two orders and the mythologies that signify them, the boy decides to balance the opposed claims by locking the python in a box: 'The python would die for lack of air, and he would be responsible for its death without being guilty of killing it, which seemed to him a very happy compromise' (p. 50). The author's sarcasm at the end of this phrase draws attention to the irony and tragedy involved in what appears, on the surface, to be a neat compromise. For to be a colonial, as Amilcar Cabral once observed, is to live with an identity that is 'incomplete, partial, and false.'[7]

It was Cabral, too, who underscored the importance of culture as an instrument of domination and liberation:

> In fact, to take up arms to dominate a people is, above all, to take up arms to destroy, or at least to neutralize, to paralyze its cultural life. For, with a strong indigenous cultural life, foreign domination cannot be sure of it perpetuation.[8]

As I have already observed, the tactic colonialism adopts is one of exposing traditional myths and symbols and depriving them of their substance. Reduced to an empty shell, or so it seems, the metaphysical systems of Umuaro can be replaced by new thought and value systems. In fact, the vulgarization of a culture is indispensable in the war for domination in a colonial situation. When building a new road to facilitate the exploitation of the land, for example, the youths of Umuaro gave an ancient python song 'a new and irreverent twist and changed it into a half familiar, half strange and hilarious work-song' (p. 81). The song may appear to be a case of 'malicious humour', but the political economy of the new regime encourages irreverence to the old gods. Earlier in the chapter, Achebe notes, the young men improvise a song to celebrate their new wages, '[a]and they sang it in English too!' (p. 76).

Indeed, as the novel progresses, we begin to realize that authority has been shifting away from Ulu and Idemili, who have become engaged in civil war, to the new idols of colonialism. While Ezeulu and other priests struggle over the authority of tradition, citing the wisdom of the ancestors and the intervention of the gods, the white man is developing a new patronage system which unwittingly parallels the old one. Like Nwaka, Winterbottom has a team of praise singers; like Ezeulu, he has created a myth of invulnerability. The new messenger class are the colonialist's intermediaries and functionaries; they are also role models who promote the worship of the new idols. As a matter of fact, the chief court messenger, Jekopu, has no identity outside his function as Winterbottom's servant; he often strives to refract the authority of the 'destroyer of guns'. Meanwhile, the messenger's escort makes what are decribed as 'desperate efforts to establish [the court messenger's] importance' (p. 136). Colonialist–messenger–escort: it is an interesting hierarchy of domination. In all cases, there is a shared belief that 'the white man has his own way of doing things' and that this way cannot be contested (p. 137).

What is surprising is that this new consensus on the power of the colonizer is shared by both the elders of Umuaro and the colonial agents: Ezeulu's friends agree with Winterbottom's corporal that the white man's footprints must be appeased with sacrifices for 'the masked spirit of our day is the white man and his messengers' (p. 154). More significantly, the white man is posited as deriving his power from his position as the chief priest of a new deity — money — and a new economy which revolves around the cash nexus. John Nwodika credits his personal *chi* to his new job as a messenger, but he also knows that the forces that drive him are very remote from his ancestral spirits. His friend and mentor, Ekemezie, resorts to tradition to explain and justify the new economic and political reality:

> He called me by name and I answered. He said everything was good in its season; dancing in the season of dancing. But, he said, a man of sense does not go on hunting little bush rodents when his age mates are after big game. He told me to leave dancing and join in the race for the white man's money. I was all eyes. Ekemezie called me Nwabueze and I said yes it was my name. He said the race for the white man's money would not wait until tomorrow or till we were ready to join; if the rat could not run fast enough it must make way for the tortoise. He said other people from every small clan — some people we used to despise — they were all now in high favour when our people did not even know that day had broken. (p. 169)

This passage is probably the most important in the novel for several reasons. First of all, the author has a keen awareness of the relationship between political economy and culture, of the intimate connection between value systems and the social structure. Money, as Nwodika aptly observes, is the new *ikenga*; the rules that matter most are not those of the ritual dance, but of the market and exchange. Thus the unwillingness of the clan to become involved in worshiping the new fetish is cause for lamentation, as far as Nwodika is concerned: 'Sometimes I feel shame when others ask me where I come from. We have no share in the market; we have no share in the white man's office; we have no share anywhere.' (p. 170). And let us not forget that in the capitalist economy, which Achebe prefigures, shares are the chief symbols of sacrifice and exchange.

Secondly, Achebe is conscious of how the new myth of the market and money reappropriates traditional language, and, as Barthes would say, colonizes it:[9] the tone and cadence of the above passage, and the stock of proverbs and metaphors it utilizes, refer to a wisdom which has been established over time and is hence taken for granted by both speaker and listener. But the tonality of Nwodika's speech conceals the vulgarization of traditional value systems by the new culture. For what Nwodika's speech tries to conceal is the fact that, to succeed in the colonial political economy, he must sell his labour at a low price; he has lost his independence as a producer and become a houseboy! However, there is an important irony in Nwodika's rationalization of the colonial situation: for he who has degraded himself for the sake of the race for the new money has more insight into the historical process than Ezeulu, the priest of Ulu. For while the priest has the illusion that he has some power over both Winterbottom and Umuaro, Nwodika has a keen sense of the character of the new power and its weapons of aggrandizement.

At the end of *Arrow of God*, Achebe draws our attention to the questions of interpretation and meaning which have obsessed Ezeulu and his rivals throughtout the novel. The final outcome of the conflict between the priest of Ulu and the community is, for the people of Umuaro, simple: 'Their god had taken sides with them against their headstrong and ambitious priest and thus upheld the wisdom of their ancestors — that no man however great was greater than his people; that no one ever won judgement against his clan.' (p. 230). But the relationship between people and the gods, the natural and supernatural, is highly ambiguous in this novel. The people's view that Ulu has joined them in the destruction of Ezeulu is not sanctioned by the narrator: 'If this was so then Ulu had chosen a dangerous time to uphold that truth for in destroying his priest he had also brought disaster on himself' (ibid.). But can we really talk of the people of Umuaro except in relation to Ulu? Does Ulu have an existence outside the desires and conscious intentions of the people of Umuaro? This is a very vexed issue in the novel. One might even argue that the relationship between men and gods, and the authority due to each, is the root cause of the cultural conflict and crisis of consciousness that has gripped Achebe's society.

Very early in the novel, we have Ezeulu meditating on the nature of his power and authority:

Whenever Ezeulu considered the immensity of his power over the year and the crops and, therefore, over the people he wondered whether it was real. It was true he named the day for the feast of the Pumpkin Leaves and for the New Yam feast; but he did not choose it. He was merely a watchman. His power was no more that the power of a child over a goat that was said to be his. As long as the goat was alive it could be his; he would find it food and take care of it. But the day it was slaughtered he would know sooner who the real owner was. *No! the Chief Priest of Ulu was more than that, must be more than that.* If he should refuse to name the day there would be no festival — no planting and no reaping. But could be refuse? No Chief Priest had ever refused. So it could not be done. He would not dare. (p. 3. My emphasis.)

Ezeulu is concerned with the origins and extent of his powers: he wonders whether he is merely an interpreter of signs or the originator of such signs; he would like to believe that his powers are more that those of a messenger, but he finds no certainty between what is and what must be. Thus when he later refuses to name the day of the festival of the new yam, he is not merely punishing Umuaro, but also testing out his power and will to dare. The priest's uncertainty about the relationship between men and gods is one which the reader is forced to share. The culture, or more appropriately Achebe's text, sends us contradictory signals. On one hand, the gods seem to have absolute control over men: people's destinies and functions are 'marked' irrespective of their will or need; and yet, on the other hand, the images of gods are carved by men, they are the projection of ideas in the minds of the mortals (p. 4–5) Why, then, is Ezeulu unhappy with his eldest son when the latter carves a diety? Because the act seems to secularize the deities, and the Chief Priest is aware of the paradox inherent in his position and that of the god he serves. He knows for example that, although Ulu is the foundation on which Umuaro is built, the god did not precede the people. On the contrary, we are told, when the six villages came together to 'save themselves', they 'hired a strong team of medicine-men to install a common deity for them' (p. 15). So when Ezeulu characterizes Ulu as the god who founded Umuaro, he is blind to the other half of the history — that it was actually the people of Umuaro who founded the god. It would seem that Ezeulu overemphasizes the centrality of the god to justify his own position and to legitimize some of his unpopular positions. At a time of rapid social change when historical developments might actually challenge the sanctity and hegemony of his deity, Ezeulu goes out of his way to dissociate Ulu from the social structures of Umuaro. Thus when many in the village decide to go to war against Okperi, Ezeulu observes that 'Today the world is spoilt and there is no longer head or tail in anything that is done. But Ulu is not spoilt with it.' (p. 27). A similar attempt to dissociate Ulu from the fate of the community destroys Ezeulu. For in reality, it is through the gods that men fight their earthly struggles, just as the gods use men as tools in their spiritual conflicts.

Myth is recognized as ideology at the point when men try to justify their own positions and their relations of power by insisting that the gods they serve are ahistorical, that they were there before the beginning of time. Predictably then, Ezeulu's chief rival, the priest of Idemili, tries to paint an image of his god that transcends Ulu and temporality: 'Every boy in Umuaro knows that Ulu was made by our fathers long ago. But Idemili was there at the beginning of things.' (p. 41). Idemili's immortality is represented in words and symbols: 'Idemili means Pillar of Water. As the pillar of this house holds the roof so does Idemili hold up the Raincloud in the sky that it does not fall down. Idemili belongs to the sky and that is why I, his priest, cannot sit on bare earth.' (p. 41). So each priest tries to undermine the authority of the other by downgrading the status of his god.

Questions about the authority of the gods are inevitably questions about language. For, as I will show shortly, gods only become real to people when they are represented through words, signs and speech-acts; their presence is realized when these linguistic symbols become intelligible, primarily through the agency of the priests. Let us remember, however, that language is itself an ambiguous and contentious issue in *Arrow of God*. It comes to us with a double character and with the power to confuse, agitate and enlighten. On one level, the language which is esteemed in Umuaro seems to spring from a well of common (or ancestral) wisdom; this language seems to speak consecrated truths, or to reflect unquestionable facts; its meaning and authority are taken for granted. But on another level, this language seems to be more effective when it conceals its determinancy, when it is ironic or ambivalent, when it seems to question the wisdom of the ancestors or truisms about human behaviour.

In cautioning his son Obika about his rashness, Ezeulu, who is proud of the youth's bravery, nevertheless questions the absoluteness of this virtue:

> It is praiseworthy to be brave and fearless, my son, but sometimes it is better to be a coward. We often stand in the compound of a coward to point at the ruins where a brave man used to live. The man who has never submitted to anything will soon submit to the burial mat. (p. 11)

Here we have a situation where proverbs are used to assert a kind of wisdom (cowardice) which revises or reverses the authority of another (bravery). But instances when proverbs are used to create doubts about the meaning of value systems are rare in the novel. More often than not, myth takes the language of proverbs not merely because they represent a 'grammar of values', but also because it is through proverbs that the ideological function of myth and language is inscribed. When common words are invested with the universal implications inherent in the linguistic protocol of proverbs, then we forget the ideology they convey and see them as primordial, representing 'universalism, the refusal of an explanation, an unalterable hierarchy of the world'.[10]

Indeed, the proverb for Ezeulu is a judicious weapon which is used not only to arbitrate, but also to pacify. Whenever any of his sons tries to question any of his decisions, Ezeulu will dig into his pool of apparently unquestionable wisdom to silence them, or as he likes to put it, 'to point the right way' (p. 13). At this point, we can begin to see how the issues of culture and domination, and the tripartite relationship between Umuaro, its gods and the colonizer, are thematized and fought out through language. Indeed, there is a sense in which *Arrow of God* is a novel about what language should be spoken or which mode of speech has more authority than all others. For whenever we reflect on the conflicts going on in the novel, whether between Ezeulu and Nwaka, or the larger conflict between Umuaro and the encroaching culture of colonialism, we are always confronted with ideologies or modes of consciousness trying to privilege their language. Specialization in the use of words is a matter of life and death in Umuaro. For example, in the ongoing conflict between Nwaka and Ezeulu, the winner always seems to be the person who can master the use of words to articulate his point of view. Wisdom, Nwaka suggests, 'is like a goat-skin bag; every man carries his own. Knowledge of the land is also like that.' (p. 16). In other words, no events have an eternal or natural meaning intrinsic to them; the meaning of things depends on our interpretation of them and the speaker's ability to represent his version of events authoritatively. Thus, in the dispute over the piece of land that sends Umuaro to war against Okperi, Ezeulu quotes the story of the ownership of the land as it was told to him by his father. But Nwaka undermines the authority of the story as told by Ezeulu's father in two ways. First, he questions the totality of Ezeulu's father's knowledge by arguing that 'the lore of the land is beyond the knowledge of any father' (p. 16). Historical events come to us loaded with possible distortions and prejudices, so Nwaka is not afraid 'to say that neither Ezeulu nor any other in this village can tell us about these events' (p. 16.) Secondly, having foregrounded the arbitrariness of the retelling of historical events, Nwaka, quotes his own father's version of events. He wins the argument not because he is able to prove that this particular version of events is truer than that of his rival, but because he is able to 'totally destroy . . . Ezeulu's speech' (p. 17).

In other instances, the failure to use words well or prudently can have tragic consequences. When Umuaro's emissaries arrive in Okperi to petition for war or peace and 'bring back the word', they find themselves in a situation where the conversation demanded by etiquette is impossible. In a moment of anger, an Okperi man, Ebo, compares Akukalia, the Umuaro emissary, to a 'castrated bull': 'Perhaps it was deliberate, perhaps accidental. But Ebo had just said the one thing that nobody should ever have told Akukalia who was impotent and whose two wives were secretly given to other men to bear his children.' (p. 24). This inopportune use of language eventually leads to war and destruction.

But the implications of linguistic protocol can have even more far-reaching consequences. In his analysis of contemporary mythology, Roland Barthes has made the important observation that myth gets hold of language in order to build its own system. The 'language-robbery' function of myth is its ability to 'reach everything, corrupt everything'.[11] This 'language-robbery' is evident not only in the power struggle within Umuaro itself, but in the community's larger struggle with the forces of colonialism. In the first instance, Nwaka has constructed himself a myth (embodied in his mask) as a 'Man of Riches'. At the height of the power struggle with Ezeulu, Nwaka's personal mask 'spoke a monologue full of boast'; and it is through 'the language of ancestral spirits' that Nwaka challenges Ulu (p. 39). In considering where Nwaka got his power from, the narrator draws our attention both to the rich man's relationship with the priest of Idemili and his command of speech: 'Nwaka was a great man and a great orator who was called Owner of Words by his friends' (p. 40). Nwaka's power is therefore thematized through speech.

In another respect, it is through words that colonial culture inscribes its presumed superiority over the African culture. Its favoured mode of speech is the cliché which confirms stereotypes that are taken for granted by the colonial set. For Winterbottom, a throb of drums in the bush signifies 'unspeakable rites'. His motive force is his 'strong belief in the value of the British mission in Africa' (pp. 29–30). In the colonial primer by George Allen, conquest is re-represented as the more benign 'pacification'. The movement of history is deprived of its complicated dynamics and reduced, in true Hegelian fashion, into a confrontation of the chosen and the damned: Nigeria 'is closed and will be closed until the earth has lost some of its deadly fertility' (p. 33); the British race 'will take its place, the British blood will tell'. Because none of these things is empirically true, their 'reality' depends on their linguistic reconstruction in books, speeches, or memoranda.

Significantly, the act of writing or retelling events is for Winterbottom an occasion for highlighting the significance of the colonizer in the new order of things. In his version of the war between Okperi and Umuaro, Winterbottom places his own role in the foreground and distorts the circumstances which brought about the conflict in the first place. We already know of the close kinship relationships between Umuaro and Okperi — they have historically been joined together through marriage and common gods. We also know that the war between them might have been avoided if it hadn't been for the personal feud between Ebo and Akukalia. Now, let us see how the story is retold by Winterbottom:

The people . . . of Okperi and their neighbours, Umuaro, are great

enemies. Or they were before I came into the story. A big savage war
had broken out between them over a piece of land. This feud was
made worse by the fact that Okperi welcomed missionaries and
government while Umuaro, on the other hand, has remained back-
ward . . . I think I can say with all modesty that this change came
after I had gathered and publicly destroyed all firearms in the place
except, of course, this collection here. You will be going there fre-
quently on tour. If you hear anyone talking about Otiji-Egbe, you
know they are talking about me. Otiji-Egbe means Breaker of Guns.
I am even told that all children born in that year belong to a new
age-grade of the Breaking of the Guns. (p. 37).

In this version of events, the colonizer is represented as the force of
order; the dynamics of the colonized cultured are vulgarized and
reduced to insignificant events.

Indeed, we can talk about a political economy of language in *Arrow
of God*: speech and narration are inevitably bound up with questions
of political and economic domination, historical progress, the division
of labour and the redefinition of human and natural resources. We
have already seen how Nwaka is described as the 'owner of words' and
how he achieves his power and influence by patronizing the priest of
Idemili. A similar expropriation of language and symbolism is at work
in the movement of the Christian church. The most influential men in
the new culture are masters of the word: Ezeulu's son Oduche no longer
looks up to his father as the custodian of wisdom, but to those among
his teachers who have mastered the white man's language. English is
slowly replacing titles as the symbol of achievement; knowledge is
posited as identical to the mastery of the colonizer's language. Thus it
is said that the West Indian missionary, Blackett, 'had more knowledge
than white men', while the teacher from the delta, John Goodcountry,
'spoke the white man's language as if it was his own' (p. 46). As we have
already seen, Goodcountry has drawn myths into the cultural war
going on in Umuaro. His determination is to deny all traditional myths
of their mystery and significance and reduce them to a *bétise*. Goodcountry knows that 'to speak a language is to own a world':[12] 'The
world will pass away but not one single word of our Lord will be set
aside' (p. 49).

Of course, the revolution of the word which Goodcountry is trying
to promote goes beyond language; it aims at the destruction of a
culture and of established thought systems which people had assumed
were natural. Colonialism challenges and the redefines what is natural.
What the colonial administration aims for, however, is not merely the
institution of a 'natural' and 'civilized' order, which are both synonyms
for domination, but a new set of economic relationships. For example,
Moses Unachukwu, because of 'his familiarity with the white man's

language', becomes the middle man between the new wage labourers in Umuaro and the colonial supervisor (p. 77); his mastery of the alien tongue also earns him unusual privileges within the traditional set-up. Moreover, Unachukwu knows that the white man's language, religion and road are connected:

> Yes, we are talking about the white man's road. But when the roof and walls of a house fall in, the ceiling is not left standing. The white man, the new religion, the soldiers, the new road — they are part of the same thing. The white man has a gun, a matchet, a bow and carries fire in his mouth. He does not fight with a weapon alone. (p. 85)

In contrast to this authority, we have the confusion of the elders. On the one hand, priests such as Ezeulu believe they are the sole source of divine and secular authority: 'Who tells the clan what it says? What does the clan know?' Ezeulu asks his friend Akuebe in a moment of immodesty (p. 131). And yet, while Ezeulu may believe he was right about the conflict between Umuaro and Okperi, he proves naïve and ignorant about his own authority and that of the adverse colonial culture. First, he fails to understand that his power derives from Ulu, and that Ulu is a creation of the community. Thus the god cannot be used against the people because, as Soyinka has aptly observed, when gods die 'the carver is summoned and a new god comes to life. The old is discarded, left to rot in the bush and be eaten by termites.'[13] The roots of the god, and his justification as a deity, lie not only in the desires of the community to establish some tangible relationship with the unknown, but are linked to basic material interests, in this case the yam. The relationship between the will of the god and the material survival of the culture is expressed succinctly by Onenyi Nnanyelugo:

> Shall we . . . sit down and watch our harvest ruined and our children and wives die of hunger? No! Although I am not the priest of Ulu I can say that the deity does not want Umuaro to perish. We call him the saver. Therefore you must find a way out, Ezeulu. (p. 207)

Of course, Ezeulu fails to save the situation, and, capitalizing on this failure, the Christians present themselves as an alternative cultural system. In the process, the new order is able to destroy the power and authority the priest of Ulu was trying to conserve. Where did Ezeulu fail? I think he essentially fails to understand that culture is a totality. He fails to acknowledge the crucial links between belief, political behaviour and economic interests, which people like Nnanyelugo and Nwachukwa understand so well. Thus he believes that he can seek accommodation with some aspects of the colonizer's culture while discarding the ones he finds irrelevant. But by sending his son Oduche to be his eyes in the colonial camp, could he have imagined that he was handing him over to the new order? Not really. The achievement of *Arrow of God* is Achebe's avoidance of Ezeulu's error of treating culture independently of the forces which sanction it. For as Cabral observed 'culture is the vigorous manifestation on the ideological or idealist plane of the physical and historical reality of the society that is dominated or to be dominated'.[14]

Myth and desire in *The Concubine*

Of course, myth has always been treated as a manifestation of a collective unconsciousness, but recent developments in the theory of language and psychoanalysis have increasingly questioned this function by pointing to the intricate relationship between language and the 'unknown'. It is no longer enough to say that myths express a community's fears, or hopes, or expectations for, as I will show in a moment, the apprehension of myth is not always uniform. While the collective dimension of myth cannot be dismissed entirely, it is also important to underscore the subjective element in mythologies. For while a community may express its identity through its mythologies, it is also true that individuals may often find themselves locked into a struggle with their community as to the meaning of such myths and their implications for personal conduct. In this respect, Myth becomes a system which tries to control and regulate the individual's desire. At the same time, the individual who, in his quest for his identity, contravenes this system is driven to madness. This is exactly what happens in Elechi Amadi's novel.

There is no doubt that myth in *The Concubine* is an important tool of self-understanding: it defines an individual's relationship with his or her community, his or her place in the cosmos; more importantly, it functions as a stable anchor in an unstable and opaque universe. For while the gods in Achebe's novel are defined by essentially secular functions, people in *The Concubine* do not seem to have any powers over their deities. In the latter novel, the gods predate men. Thus in Omokachi's myth of creation, the founder fathers did not create a god to sanctify their union, but obeyed a 'terrible omen' from the gods.[15] Furthermore, the gods are a powerful presence over people and objects, always crying for sacrifices. Since the gods are perceived as unpredictable, the role of the *dibia* as an interpreter is crucial: he is the only person who seems to have direct access to the universe. Thus, when Emenike visits the *dibia* Nwokekoro early in the novel, we are told that between the medium and the gods 'there was great understanding' (p. 17). He also has the power to read invisible signs and pre-empt what is going to happen: Emenike reads his own death written on the *dibia's* face.

Death is not merely the cessation of life: in Amadi's novel, it is the great unknown, the most important sign which the gods send down to earth as as a manifestation of their power over people. Furthermore, the power of death is exacerbated by its ambiguity; it never seems to have one clear-cut message, and the thoughts of many characters seem to revolve around what death really means. What is the meaning of Emenike's youthful death, for example? His rival, Madume, at first sees it as a prefiguration of his own, fearing what 'retributions the gods had in store for him' (p. 53). But soon after, he interprets this death as an act sanctioned by the gods: 'people did not just die without reason. Invariably they died either because they had done something wrong or because they had neglected to minister to the gods or to the spirits of their ancestors'. In other words, death cannot be apprehended with any certainty. On his way to woo Ihuoma, Maduke hits his foot on the ground; his eyes pass from the dead man's grave to his bleeding toe, and a 'vague fear came over him and he shivered' (p. 57).

It is when Maduke goes to Anyika, the *dibia*, for consultation that we begin to realize how important mythology is to decorum and social control in the community. For the *dibia*, Maduke's 'toe disaster' is no ordinary act but a 'premonition': several spirits have sworn to kill Maduke because they don't want him 'to have anything to do with Ihuoma. They have been on the lookout for you.' (p. 58). Thus the gods have intervened to proctect the widow from an avaricious suitor, and what may just be the *dibia's* sense of propriety and consciousness of established social rules is endowed with divine authority. Madume returns home feeling 'the presence of the spirits around us' and an awareness that he cannot just pick up Ihuoma like meat from a carcass: 'He must give her up if only to spare his life.' (p. 67). But Maduke's greed knows no bounds, and when he decides to take over the piece of land which the elders and priests have arbitrated in favour of Emenike, he has decisively contravened the rules of the gods. The snake that spits into Maduke's eyes is therefore seen as 'the act of a god, probably a very powerful god' (p. 70). Furthermore, in Maduke's abominable death by his own hand, we see the double character of the gods neatly balanced. They are, first, the instrument of punishment and retribution: 'It was impossible for the wicked to go unpunished, thè everwatchful gods of retribution, Ofo and Ogu, always made sure of that.' (p. 77). And yet, on the other hand, this retribution is intended to protect the weak and powerless.

However, the problem with control, whether secular or spiritual, is that it assumes that there is some consensus on what is acceptable and what is undesired. When such control no longer serves the interests of certain individuals or groups, then it is perceived as a repressive force which must be rebelled against or discarded. But does myth then function as a repressive force when it comes up against fantasies or desires? Wole Soyinka, who sees myth as a manifestation of the collective vision or world-view of a culture, is adamant in his dissociation of myth and fantasy. His argument is that

> To describe a *collective* inner world as fantasy is not intelligible, for the nature of an inner world in a cohesive society is the essentialisation of a rational world-view, one which is elicited from the reality of social and natural experience and from the integrated reality of racial myths into a living morality.[16]

While the whole definition of myth as the expression of collective fantasies is itself questionable, there is no doubt in my mind that myths do in fact repress desire. On a simpler level, they achieve this repressive function by denying the individual responsibility for his own needs. Thus Ekwueme's lack of interest in Ahurole is not explained in terms of his likes or dislikes but in terms of an external agency: 'What had come over Ekwe? Someone must be involved. He must have been bewitched.' (p. 105). If he has not been bewitched, then someone else must be to blame, most likely a woman.

At no stage in this continuous search for scapegoats is it suggested that Ekwe's problems are within him. More significantly, it is the woman who takes on the ritualistic role of the scapegoat and is forced to sacrifice her own inner needs. Thus, after Ekwueme marries another woman, Ihuoma is relieved that things will return to normal; but this normality is not real; she has to put on appearances and pretend that things are going well for her; she locks up her feelings and emotions:

> Whatever she felt was safely locked up in her mind. Not even her mother could probe into its depths and wrench its secrets. She had admitted to herself that she liked Ekwe very much. But what woman does not like some man? Her liking for Ekwe was not frantic nor was it sudden. It had grown gradually over a long period. Since it did not take her by storm she was able to keep it firmly under control. (p. 127)

In the paragraphs that follow, Amadi shows how and why repression is represented as the thing desired in this community. The traditions of Omokachi are rooted in propriety and decorum: 'Excessive or fanatical feelings over anything were frowned upon and even described as crazy. Anyone who could not control his feelings was regarded as being unduly influenced by his *agwu*.' (p. 127)

But who determines what is normal behaviour and at what point does dissent become madness? This question does not arise in Amadi's community because what is normal is also assumed to be natural. In other words, human activities are judged against an unquestionable standard which is sanctioned by the supernatural. Thus a woman's desire for a man is described as 'a subtle reflex action, a legacy of her prehistoric ancestors' and love is described as deep and eternal; it has nothing to do with material interests or sexuality (p. 127). For this reason, Ihuoma feels obliged to control her desires, 'to avoid behaving in a way that might disrupt this perfect setting' (ibid.). However, Ekwueme finds it difficult to enforce the same kind of control. At first he reconciles himself to his marriage to Ahurole because tradition dictates it, and 'Ihuoma's image gradually sank into his subconscious but after a hard struggle' (p. 129). But his desire for Ihuoma cannot be repressed for ever because it is indeed the projection of a more dangerous desire, an attempt to transcend the greatest sexual taboo of them all — his attraction to his mother.

There is no doubt that Ekwueme suffers from a deep-rooted Oedipus complex: his thoughts and desires revolve around his mother; his efforts are directed towards pleasing her, and he prefers her company to that of any other woman. Indeed, he is not keen on other women, except for Ihuoma. Why Ihuoma? Because he sees her as a projection of his mother: 'She was so understanding, motherly and beautiful. Ahurole was beautiful. He hoped she would be understanding and perhaps motherly as well' (p. 132). Ekwueme's mother is a model of conduct which every other woman is supposed to emulate, therefore he characterizes Ahurole as abnormal solely because she does not meet this standard: 'Often he compared his mother to Ahurole and each time his wife fell far short of expectations.' (p. 140).

The problem for the hero who suffers from this kind of Oedipus complex is that no other woman can be exactly like his mother. Ihuoma approximates to the hero's standard, but she is beyond his reach. The result is disturbance, confusion and a sense of entrapment. A 'vague oppressive blanket of sadness' envelops him whenever he comes across Ihuoma, and his thoughts turn to the rules that have denied him the fulfilment of his desires. Ihuoma has a remarkable insight into the strong feelings repressed inside her would-be lover: 'She knew that he was like an animal at bay looking for a way out.' (p. 148). But she also realizes that he can only be tamed if she submits to his needs. The irony is that there cannot be such a submission without contravening the most sacred rules in the community.

There is even a further paradox: such rules can only be broken beyond the confines of what is considered to be true and real, in a world of fantasy and madness. For in madness a subject can express his or her true self without fear of rules. This is why the community explains Ekwueme's desire for Ihuoma as the preference of a 'madman', thus making it forgivable. But in reality, the open expression of desire is the only cure for madness: this is why the madman is allowed to have Ihuoma. And for a time, it seems that Ekwueme has acquired what he has always desired by virtue of his madness. But then the mythical intervenes in a lethal way: it is discovered that Ihuoma is the wife of the water spirit, and her earthly lover is killed trying to supplicate the deity, and the rules of the community remain intact. What this means in ordinary language is that uncontrolled desire will not be allowed to have its own way, because this would be a recipe for chaos. Thus myth, and its most potent agent, death, become an important force for equalizing the scores and restoring the sense of balance which Amadi's community needs to survive.

Notes

1 For a discussion of language as a form of practical consciousness, see Marx and Engels 'The German Ideology' in *The Marx–Engels Reader*, ed. Robert C. Tucker (New York: W. W. Norton), p. 158.
2 *Myth, Literature and the African World* (Cambridge: Cambridge University Press, 1976), p. 15.
3 See Claude Lévi-Strauss, 'The Structural Study of Myths' in *The Structuralists from Marx to Lévi-Strauss*, ed. Richard and Fernande DeGeorge (New York: Doubleday, 1972), pp. 170–74.
4 Roland Barthes, 'Myth Today' in *A Barthes Reader*, ed. Susan Sontag (New York: Hill and Wang, 1982), p. 93.
5 Soyinka, p. 88.
6 *Arrow of God*, 2nd edn (London: Heinemann Educational Books, 1974), p. 1. All further references to this edition are in the text.
7 Amilcar Cabral, 'Identity and Dignity in the Context of the National Liberation Struggle' in *Return to the Source: Selected Speeches of Amilcar Cabral* (New York: Monthly Review Press, 1973), p. 65.
8 'National Liberation and Culture' in *Identity and Dignity*, p. 49.
9 Barthes, p. 120.
10 Barthes, p. 144. For other discussions of proverbs and language in *Arrow of God*, see Bernth Lindfors, 'The Palm Oil with which Achebe's Words Are Eaten', *African Literature Today* 1(1968): 2–18; and Gareth Griffiths, 'Language and Action in the Novels of Chinua Achebe', *African Literature Today* 5(1971): 88–105.
11 Barthes, p. 120.

12 See Frantz Fanon, *Black Skins, White Masks*, trs. Charles Ian Markmann (New York: Grove Press, 1967), p. 38.
13 Soyinka, p. 86.
14 Cabral, p. 41.
15 *The Concubine* (London: Heinemann Educational Books, 1966), p. 14. Further references to this edition are in the text.
16 Soyinka, p. 34.

Index

Index